Running a Successful Franchise

Kirk Shivell

Kent Banning

McGraw-Hill, Inc.
New York San Francisco Washington, D.C. Auckland Bogotá
Caracas Lisbon London Madrid Mexico City Milan
Montreal New Delhi San Juan Singapore
Sydney Tokyo Toronto

Library of Congress Cataloging-in-Publication Data

Shivell, Kirk.
  Running a successful franchise / Kirk Shivell, Kent Banning.
    p. cm.
  Includes index.
  ISBN 0-07-056987-8
  1. Franchises (Retail trade)—United States—Management.
I. Banning, Kent B. II. Title.
HF5429.235.U5S55 1993   92-39117
658.8 ' 708—dc20   CIP

1 2 3 4 5 6 7 8 9 0   DOC/DOC   9 8 7 6 5 4 3 2

ISBN 0-07-056987-8

*The sponsoring editor for this book was David Conti, the editing supervisor was
Fred Dahl, and the production supervisor was Donald Schmidt. It was set in
Baskerville by Inkwell Publishing Services.*

Printed and bound by R. R. Donnelley & Sons Company.

This book is printed on recycled, acid-free paper containing a minimum of
50% recycled de-inked fiber.

Contents

Foreword

Franchise consultants and others involved in franchising usually have extensive libraries on the franchise process. I have probably 50 franchise books in my reference library. When a client asks me for information on franchising, I can usually recommend a book after I have targeted the particular area of the franchise process that the client is inquiring about—advertising/promotion, site selection, financial management, and so on. However, when I have been asked to recommend a book that covers the entire gamut of franchising, I have been stumped.

That is, until now.

Kirk Shivell and Kent Banning, in their book *Running a Successful Franchise,* have hit the jackpot in terms of providing a book that covers all the business of franchising. This book is a must-read for the franchise professional, as well as for the individual who simply has an interest in franchising and would like to gain a better understanding of the process. Subjects ranging from the legal requirements to franchise a business, properly managing a franchise, franchisor/franchisee relationships, aspects of franchise training, ongoing franchisee support, and many other important subjects are all covered in this exciting publication. It is written in easy-to-understand language, so that the lay person, as well as the professional, will find this book readily useful.

I heartily recommend that anyone interested in a broad understanding of this fascinating subject read and study this publication.

Richard A. Beuzekom
Franchise Consulting Services
Tucson, Arizona

Preface

We are witnessing, in the early nineties, massive changes in the American economy. After over five decades of defense-driven business activity, the fall of the Berlin Wall and the collapse of the communist-dominated countries in Europe have changed our direction and our purpose. As America adjusts to new priorities, many of the major corporations and institutions are downsizing and developing new business strategies to cope with a shrinking market for defense-related products. As a result, an unprecedented number of skilled employees and middle- to upper-level managers have been forced to reenter the labor market. Many have decided that the uncertainty and the stress of life within the large organization are no longer attractive, and they are looking to own their own small businesses.

In fact, small business, during the past decade, has been the source of most of the growth in products, services, and employment in the United States—and a significant amount of that growth has come from businesses that are part of a franchise network. The concept of owning a franchised business has expanded rapidly, and now franchises are responsible for over 30 percent of retail sales nationwide.

To many, owning their own independent small businesses and owning businesses that are parts of a franchise network are the same, an assumption that, in reality, is incorrect. Although owning and managing a franchise will take the same long hours, hard work, and attention to detail that the small independent businessperson must commit to in order to be successful, there are many very important differences between the two roles. Unlike the independent entrepreneur, the franchisee is a member of a team whose reputation and success depend on the consistency and the management ability of everyone within the franchise network. The franchisee must know what management functions are controlled by the franchisor and what functions are his or her sole responsibility. The franchisee must also know how much latitude there is for independent judgment in those areas controlled or influenced by the franchisor, particularly in the areas of marketing, sales, advertising, accounting, purchasing, and quality control. In actuality, almost every aspect of managing a franchise is affected by the franchise agreement, even though on the surface it appears that it is the sole responsibility of the franchisee.

The relationship between the franchisor and the franchisee is complex and often misunderstood—even by those currently in a franchise. Those people who are beginning the process of obtaining a franchise and those currently owning one often assume that the franchisor will train or advise them in every aspect of managing a franchise—an assumption that is far from reality. In most cases, the franchisor's training program is limited to product information and techniques, sales and marketing, purchasing, and quality control. The franchisor expects that the franchisees will supply their own management expertise in the areas of personnel selection and supervision, accounting and financial statements, resource management, and organization. Yet often both potential and current franchisees have little knowledge of management techniques, or they have experience that is not appropriate to franchise operations. Consequently, they fail to reach their full potential.

The authors of this book—with over 50 years of combined experience in managing and consulting with various types of franchises, dealerships, and cooperatives—are thoroughly familiar with the demanding role of the franchisee. They cover, in detail, the most important elements of managing franchised operations including those areas most often the cause of conflict between the parties involved. Some of the other topics covered are:

Understanding the franchise agreement.

Business structure options for franchisees.

The legal aspect of franchise management.

Developing human resource policies to reduce employee turnover.

Controlling nonoperational losses.

Enhancing franchise advertising and marketing programs.

Fiscal management and policy.

How to read and analyze financial statements.

Business organization and communications.

This book contains valuable information of interest to several groups of people involved in the franchise industry.

Those contemplating or in the process of purchasing a franchise: The book provides a greater understanding of the franchisor/franchisee relationship and the expectations of both parties. It also provides detailed information on those aspects of managing a franchise that are normally not provided by the franchisor.

Persons currently owning and operating a franchise: You will find many valuable tips on how to manage a successful franchise operation. The book identifies areas of potential conflict and how to avoid them. It also explores the advantages and disadvantages of various business structure options as the franchise matures.

Franchisor executives responsible for franchisee training: Because the book encourages a greater understanding of the franchisor/franchisee relationship and provides much needed information about operating a successful franchise, it is an ideal supplement to franchise training programs.

Franchisees who are expanding by purchasing additional units: Considerable information is available about transitioning from single-unit to multiunit or corporate-style franchising in the areas of marketing, business structure, and effective communications.

Former corporate executives and managers considering franchising: You will find a discussion about the transition from the large organization to managing a franchise, including the description of personality profiles used by franchisors to screen potential franchisees and the adjustments necessary for former employees of large organizations to become successful in franchise operations and ownership.

There can be little doubt that the franchise concept will continue to grow in terms of the percentage of retail sales. In fact, it is projected that the franchise industry will provide over 50 percent of the total retail sales of products and services by the end of the nineties. For those interested in being successful in franchising, it is important to understand the need for teamwork and consistency. Franchising may not be the place for the fiercely independent entrepreneur, but it can offer many opportunities to those willing to work hard for a common goal.

Kirk Shivell
Kent Banning

Acknowledgments

This book developed from studying, visiting, questioning, surveying, and exchanging information with many hundreds of franchisees from coast to coast over a period of more than a generation, during which time the franchise industry grew from infancy to its present degree of maturity. We are grateful for the friendships we have made, for all we have learned, and for the opportunity to share the information in this book with all who are, or who contemplate being, in franchising.

Two individuals were especially pertinent in their observations while the manuscript was in preparation. Therefore we want to express special thanks to them: Ms. Brook Carey, President, Advanced Franchise Concepts, and Richard Beuzekom, President, Franchise Consulting Services.

We are grateful also for all the help we have always received from both private and public organizations concerned with franchising. These include particularly the International Franchise Association, the Federal Trade Commission, and the United States Small Business Administration.

The world of franchising is indeed a fascinating new world, filled with prosperous opportunities for men and women who are courageous, prudent, and industrious. This book is written because we earnestly want them to succeed.

Kirk Shivell
Kent Banning

1

Behold,
a New World
of Business

The Fortune 500 companies may get the publicity, but a close look at the American economy will reveal the true heroes: Franchises are the most rapidly growing kind of enterprises in the country. John Naisbitt, author of *Megatrends* and *Megatrends 2000,* predicted that franchising will account for more than half of all retail sales by the end of the 1900s. Between 1987 and 1989, franchises added over 400,000 new jobs to the U.S. economy, while the Fortune 500 companies added only 10,000. In addition, by 1990, the total number of franchises in the U.S. had topped a half million. The annual sales of goods and services by franchising networks is expected to top 758 billion. All these statistics point to one compelling fact: Franchising has become the big new American way of doing business.

Of the many kinds of franchises, a venture usually will fall into one of two general arrangements:

1. *Business franchise:* In this arrangement, the franchisee buys the right to use the franchisor's methods of marketing, operational systems, logos, trademarks, architectural styles, and other features. The franchisor will dictate many of the details of the business such as prices, quality, product and equipment specifications, and the methods and hours of operations. The franchisor derives income from up-front fees, royalties, percentages of gross sales, and advertising pools.

2. *Product franchise:* In this, the franchisor is a manufacturer or distributor of a product or products, and the franchisee is usually a

retailer or wholesaler. The profits to the franchisor come from price markups at the various marketing levels. The question of whether the relationship between the parties is that of a true franchise or a distributorship depends on the amount of control exerted by the manufacturer or the primary distributor on business operations and on the product lines of the retailer or subdistributor.

The key difference between a completely independent small business owner and a franchisee lies in the degree of influence and control. The independent small business owner has total control over site selection, architectural style, hiring and training of employees, general business practices, accounting systems, marketing, advertising, hours of operations, pricing, and kinds of products or services to be sold. In other words, he or she is responsible for all aspects of business operations. The franchisee, by comparison, may be controlled, or at least influenced, by the franchisor in any or all aspects of operating a business. Consequently, despite the tendency of some observers to combine both the individual entrepreneurs and franchisees under the label of "small businesspersons," there are marked differences between the two in the managerial responsibilities and the opportunities for creativity.

Currently, franchisees are gradually separating into three distinct categories:

1. Persons who buy a single unit within a franchise network with the intent to actively manage that unit as a means of making a living.

2. Persons who buy or expand into a small multiunit franchise ownership, which they still manage personally.

3. Persons who have an extensive multiunit franchise requiring a formal management organization.

Some multiunit owners may own more than one type of franchise—for example, two or three car rental agencies, some photo processing shops, and a temporary personnel office. The number of multiunit franchises is growing rapidly, particularly in urban areas, and is an increasingly significant force in retailing. In one sense, multiunit ownership can be called "corporate style franchising" because the growth patterns are similar to corporate expansion. The growth patterns, however, can take two entirely different forms. In the first, the corporation may buy numerous franchises in a variety of businesses, and in the second the corporation may buy exclusive rights to specific territories and become a subfranchisor or distributor with the right to sell franchises within that area and collect a portion of the fees and royalties.

How significant is the multiunit trend? A few phone calls to local franchised businesses can reveal whether this trend is important in any given area. If you own a single-unit franchise or are contemplating buying one, you should consider making several calls to determine the extent of multiunit ownership nearby. Whether the existence of multiunit ownership is a plus or minus must be judged on a case-by-case basis but several assumptions can be made. First, control of all units of a specific franchise within a territory may provide the owners with a pricing advantage because of the lack of competition. Second, because the subfranchisor controls the territory, the franchise fee could be higher than it would be if the franchise were offered on the open market. Third, the number of quality franchises available to individual franchisees will be diminished because the primary franchisor will prefer to sell units to an established multiunit owner rather than to an unknown and untested individual. In fact, many franchisors will offer reduced franchise fees to those who buy more than one unit.

There is another method by which one may enter an existing franchise network called *conversion franchising*. An owner of an existing independent business may feel that joining a franchise involving the same type of business may offer some advantages in marketing, name recognition, and supply and equipment costs. Franchisors often welcome conversion franchisees because they are dealing with a demonstratable record; consequently the risk on their part is reduced. But often some franchisors are wary of conversions because owners may have difficulty in adjusting to a situation in which they have given up a substantial amount of control.

Another trend in franchising is international expansion. McDonald's, Burger King, and Merle Norman Cosmetics are just a few of the major franchisors that are setting up units in both hemispheres, and it appears that changes in the political and economic structures in Europe, Asia, and South America will, in the future, significantly expand the franchising potential. Franchising holds considerable appeal to persons in countries just converting to a free market economy because of the support and expertise offered by the franchise network, particularly to men and women not accustomed to operating a business in the private sector.

Regardless of the locality, whether in your hometown or overseas, the amount of support is one of the most controversial elements of the franchisee-franchisor relationship. Franchisees often take the position that the franchisor is providing less support than was promised, and the franchisors argue that their basic responsibility to the franchisee is limited to product or service information and training, site selection, and marketing assistance. The basic knowledge and expertise to manage a business, they declare, must be furnished by the franchisee. *The fact that most franchisors do legitimately and purposely limit the support given to the franchisees is a reality that many potential or existing franchisees do not understand.* They go into a franchise relationship with the expectation that franchisors are going to hold their hand and offer directions every step of the way. Unfortunately, and sometimes tragically, they fail to realize that they, as franchisees, are responsible for most of the tasks of operating the business.

Franchising places special demands on the franchisee because of the nature of the relationship. Some persons have said that the role of a franchisee is somewhere between an entrepreneur and an employee, but current trends in franchising are changing that role because these trends are changing the nature of the franchise industry. A decade or two ago, when someone mentioned a franchise, the image that first came to mind was that of a "Mom and Pop" team operating a fast food outlet. Now, however, in some market areas it is difficult to find a franchisee who owns and manages just one location. To repeat, multiple ownership can pose some problems for would-be franchisees, but to those who already own a franchise or are in the process of obtaining one, the multiunit concept must be considered as at least a possibility. Recognize, however, that multiunit ownership could change your role from that of a hands-on manager to a role similar that of to the corporate manager who oversees numerous operating branches. Multiunit operations require more sophisticated management skills.

Some Franchisee Profiles

To help you understand the differing roles and demands on a franchisee, here are profiles of three successful franchisees. The first owns and manages just one franchise and has decided to grow through the expansion of his current operation rather than buying other units. The other two own multiple units within the same franchise business.

Auto Body Shop

Mike Wilenchek owns an auto body paint shop franchise, one of approximately 500 within the franchise organization. The franchise originated about 20 years and has grown steadily ever since. Much of its success is based on the fact that the originator developed advanced technology in auto painting and has managed to keep pace with new developments ever since.

Mike graduated from an eastern university in 1970 with a degree in business management and went to work for a major oil company. Finding that working for a large corporation was not to his liking, he joined his father's business, an independently owned heating oil distributorship. After three years with his father, he moved West and, with another relative, started a veterinary hospital supply business. After awhile, this business broke up and Mike began to look for a small business to purchase on his own.

At first, he did not even consider buying a franchise. After almost a year of looking around, however, he began to observe an auto body and paint shop, and for several weeks he watched the amount and the type of traffic going in and out of the shop. It became apparent that the business was thriving and, upon investigation, he found that the shop was part of a growing franchise network. Upon contacting the franchisor, he learned that another franchise unit across town was available and, after reviewing the operation and the financial records, he purchased it. Looking back, now 14 years later, he admits that he was very fortunate.

> I know now that I should have consulted an attorney and an accountant to review the franchise agreement and the books. Even though everything turned fine and I had few difficulties, buying the franchise without the help of an advisory team was very risky. Some of my friends have bought other franchises without professional advice and they can tell some real horror stories.

Because Mike had been involved in the management of small businesses twice previously, he had gained an excellent grasp of the management skills necessary to operate a profitable company. He had enjoyed being his own boss and escaping the confusion and the stress of working for a large company. However, he found that being responsible for every aspect of the business's operations, particularly the marketing and advertising, was very time-consuming. It seemed that there never were sufficient hours in the day to tend to all the demands and the details that needed his attention. In each of his previous small business involvements, he also had to learn the in's and out's of that particular industry by trial and error, a process that often was responsible for expensive mistakes. When he turned to franchising, one of his first steps was to attend the franchise training program. Mike comments:

> I think that training is one of the most important advantages of operating a business within a franchise network. My franchisor had a four-week training program that covered all of the technical aspects of operating an auto body and paint shop. The course included sales and telephone tracks, estimating, operating the shop equipment, and all the technical information necessary for painting and auto body repair. They assumed that I had the basic management knowledge, such as

employee supervision, scheduling, understanding financial reports, handling an organization—areas that I had majored in at college and obviously had been involved in while managing the previous businesses.

Even though I had no experience in running this type of a shop before, I was able to walk into it that first morning and hit the ground running, estimating and setting up jobs and working immediately with the customers. As in any business start-up, I had some problems in the beginning but these were problems involving my own management style and control. It took me awhile to get a handle on all aspects of the business and set up the necessary management control systems. Another part of the job that took time was the building of the amount of confidence in my employees necessary to turn them into an effective team—confidence in both me and themselves. As a manager, I have always been strong in the areas of problem solving and customer service, but my weakness was and still is in the area of delegating. I still try to do or become involved in everything and, in this business, that is impossible. I have made progress, however. For example, my shop manager is now responsible for hiring and firing shop employees.

Although Mike was very pleased with the training he received, he did think that the program could be improved by adding more information about finance, accounting, personnel, and certain legal matters such as wage and hour law and contracts. He did realize, however, that laws of this type can vary from one region or state to another and that, generally, obtaining this information is the responsibility of the franchisee.

When asked if he was considering buying another franchise unit, Mike replied:

Although I realize that multiunit franchise ownership is increasing, it is not a trend that impacts this industry to any great extent. Usually an auto paint and body shop is larger than most franchises in both size and the number of employees. My franchisor believes strongly in hands-on owner management, therefore the number of multiunit franchisees is limited.

Print Shop

Marcia Bestor and her husband, Bill, own three print shop units in a community of approximately 125,000. Although the community does not have a large industrial employment base, there is a substantial number of small to medium-sized businesses involving both products and services, and the area also is a prominent tourist destination. The locale is excellent for quick print shops because most of the surrounding businesses are not large enough to have their own graphics and print capabilities.

Marcia and Bill bought their first unit approximately eight years ago when the franchise was in the process of expanding. Two years later they purchased their second store and within three years added the third. The franchise itself was started in 1970 as an independently owned store, and after the founder expanded the number to seven stores, he decided to franchise his knowledge and experience. Since then, the organization has expanded to approximately 330 units in the United States and elsewhere.

Marcia has a BA degree in merchandising and some master's level courses in education. Her previous work history includes a stint in the restaurant business, several years in department store sales, and two years in nationwide promotion work for a cosmetic firm. Bill had considerable restaurant management experience. After they moved to their present city, she went to work for the franchisor as an employee. Since her franchisor has a policy of giving employees an option to apply for a franchise, she and her husband decided to purchase an existing store within the system. As a former employee of the franchisor, she understood the system and the relationship between the franchisee and franchisor. Consequently, she and her husband had little difficulty in making the transition despite the fact that neither had any previous small business ownership experience.

The Bestors' successful record as franchisees holds several useful lessons for a current or potential franchise owner.

First, when they first began thinking about going into business for themselves they considered buying a restaurant. They took the time to carefully consider this and came to the conclusion that it was too much of a gamble. While their financial resources were comfortable, they could not afford a sustained period of losses and, through various sources, they learned that the restaurant industry sustains higher-than-average business failures. Second, through Marcia's prior experience with the franchisor, they knew the success rate was much higher with an already tested business system. Third, again through Marcia's experience, they completely understood the basic rule of the franchise game—that they must forgo some of their autonomy to become a member of the franchisor's team. Fourth, both of them, particularly Bill because of his experience the restaurant business, understood the value of personal customer service. Fifth, and perhaps the most important element in their success, was the fact that they had taken a careful look at themselves and their own relationship. They realized they were not really comfortable taking large risks, that they were both basically conservative. They analyzed their own individual strengths and weaknesses and found that the differences were complementary, not adversarial, and that they could share the business responsibilities according to his and her individual strengths. They also knew that they both disliked working for large corporations because of the lack of personal contacts within the organization and with the customers. Now, even with three stores, they know each of their thirty employees personally, and the demands of the business keep them constantly in contact with their customers.

Fast Food

Mark Roden owns 16 fast food franchise units and has plans to open seven more this year. He bought his first unit in 1987, another in 1988, and 14 more in the next three years. His background is primarily in food retailing. He worked in fast food restaurants and supermarkets while going to college; after receiving his BS degree in marketing, he went to work for a local supermarket chain. He soon was promoted to grocery manager and worked in that position for several years. But, although he enjoyed some aspects of his job, he felt buried in the corporate bureaucracy and began to look for another career direction.

His first contact with the fast food franchise was as a customer, and after several visits he became interested in purchasing a franchise.

> I did not consciously make a decision between owning a franchise or starting my own independent store, although I probably was at the time aware that buying a franchise involved less risk. It wasn't the idea that it was a franchise that sold me. I bought because it looked like a growing business, had the best product and a real presence in the market place. After I became involved, I realized that, if you start your own business, you are the one who has to set up the marketing plan and the control systems. Being part of a franchise lessens the amount of time and effort to be spent on details. I prefer owning a franchise because of the support and control mechanisms and the sharing of ways to improve. When you own your own business you make a lot of mistakes that can be costly, while in belonging to a franchise network and sharing experiences, you can avoid many costly goofs. You also have standards to measure up to.

Mark started with a management background in direct supervision of employees and had a strong sense of marketing and sales. He was, however, not experienced or knowledgeable about the backroom—the bookkeeping, the necessary personnel and inventory controls, and how important it was to control all categories of costs. Like most beginning franchisees, he wanted to control everything, know everything, and make every decision. He also was inexperienced in hiring and made some mistakes in the beginning. After about a year, he reevaluated his position and his goals and realized that to prosper he must build an good employee team.

Asked what his management strengths are, Mark says:

> I am people oriented. In this business, you must deal effectively with three groups of people: the customers, the employees, and the vendors. The bulk of my working day is spent in constant contact with one or more of these three groups. My biggest weakness is to avoid something that I don't like to do. I don't like details, yet details are a necessary part of business. The first year that we added seven stores, I realized that I was getting so bogged in detail I no longer enjoyed my work. I had lost track of my basic business, and I knew that I had to put together an organization and hire people to do the things that I was avoiding. At that point I hired someone to handle sales and marketing, another person to be a combination of controller and office manager, and some support staff. Now I'm in at least one store every day, sometimes three or four. I'm back working with people again, something I'm good at.

Listen to the Franchisees Themselves

Here are the opinions of these franchisees concerning some of the important aspects of managing a franchise.

Question *What are the advantages of franchising over operating an independent small business?*

Mike

> The most important advantage is the training. I had never been involved in the auto body and paint business before, and yet I was able to function effectively from the first day. The second important aspect is the risk reduction. Although I wanted to own my own business and be my own boss, I was not and am not a risk taker.

Marcia

> First of all, if you want to buy an existing business, finding the right deal is difficult. We searched for over a year for something that appealed to us and made sense financially, and never did find the right one. In every case the risk was too great. After we looked at the quick print franchise, we knew the risk was less and that the franchisor did a lot for the franchisee. The franchisor had developed a technology and

a format that were very marketable, and we thought we would be crazy to buy anything other than something that had worked for other people.

Mark

I prefer to work within a franchise network for a number of reasons. First, the support and control mechanisms that enable me to closely control product cost. Second, the sharing of ways to improve through contact with the franchisor and other franchisees. We have a monthly conference call among several franchisees like me, and we learn a great deal from sharing both mistakes and accomplishments. Third, I think the standards are higher than those found in many independent businesses.

Question *What were the most serious problems that you encountered during your first year?*

Mike

Although I knew the technical side, I didn't know the management end. I tried to do everything because I was reluctant to delegate even some of the simplest tasks. I had to be involved in or know everything. My other problem was that I had not yet built a team spirit among my employees. I also had another problem that tested the strength of a franchise system. Both my parents died within a short period of time and despite the amount of time I lost and the emotions involved, the business survived because of the structure of the franchise and with the help of some very loyal employees.

Marcia

The biggest problem was wearing so many hats. We couldn't afford to hire people to do everything. So consequently we were running the equipment, doing the books, dealing with the customers, and being pulled so many ways. I thought I knew the printing business, but every day I found something else that I thought I knew but didn't. So, even though we joined a franchise, the first year was a learning experience. And it still is.

Mark

I wanted to control everything, and hire everybody, partly because of my background. In a large company it is often the case that you are responsible for things that you really do not have full control over, and, when I went on my own, I reacted to that feeling. I was good at increasing sales but not good at controlling costs and, of course, that is part of the equation. Making money equals increasing sales and decreasing costs. I also had problems in my choice of employees. At first I wanted to hire people that I could control. I wanted to make every decision and the first people I hired were terrible hires. After a short time, however, I reevaluated what I wanted and where I wanted the company to go. I changed my criteria for hiring and consequently got some terrific people.

Question *What areas of management do most franchise training programs fail to address?*

Mike

Mostly personnel and financial matters. I realize that it would be difficult to put together a program that would apply in all parts of the country, but I think that some general information would have been helpful. There are also some legal issues that could have been covered such as wage and hour laws and some OSHA information. Again, these may differ from state to state but some information should be included.

Marcia

My franchisor's program was quite comprehensive, but they tried to give too much too fast. Shortly after I went through the program, they did lengthen the course to allow the franchisees time to absorb the details. While it is true that they did not cover many of the details involving general management techniques, Bill and I had already been involved in managing several different kinds of operations, and the restaurant business is a good hands-on training program.

Mark

I think that more information on personnel, delegating, supervising, prioritizing, and scheduling might be helpful. Certainly, the financial side, such as cash flow requirement and cost control, is an area for which you always need more information even though they strongly advise that you have an accountant and an attorney.

Question *Will strong-minded, independent entrepreneurs make good franchisees?*

Mike

No, not unless they are willing to cooperate with the franchisor. I know of franchisees who fight the franchisor every step of the way, franchisees who think that they are the only ones who know it all. But if a franchisor has been around for 15 or 20 years, they must be doing something right and the franchisee is paying to know what it is. Why pay for advice if you are not going to take it?

Marcia

I think in some cases they do, although the franchisor must know how to handle them carefully. You can't meet a dominant person head-on. The franchisor must also be very careful in selecting this type of a personality because they must be receptive to training and some restrictions. Personally, I like the barracuda type. They don't become dejected if they have had a slow day. They pick themselves up and get ready to fight again.

Mark

No, unless they can recognize that, in this business, the franchisee needs to be creative and innovative in the promotion and marketing area but must be supportive of the strict guidelines of the franchise. My managers often say that they want to be more creative, and I agree as long as they are creative outside the store in their advertising and promotions but don't change the standards inside the store. When I hear someone say that they are going to change this and that, I wonder why they bought the franchise. There is a place in this world for people that can do things the best, but their place may not be within a franchise because they don't conform to a standard.

Question *What types of personalities make the best franchisees?*

Mike

Today's franchisee has to be easygoing but strong-willed. Relaxed enough to cope with changing markets and customers but confident enough to attack problems quickly and with considerable control. They must be excellent negotiators because they will be put in a negotiating position many times each day. They must be willing to compromise because that ability is the key to customer service and repeat customers. Depending on their location, they must also be ready to deal with the culturally diverse, even to the extent of learning another language. In many areas, both the customers and the employees come from a variety of races and ethnic backgrounds. Being able to communicate with them in their own language is a real plus.

Marcia

Our franchisor uses a personality profile questionnaire as part of the franchisee screening process. The ideal, according to the designer of the test, is someone that is somewhat dominant but not to the extent that they refuse to compromise or conform to standards; someone who is highly influential and comfortable within that role; someone with a high energy level and has no problems with change. Being adaptable to change is very important because the business environment changes every day. Today I own a print shop. Tomorrow, who knows, I may be selling popcorn. But if that is what it takes to be successful, I will do it.

Mark

To be a successful franchisee, you need to be highly motivated, a person who puts work, not above everything else, but near the top. Typically, a franchisee can burn out if they continue to put those 80 to 110 hours per week. They have to achieve some sort of balance. They have to delegate more and learn to stop and enjoy other activities or events. It makes little sense to work hard to be able to afford to do things but not have the time to do them.

Question *What areas of the franchisor/franchisee relationship most often lead to conflict?*

Mike

I can think of several. First, you must lose part of your individual identity when you join a franchise. On the surface it appears that the company logo is the symbol of success when, in reality, the identity and the reputation of the franchisee are responsible for much of the business. Another problem often involves having to conform to pricing when a franchisor sets up a promotion. There are also often questions concerning the advertising fee. Is it being spent to everyone's advantage? Is everyone contributing?

Marcia

There are several areas in which potential conflict exists and most of it is due to problems in communicating.In many ways, running a franchise is like cooking. The recipe is successful only if you use all the ingredients, and the franchisee and franchisor must agree on what ingredients are necessary. Consequently, there must be a mechanism to ensure that both parties can communicate in good faith. Another area of conflict in many franchises in the choice of equipment, principally because the markets are different from one location to another.

Mark

Of course, there is always disagreement about site selection and the distance between sites, but the principal disagreement involves a question of orientation—where each side is coming from. Theoretically, both sides have the same objective—to be successful. Realistically, however, the franchisor's idea of success is constantly increasing sales because that is the basis of the royalty payment. The franchisees, however, are focused on the bottom line—profitability; and increased sales and profitability do not necessarily go hand in hand. If increased sales disproportionately increases expenses, then the franchisee has less to take to the bank.

2
Study Yourself and the Franchise World

The first function of management is to prevent mistakes. And the first mistake for you to prevent is getting into a franchise that isn't right for you. In fact, you may learn that no kind of franchise is right for you. To find out, there are three measurements to apply, and there are well-defined processes for applying them. What you need is the answers to these questions:

1. Are you suited for franchising?
2. Is a congenial franchise available?
3. Do you have the money to be a franchisee?

Fortunately, the experience of franchisors can guide you in determining whether you are suited for franchising at all. And if it should become clear to you that you are not, don't be discouraged. Much of the information in this book could help you succeed in an independent business of your own.

Franchisors are very familiar with the fact that being a franchisee is not appropriate for everybody. If a franchise is sold to someone who cannot make it a success, the franchisor will suffer almost as much as the franchisee who fails. Not only does the franchise unit fail to produce its potential income, but a failing franchise can also consume a tremendous amount of time and effort on the part of the franchisor to either save the unit or try to sell it to someone else. A failing franchise is a no-win situation for everyone.

Reputable franchisors will go to great lengths to ensure that they have a good match between their organization and their franchisees. In fact, if a franchisor that you are considering does not thoroughly investigate potential franchisees, be very cautious. The absence of a thorough screening process usually means that the franchisor is after a fast buck and has no real regard for either you or your future.

A typical franchisee screening process will encompass at least a half dozen components of an applicant's resources, background, and character. Obviously, because of the fact that a franchise sells for anywhere from five thousand to several hundred thousand dollars, the first thing franchisors will investigate is your financial resources. They will look closely at your net assets and your liquidity. If, for example, your cash and other ready assets are used to purchase the franchise, leaving you with inadequate working capital, most franchisors will be very reluctant to do business with you. Even if the franchisor has financing help available, the strength of your own financial statements will be the initial test. A franchisor will also examine your general credit rating to determine your attitude toward financial obligations. From a franchisor's point of view, the payment of royalties and other fees should occupy first place in your priorities.

Second, a franchisor will review your business experience. The nature of the desired experience varies greatly among franchisors, but each has an image of what it considers to be the best experience for one of its franchisees. Many franchisors will say that experience in the same type of industry as the franchise may not be necessary—that they will do all the necessary training. In fact, some franchisors prefer that their potential franchisees do not have any experience in their line because they feel that learning the franchisor's system is enough of a load without having to unlearn different procedures learned elsewhere. Franchisors also will look at the type and level of an applicant's experience. Later on in this chapter we will discuss in greater detail some types of persons who consider becoming franchisees and how their occupational backgrounds are regarded by franchisors. At this point it is enough to say that franchisors differ considerably on the ideal background for their kind of businesses.

Next, franchisors will attempt to determine whether your general behavior and attitudes are compatible with their standards. These usually will be determined by two methods; written answers to questions on the application and other documents, along with verbal answers to questions asked during preliminary and secondary interviews. Secondary or final interviews are usually conducted by senior officers of the franchise corporation.

In addition, a franchisor will try to identify or measure the depth of your commitment to a franchise, especially if you wish to include your spouse or children as owners of the franchise. In many franchise networks, over half of the owners are husband and wife teams and, in such cases, the franchisors are looking for proven compatibility and a sense of commitment by both parties. Franchisors are very aware of the fact that, despite the depth of their relationship, many wives and husbands simply cannot work together.

Perhaps the most difficult part of a franchisor's investigation is the evaluation of a potential franchisee's managerial ability. Many applicants have had little or no true managerial experience. Others may have had considerable experience in management but of a type that is not applicable to franchising. This problem is discussed later in this chapter, but at this point it is enough to say that much of the managerial experience in large corporations or organizations is not applicable to franchise management and in fact can be detrimental.

Because of the size of most franchise units, the owner is expected to have considerable direct contact with the customers. If owners begin to add to the number of units they own, direct customer contact will diminish but the training of employees in customer service will increase in importance. As a result customer service experience is a must in the granting of most franchises.

The Psychological Profile of the Ideal Franchisee

A very pronounced trend in franchisee investigations is the use of psychological-personality testing. Many franchisors now use these tests to produce a psychological profile of an applicant, and in some cases similar tests are available to current franchisees for use in screening their potential employees. The developers of these tests have found that the psychological-personality profile of the ideal franchisee is remarkably similar for all types of franchise. The ideal profile for a franchisee's employees, however, will differ according to the type of franchise.

The investigation of potential franchisees is an expensive and time-consuming process, a fact that at least partially explains why many franchisors give priority, and originating fee discounts, to current franchisees who wish to own additional units. A current franchisee has a demonstrable record and is familiar with the system, and consequently selection and training costs are virtually eliminated.

As you may know, psychological-personality testing is somewhat contro-versial, and some state laws restrict its use. It is stated, with considerable justification, that tests of this kind may be unfair to persons who seek jobs. The situation is different, however, when the stake is a substantial in-vestment of time, money, and reputation by both parties who contem-plate a franchise. This is more a matter of marriage than of employment. Numerous persons or companies now provide psychological-personality tests, but TIMS Management Systems, Inc., is presently the only one endorsed by the International Franchise Association and listed in its Directory of Suppliers. (The word TIMS is an acronym for Thomas Inter-national Management Systems of which TIMS is a part.)

1. TIMS Management Systems, Inc. P.O. Box 36360, Tucson, AZ 85740 (1-800-528-5153)

2. Franchise Opportunities Guide, IFA, 1350 New York Avenue, N.W., Suite 900, Washington D.C. 20005 (202-628-8000) $20

The head of TIMS is Thomas M. Hendrickson and, under his direction, two kinds of tests have been developed for the franchise industry. The first kind is designed to be taken by present franchisees or by their key executives so that the profile of the ideal franchisee for that business can be established. The second kind is to be taken by potential franchisees to show how their profiles compare with the ideal.

It is now very probable that, if you apply for a franchise, you will be asked to fill out a profile questionnaire. But you do not have to be en-tirely in suspense until then. TIMS now provides, for a modest fee (under $100 at this writing), a service that enables a prospective franchisee to take this kind of test in advance. Get in touch with TIMS, state the kind of franchise you are interested in, and appropriate forms will be sent di-rect to you. Then, normally within five working days after you return the completed forms, TIMS will send you a confidential report.

Do not be surprised if you are less than perfect, and do not be too eas-ily disheartened. Remember, the important goal at this point is not to get a franchise but to prevent a mistake. Unless the disparities of your profile are vast, get in touch with the franchisor anyway, preferably by phone, and ask to speak to an executive. The fact that you have had the foresight and concern to voluntarily be tested should enhance the impression you make and encourage them to consider you.

Bear in mind that a personality test is only one part of the franchisor's investigative process, just one kind of evidence to aid the selection com-mittee in arriving at its decision. Many other kinds of evidence, such as the personal impression you make in interviews, the references you give, and the business and financial history of your life, will also influence the committee.

But, you may ask, what does a franchisor look for in the psychological make-up and the personality of a franchisee? It could be the right proportions of each of numerous characteristics, such as adaptability, meticulousness, self-confidence, self-discipline, and sociability. But Dr. Hendrickson is one of those who focus on four comprehensive measurements in constructing a profile. The following is a composite of those for several different types of franchises:

1. Dominance (D). Understandably, franchisors seem to prefer people who score 50 to 75 percent in this measurement; that is, they are moderately dominant. Highly dominant persons have the drive to push forward against opposition, but they also tend to be openly critical of those they see as hampering their progress and do not measure up to their high, sometimes unrealistic, standards. They seldom phrase their demands diplomatically, nor do they worry much about their impact on others. When tasks or situations become routine, they tend to lose interest and look elsewhere for challenges. They will want room to advance themselves, along with the power and authority to act on their own. They aspire to be judged on their achievements and want to select their own way to success. They easily become frustrated and impatient and find it difficult to pace themselves. They have a wide range of interests and like to explore new approaches and ideas. They are not reluctant to take risks.

It is easy to understand why the franchisors want moderation in the dominant side of personality. A high dominance score is characteristic of the small independent entrepreneur who may tend to be a maverick, not a team player. Franchisors want people who may be strong-willed but are disposed to sacrifice some of their ego and play within the rules of their game.

2. Influence (I). Although high scores in the influence dimension in personality is typical of people who excel in sales and customer relations, franchisors prefer persons with moderate scores here also. A rating of 50 to 75 percent or perhaps slightly more and slightly above the D rating is considered the best influence score for a franchisee.

High influence persons are characterized by their outgoing and enthusiastic nature. They enjoy meeting people and sharing with them their positive outlook and motivation. People respond to their warmth and usually trust them. They generally tend to gain high visibility because they like the spotlight, but they also may try to charm rather than perform when in a tough predicament. They also may become absorbed in their relations with people and lose focus on business goals. When dealing with people, they may come across as shallow or superficial because of their tendency to move quickly from one person to another. Often they are trapped by their own trust and acceptance of people. High influence people often need close supervision to meet their objectives.

Most franchisors feel that, although sales, promotion, public relations, and customer service are essential skills in franchising, the disadvantages and the lack of independent direction of the high influence person are too much of a trade-off. Consequently, the desired moderate score is, in reality, a compromise to avoid some serious potential problems in dealing with franchisees who are so wrapped up in sales and popularity that they lose sight of the bottom line.

3. Steadiness (D).   Franchisors prefer applicants who score 25 to 50 percent in steadiness. Persons with a high steadiness score have some characteristics that might seem to be valuable, but the disadvantages far outweigh the advantages. Persons with a high steadiness personality tend to be calm and easy to talk to. Their emotional patterns are low-key but communicate a sense of sincerity and interest in others. They are sensitive—so much so that they may interpret remarks or actions as offensive or derogatory when no affront was intended. Their basic style is that of a team player who is calm, stable, and dependable. Unfortunately, the high steadiness personality cannot easily cope with change. Stability and predictability are important because they prefer events to follow the same patterns as in the past. They want the assurance that hard work and loyalty will pay off. It is difficult to convince them to change their positions or attitudes to meet changing conditions because they like a clearly defined structure and feeling of security. Usually they are steady, hardworking, and sincere.

At first glance high steadiness persons would seem to have the characteristics necessary to become good franchisees, but there are two reasons why they are not.

First, in most franchises, the owner of the franchise unit has to be on the front line of the marketplace—the one, more than anyone else, who is directly involved with the consumer. Consumer inclinations are constantly subject to change because of competition, fads, traffic patterns, and countless other potential influences. The franchisee as a retailer must be able react quickly to changes in order to maintain a profitable business. If the franchisee is highly resistant to change, the chances of survival can be slim.

Second, creativity and the ability to quickly solve problems are attributes that the high steadiness personality simply does not have. Successful reaction to changing conditions and markets requires imagination, resourcefulness, and foresight. Franchisees should be able to accurately project the probable outcome if they decide on a certain course of action and have the will to take that course as quickly as possible. High steadiness personalities are neither decision makers, planners, nor moderate risk takers; yet all of these attributes are crucial to the success of a franchisee.

4. Compliance (C). Franchisors disagree widely in what they consider to be the right amount of compliance in a franchisee. The scores desired by franchisors range from just above 50 percent to very strong—that is, 75 percent and above. The range appears to be based on the degree of technology required in the operation of the franchise. The sophisticated technical service franchises (such as quick prints, computer, and dental/medical service businesses) tend to require higher compliance scores than those involved in retailing.

The high compliance personalities wish to avoid antagonizing others. They tend to use tact and diplomacy when dealing with persons in authority. To avoid conflict, they will use caution and conservatism. They make decisions slowly because they feel the need to check and recheck data. This attention to detail makes them excellent troubleshooters and, in some cases, problem solvers. Although they will go along with change, they usually will not take unpopular positions or act independently. They are methodical and systematic and are most comfortable working within a highly structured organization.

Franchisors who prefer a strong compliance personality do so because this type of a person will not fight the system, particularly when the required procedures are complex. Their attention to detail is a plus when managing a system involving sophisticated equipment or procedures. Franchisors who prefer a lower compliance rating have operations that require people who are more flexible, assertive, and imaginative, people who are able to think on their feet and act more independently. These franchisors want someone who will conform to the standards and the requirements of their franchise system, but they also want creativity because of the nature of the retail product/service business.

3

Ease the Transition
to Life
as a Franchisee

If You Are an Entrepreneur

Those who do not fully understand the relationship between the franchisor and the franchisee often assume that the small independent business person, the true entrepreneur, is best qualified to become a franchisee. This is far from being necessarily so. The profile of the ideal candidate described in Chap. 2 reveals some marked differences between the profile of an entrepreneur and that of a franchisee. Based on the descriptions of Dr. Hendrickson, the profile for a successful entrepreneur would be very high in dominance, almost as high in influence, low in steadiness, and also low in compliance. These differences are substantiated by the opinions of many franchisors who are reluctant to enter into conversion franchise agreements. You will remember that a conversion franchise is one in which an existing business joins a franchise network, for example, an individually owned successful hardware store that joins a franchise in the same industry. According to many persons familiar with conversion franchising, it can be very difficult for an owner who has been operating with complete independence to suddenly have to conform to the procedures and style of a franchise. This kind of marriage can be anything but satisfactory for either party.

Many franchisors are reluctant to deal with some present or former small business owners because of their motivations. As one franchise marketing manager says:

Small business owners are driven by either profit or ego. The ones driven by the profit motive are usually quite flexible and are willing to concentrate on what we believe are the necessary ingredients for success. For example, we believe very strongly that the customer is always right is a sound long-term policy and strategy. The profit-minded small business person is usually of the same conviction and easily adapts to our procedures and requirements. The ego-driven small business person is a different story. Profit is secondary to personality needs—the need to dominate and control to the extreme. With this type of person, employee turnover is always excessively high, and customer service is given a low priority. In fact, one of the features common to this type of management is the lack of repeat customers.

If you are a small business owner and are considering going into franchising or if you already are now a franchise owner with a small business background, we suggest that you carefully study the personality of a successful franchisee. The need for you, as a franchisee, to conform to the franchisor's format and procedures is crucial to your success and is your responsibility to the entire franchise system of which you are a part. The success of a franchise system depends on consistency and uniformity. A customer doing business with a recognized franchise expects certain levels of quality in both the service and the product. If any franchisee fails to provide these, that lack of performance reflects unfavorably on the whole system. If your personal need to control and to dominate is extreme, then franchising probably is not for you.

If You Are an Employee

The franchise industry is reporting a fact that should not be surprising: a dramatic increase in former corporate managers and executives who would like to start their own businesses or buy franchises. Some of these potential franchisees have lost their jobs and the rest have left voluntarily. If you are in either of these two groups, you should be aware of the fact that there are some very significant differences between the two, differences that can be either advantageous or disadvantageous, depending on your ultimate goals. If you are someone who is thinking about acquiring a franchise, the recognition of your own motivations and personality traits may help you decide whether being a franchisee or a small business owner is the right kind of a career for you. If you are already involved in owning a franchise, knowing more about the requirements of franchise or small business ownership should help you recognize your strengths and weaknesses. And, since the role of franchisees changes significantly when they become a multiunit owner, an introspective look at your own character and personality traits can help you decide whether or not expansion would be right for you.

Men and women who were involuntarily terminated are likely to be persons who were most comfortable in the corporate environment and, in many cases, were very successful. Since their termination was caused not by any lack of satisfactory performance but by economic conditions or other uncontrollable occurrences, their first step is to try to find another position in their field at their former level and salary. The economy of the early nineties greatly constricts the chances of finding such a position, therefore in many cases the involuntary terminee begins to consider small business or franchise ownership.

Many franchisors view the involuntary terminee with some skepticism. The marketing director for a franchisor with several hundred locations worldwide offers at least a partial explanation. He reports that in 1991 over two-thirds of the applicants for a franchise were former corporate employees. Between 25 and 35 percent of these applicants did not pass the initial screening process and therefore were not eligible to purchase a franchise. This particular franchisor uses a personality profile match test as part of their screening process. The results of the test are reviewed by all members of the franchisor's executive staff who also are responsible for interviewing the applicants. According to the interviewers, a significant number of the involuntary terminees display the following characteristics:

1. They were too comfortable within the corporate "cocoon." They are accustomed to functioning within a very narrow sphere of influence and control. Decision making is based on staff input and is often politically influenced, with little regard for the bottom line.

2. They have a nine-to-five mentality. If their work is not completed by 4:45, it is put aside until tomorrow.

3. They have always had a clerical and support staff to "run and fetch." They do not seem sufficiently flexible to function independently and carry the responsibility for wearing all the hats necessary when operating a franchise with few or even no support employees.

4. They are not profit-oriented. Their principal involvement with cost control was to ensure that their department or section operated within "the budget." They were too far removed from the production end of the business to understand the cause-and-effect issue of profits, that is, the impact of their decisions on profits.

5. They do not have the necessary high energy level and drive to succeed. Their concept of success was to play the right game to climb the
corporate ladder. They were completely comfortable within the structured environment and were not psychologically suited for the sometimes chaotic existence of a franchisee, particularly during the
start-up phase of a franchise.

Corporate employees who left voluntarily fare significantly better during the screening process. But their chances to purchase a franchise still
depend largely on the particular reasons for leaving the corporate world.
Most applicants cite stress as one of the principal reasons, but if stress
came from workload, then this may be an immediate disqualification. A
franchisee will normally work 70 to 90 hours a week during the start-up
phase, and, even after owning the franchise for years, a work week of 60
to 70 hours in some cases is not uncommon. But if stress came from frus-
tration with the lethargic pace of the corporation, then perhaps the applicant is the type of person usually willing to pitch in to get the job done as
quickly as possible.

Voluntary terminees also often say that they had reached an income
plateau and that they want to buy a franchise to make more money. We
believe that anyone who seeks to buy a franchise for that reason alone
would be well advised to thoroughly investigate the net earnings of other
owners within the franchise. In many cases, franchisees coming from the
corporate world make less money and work much longer hours then they
are used to. The opportunity to make more money may be there, but
when and how are the questions to be answered.

Another reason given by both the involuntary and voluntary terminees
is that they want to be their own bosses, that they are tired of having
someone continually looking over their shoulders. Franchisors will take a
careful look at this type of a person, because someone who can't live by
certain rules, who will not take instruction, who cannot suppress personal
inclinations for the good of other team members will not make a good
franchisee. Granted, a franchisee is not subject to much direct supervision and does have direct control over many aspects of the business. But
when you look at a franchise agreement, you will soon see that there are
many things that a franchisee is contractually obligated to do.

As an example of what it can mean to move from corporate executive
to franchisee, here are some words from a former personnel director of a
large financial organization, now the owner of an executive placement
franchise:

It has taken me over two years to become adjusted to my new life. The first thing I missed was not having a support staff or departments that I could turn to for information or help. I had no purchasing department to buy my materials, no personnel department to screen prospective employees, no accounting department to do the bookkeeping. In two months, I went from having an office staff of 23 to having one clerical employee. During my first year, I stuffed mailers, I repaired shelves, I swept the floor, I typed, I did it all and still do most of it. I went from a 10- to 12-hour day once in a while to the same day every day. I never worried about collecting receivables; I do now—every day.

Perhaps most important change was the eventual realization that the business depends solely on me. If I don't make it successful, it will not survive. Although the franchisor can offer help in certain areas, operating the business is entirely on my shoulders.

Interestingly, the trend towards multiunit franchising is having a favorable effect for former corporate managers and executives in the role of franchisees. Those franchisors who encourage multiunit franchisees are just starting to realize the fact that, when franchisees begin to accumulate additional units, their role evolves from that of a hands-on owner/manager to that of a corporate chief executive officer. They must have organizational and communication skills that were not so necessary when they owned a single unit, but that are the ones used in their former corporate positions. Consequently, the transition to multiunit ownership can be much easier. This possibility calls for broader thinking and measurement by the franchisor. The very personality characteristics that made the potential franchisee a rather unsuitable prospect for a single franchise may be of enormous help if that franchisee is to become a multiunit owner. The franchisor must give priority to franchise characteristics that will foster initial success. Yet, if expansion seems likely, executive capabilities may become an important factor in deciding whether an applicant is to be welcomed into the franchise family.

As referred to previously, as an actual or potential franchisee, you may have to modify some of your behavior. Although most psychologists agree that personality is largely genetic, this fact does not preclude the possibility that you, being aware of your own personality profile, can make some adjustments in the way you communicate, the way you manage, and way you arrive at decisions. Throughout the remainder of this book, we will make suggestions about communicating, managing, and making decisions within a franchise network. Consider these suggestions carefully because they convey the opinions of many franchisees who are successful in balancing their business and personal lives.

Try for the Most
Satisfactory Situation

You may have heard the anecdote about the late Ray Kroc, founder of McDonald's, who, when asked to name the three most important elements in a franchise, replied, "Location, location, and location." Location may already be much in your mind. It may now be part of your ambition or dream to start life afresh in a business in a certain preferred place. This could be the Northwest, the Sunbelt, a particular state, or perhaps even a county or town within that state. It might even mean a specific corner on which you have your eye or possibly even control.

Whether this is so, it assuredly is true that you will be more satisfied, motivated, and rewarded in some locations than others. In some locations you could toil for only a meager return, and in others have less wear and tear while making more money. Accordingly, do not leave location to chance. Early in the game, and in thorough discussions with your family and other allies, consider the pros and cons of various locations and decide on the one (plus one or two alternatives) that you would like to have, subject to market study. Then you can make a better focused approach to a franchisor. For example, "I am interested in obtaining a franchise, preferably but not necessarily, in such and such location." With this kind of approach you will have established the fact that location is important to you, but you have not boxed yourself into a corner.

Location should be important to you, not only by the measures of work and income, but also by the measures of compatibility and convenience. You should be able to comfortably relate to the customers you will be serving, and your franchise should be situated reasonably close to your home and other principal interests. If not, you may have to dissipate too much of your life to being a commuter.

With all respects to Ray Kroc (indeed a great man in franchising), there may be other elements more important to your well-being than location. One rightly may be the kind of a franchise. You certainly are going to be happier, and therefore motivated to do better, in some kinds of businesses than others. Accordingly, you should do enough self-searching and discussing with family and advisers before you decide on what will be cheerfully satisfying. Perhaps you will be happy to repetitively purvey some of the world's best pizzas, or be ever patient in helping neighbors who come to your hardware store to select the right screws and bolts. Today there are a great many kinds of franchised goods and services. Isn't it advisable to go for one that you genuinely like, even though it may not bring the greatest amount of money?

Another important element is the franchisor, who will judge you strictly. Have the mettle to apply equal judgments to the franchisor. They operate within certain rules and practices, but nearly all of these guidelines are, or should be, subject to judicious interpretation and application. Do the franchisor's people have both the authority and the flexibility to be thoughtful and considerate? Before you pledge yourself to a franchisor, become acquainted with as many members of the franchisor's organization as you reasonably can. Visit as many franchisees over as wide an area as seems suitable, and ask every kind of question.

If you are not soon invited to a franchisor's office (a fact that itself may be significant), ask for an invitation. And when you are there, note the job levels of persons to whom you are introduced and how you are received by each one. Again, do not be daunted in asking questions. As long as you are serious and respectful, you should be accorded the same courtesy.

It is only sensible and fair that you apply to a franchisor the four measures of dominance, influence, steadiness, and compliance. Is the franchisor sufficiently dominant in the marketplace: Does the name have the reputation, brand recognition, and promotional prominence that you want? At the same time, is their approach to you overbearing? Do you feel confident that their name and products will sufficiently influence customers to come to you? Are they steady and predictable in their programs and requirements, or are they likely to suddenly come forth with some disturbing idea? Are they at the same time foresighted and adventuresome in research and development? And are they likely to have an attitude of consideration and compliance toward you? Dig out the answer to this crucial question: *In those matters that come down to a borderline judgment, is the franchisor inclined to give a break to the franchisee?*

Presumably, without too much difficulty, you and the franchisor will arrive at the point where you believe the joining will be beneficial to one another. But before you dig down for the franchise money, draw back a little and reflect on one more question: Do you feel confident that, if necessary, you could be contented to remain in this business for the rest of your life? To be sure, you may not have to. On the other hand, events may require it. Consider, as an old clergymen once said, "So many events can happen in a marriage, it is best to enter into it with enthusiasm."

The Money You Need

When you first contact a franchisor, a figure to ask for is an estimate of the amount of capital you will require. The franchisor's executives, in turn, probably will be curious to know how much capital you have available. This may well be a figure you cannot give them because of factors still unknown. It may well depend on whether you will have co-owners, investors, lenders, or even all three. This, in turn, depends on the kind of franchise proposal and financial projection that you, with the franchisor's help, put together. Perhaps the best answer you at first can give about your available capital is, "I hope it will be ample, but at this time I need more facts to help me find out."

The franchisor may want a financial statement right away. You must not in any way be evasive but reiterate that some information from them will expedite your being able to obtain capital commitments. For immediate information about your personal financial record, your responsibility, and the alacrity with which you pay obligations, invite the franchisor to obtain a report on you from one of the leading credit agencies. Also be ready to give references if the franchisor asks for them. Make it clear that you are a solid kind of a person. Let the franchisor know that you are aware there can be many items in a franchise requiring capital and that you would appreciate even rough estimates. Here is a typical list:

Initial licensing fees: Most franchisors will charge an initial licensing fee for the use of the trademark, business format, and/or distribution rights. This fee may be due in a lump sum or payable in installments.

Training costs: The cost of the training program may or may not be offered as part of the initial franchise fee. The costs associated with the training, such as transportation, room and board, and incidentals, are almost always the responsibility of the franchisee, and often the franchisor will require that the managers employed by a multiunit franchise must also attend the training program.

Start-up and promotional fee: This also may or may not be included in the initial fee. In some cases, a part of the start-up and promotional cost is included.

Facility leases: A franchisee may be a tenant, a sublessee of the franchisor, or required to purchase a location. In any case, the cost of the lease, the rent, or the purchasing and improvement of the property will be paid by the franchisee.

Improvements or build-outs: Many franchisors require that all franchise locations must contain certain design and/or architectural elements. The cost of these build-outs or improvements will be paid by the franchisee.

Equipment and fixtures: Most franchisors will require that equipment and fixtures be either leased or purchased from them, or they will provide a list of authorized suppliers and vendors. The purchase price or the lease security payments will be a start-up cost for the franchisee.

Inventory: The franchisee usually will be required to buy a basic inventory of products and supplies.

Insurance: The franchise agreement usually will stipulate the type and amount of minimum insurances to be carried and paid for by the franchisee.

Fees and licenses: An assortment of fees and licenses is usually required by local and state governments, such as zoning and building permits, business registration, sales tax permits, and the like. These normally are considered to be costs to the franchisee.

Working capital: Few businesses generate enough cash flow during the early years to sustain themselves. Therefore, a franchisee must allow for the fact that periodic infusions of additional capital will be necessary during the first year and probably longer. The source and availability of these infusions must be considered.

Usually it costs more to buy and get started in a franchise than to get started in an independent business. But the franchise includes, among other things, the benefit of advice and experience in forecasting costs and projecting income. Some franchisors even will assist in financing a franchise, but most will leave the job of getting up the money to you.

It is possible that, after all the capital requirements are totaled, you may see that you have on hand sufficient assets to provide all that is needed. But even if you do so, it might be preferable to attract some co-owners or investors or to borrow some of the money needed. For help in doing any of these things, read the chapters on business structures and financing.

Although there is little doubt that loans are more difficult to obtain during a recessionary period, particularly from banks, franchisees have an advantage over independent business owners because the franchisor's reputation and record can be very influential with a lender. Today, all types of lenders will carefully investigate an applicant's credit history, financial resources, and ability to run a business, but the fact that the applicant is buying into an established and successful franchise network will be a definite advantage when a loan application is evaluated.

Whatever type of lender you go to, realize that usually any lender will require you to provide approximately one-third of the funding for start-up and working capital. For example, if a total of $150,000 is needed, you will have to provide at least $50,000 from your personal savings, property, stocks, or bonds or perhaps funds from co-owners or investors. This ratio of one third will, however, vary with the nature of the franchise. A franchise that requires little ownership of land or buildings will have less value as collateral than a franchise that does own real estate. Anyway, if you are going to require a loan, you should find it encouraging to contemplate the number of sources through which loans may be obtained.

Banks. Recent upheavals in the banking industry have resulted in very tight lending policies. In most cases, 100 percent of a loan must be secured by your own personal assets, including any real property involved in the franchise. A tough requirement? Yes, but still one that you may be able to meet.

The Franchisor. About 30 percent of franchisors will offer some type of financial assistance such as loan guarantees, direct financing, or leasing programs on necessary property and equipment, but again such assistance must usually be secured by your personal assets. Most franchisors will offer assistance in finding a bank or nonbank lending source.

Small Business Administration (SBA). Although the SBA only makes direct loans under certain circumstances, the SBA does guarantee loans made by banks and other nonbank lenders to qualified applicants.

Small Business Lending Companies (SBLC). These are companies licensed by the SBA to make loans to qualified small businesses. They are active lenders in the franchise industry.

Small Business Investment Companies (SBIC). Also licensed by the SBA, SBICs specialize in equity capital and long-term financing. Usually, they will require an equity position and some input into the management process.

Business and Industrial Development Corporations (BIDC). These corporations usually are operated by the states and are underwritten by federal guarantees. Generally, they are limited to long-term financing.

Venture Capitalist Groups. These groups are privately funded and usually are interested only in large expansion projects. They will demand an equity position.

Individual Investors. A growing source of capital because of the current low rates of return on bank certificates of deposits and government investment instruments, individual investors will usually require that the loan be fully collateralized and also will often demand an equity position in the franchise, subject to buyout within a specific time period.

A Couple of Additional Words

Do not move too fast in contacting a potential co-owner, investor, or lender. Plan carefully and present an attractive proposal. And be persistent if necessary. Even when someone turns you down, try to leave the door open so you can come back. Sometimes people change their minds, and on some days people have on hand more funds than on others.

4
Use Foresight
to Prevent
Franchise Conflicts

It has been said again and again that entering into a franchise relationship is like getting married. Each party goes into the relationship with certain expectations, and the chances of success really depend on how much these expectations are met. This is especially true after the honeymoon is over. Often in a marriage both parties have to learn to compromise if they want to stay together, and an essential element in reaching agreements is the ability of both parties to communicate successfully.

A franchise relationship demands the same ability to communicate. Both the franchisee and the franchisor have certain expectations about the other's role, and, when their honeymoon is over, the degree to which they meet each other's expectations will determine the quality of their long-term relationship. The franchise agreement, however, has one more element that a marriage certificate does not: It is a contract for a specific period, and 5, 10, 15, or even 20 years is a long time to work together if one party distrusts the other.

Although some of the common causes for conflict will be discussed later in this chapter, it is advisable to first consider the expectations of the parties to the franchise agreement and explore their origin. Are they valid? How were they communicated? Are they usually the result of the franchisor being overzealous in describing the advantages of the proposed relationship, or the result of a franchisee's lack of maturity and common sense? The exact answers to these questions will probably differ in each situation. Yet it is crucial to the existence of the franchise relationship for both parties to understand that expectations do exist, and, if they are not met satisfactorily, disharmony and distrust will most certainly follow.

Franchisee Expectations

Discussions with current franchisees indicate that before they signed their first franchise agreement, their understanding of the franchising concept ranged from almost none at all to an excellent grasp of the elements of a franchise network. In general, however, most knew a little about franchising from reading generally favorable articles in magazines and newspapers and from talking with friends who were either employed by or who owned franchised businesses. Usually franchisees have previously done business with a franchise but did not know whether the business was part of a company-owned chain or a true franchise until they became interested in owning a similar business. Others, when thinking or inquiring about going into business for themselves, were advised to investigate the franchising concept and therefore bought or borrowed one of the many books available about selecting a franchise. Consequently, they had at least a general understanding of how a franchise differed from an independent small business and what the franchisor typically offered. Franchisees who did even a minimal amount of investigating have tended to be more realistic about the franchising relationship, but many of them still have formed their expectations from the representations made by the franchisor's salespersons.

Even a brief look at the amount and the nature of current litigation between franchisees and franchisors will show that much of it is based on claims of misrepresentation by franchise sales representatives. These claims take many forms and may involve alleged misrepresentation of potential income, support services, territorial rights, and other elements of the agreements. In this type of litigation, the franchisee, rightly or wrongly, made certain assumptions about income projections and other aspects of the franchise relationship based on the literature and the sales presentation of the franchisor. These assumptions were, in the minds of the franchisees, their level of expectations—a level that in many cases was far beyond the intent of the franchisor. The resulting litigation therefore is based on three possibilities:

1. A lack of effective communication between the two parties.
2. A tendency for some franchisees to hold the franchisor responsible for their own lack of ability to manage a business.

3. Exaggeration by a sales representative who is likely to be compensated on a commission basis.

Conversely, some of the litigation involves franchisors who are terminating or refusing to renew the franchise agreement because the franchisee has failed to meet the quality standards or operating procedures of the franchise. Again, this situation involves the failure of one party to meet the expectations of the other; however, in this case the expectations of the franchisor are usually more clearly defined. Since the franchise agreement is invariably prepared by the franchisor's attorney, there is much greater emphasis on what the franchisor expects from the franchisee than what the franchisee can expect from the franchisor. Obviously the goal of the franchisor's attorney is to develop a document that will describe the franchisor's expectations in very explicit terms but will define the franchisor's obligations in only very general terms, thus giving the franchisor the greatest amount of flexibility possible.

Since the franchisee's image of a franchisor can be formed by many different sources of information, those considering franchising or already in it will benefit exploring what a franchisee can *reasonably* expect from a franchisor in a variety of situations. In other words, try to separate fact from fancy. In general, you as a franchisee will expect:

A High Degree of Independence

Most of you have migrated from either the corporate world or some other type of large organization where you were constantly under the thumb of a manager or supervisor and worked within a highly structured work environment. Why you left the organization or corporation is immaterial. The fact that you are anticipating buying a franchise or are already in one indicates a desire to be your own boss—to escape the confinement and limitations imposed by a bureaucracy and be more in charge of your own destiny. Realistically, however, if you are involved with a reputable and successful franchise, you have exchanged one structured organization for another. The success of a franchise depends on the consistent and continuous quality of the product or service provided, rapid and repeat customer response, and name recognition. In fact, franchising is logo- or trademark-driven, and any franchisee who fails to live up to the standards of the franchisor detracts from the credibility of that trademark. For this reason, franchisors will impose product and operational standards and other requirements on their franchisees. Although these will differ from one type of a franchise to another, they will limit your independence. In some cases, they are so restrictive that you actually will be more like a contract employee than an independent business owner. Considering the nature of franchising, it is not reasonable for you to assume that you will be completely your own boss. Realistically, you are a member of a team, whose members are mutually dependent for their success—and yours.

Considerable Aid in Site Selection

Many of you as franchisees will expect either to get considerable assistance in selecting a site or to have the site selected for you by the franchisor in a turnkey situation. Since most of the franchisors state, in their brochures and sales presentations, that they provide this type of assistance, it is reasonable for you to assume that such assistance is available. The questions are, however, how much help will the franchisor *actually* provide, and is their input based on a thorough market study? These questions are particularly relevant when the franchisor demands the right to approve a site before the franchise is granted, a stipulation that is in most franchise agreements. In essence, then, although it is your responsibility to select the site, the franchisor has the right to disapprove your selection.

As noted in the section on market surveys in Chap. 6, most product and service franchises are targeted at fairly narrow markets with specific customer profiles. Since the demographics will vary significantly from one population base to another, a market study for a particular franchise must be very thorough in its identification of the composition of the market area. It is seldom sufficient to say, for example, that a market population of 30,000 for each franchise unit will provide an adequate number of potential customers. The study must also identify the number of people within the market area who match the customer profile. The crucial figure is the number of potential customers, not the total population.

Did the franchisor do a complete market survey of the area surrounding your proposed site before approving or rejecting your selection? Probably not. A complete market research project is very time-consuming and expensive, and few franchisors have either the staff or the resources to do a comprehensive study for each franchised unit. What they may be able to provide is an accurate customer profile and some information about time-distance contours. If you are expanding from one or more units, then you have the opportunity to study your own customer base and make comparisons in terms of age, apparent income levels, ethnic background, family status, sex, household location, and other factors. But in terms of the amount of actual assistance that you can reasonably expect from a franchisor, the fact is that site selection aid will be quite limited from most franchisors. Therefore expect to make most of the demographic studies yourself, particularly if you are expanding.

There is a marked trend toward the leasing of a site by the franchisor who, in turn, will sublease it to the franchisee, or in some cases the franchisor will actually buy the property, build the facility, and then lease it to the franchisee. In these situations, even if the franchisee had originally selected the site, the odds are that the franchisor will do a more thorough preliminary market study.

Territorial Rights

If the franchisor offers an exclusive territory in the franchise agreement, most franchisees will expect that:

1. The franchisor, during the term of the agreement, will not sell another franchise or open a company-owned unit within the boundaries of the assigned territory.

2. The potential customers within the territory come with the rights to the territory.

3. The boundaries of the territory cannot be changed without the written agreement of both parties.

4. The population density of the assigned territory will be sufficient to support the franchise location.

Expectations 1 and 3 are certainly reasonable if the franchisor is offering an exclusive territory. Expectation 2 is neither reasonable nor enforceable. Neither you nor the franchisor can exercise any control over where the customer decides to do business. The granting of a territory, in most instances, refers to the location of the franchise, not to the origin of the customers. Granted, the boundaries of the exclusive territory should conform to the market area's time-distance contours, but if you are fortunate enough to have your contours and your customer base extend beyond your territorial boundaries, the customers from those areas outside your territory can still be yours. Unfortunately, the reverse is more often the case. A franchisor will sell a territory adjacent to yours but will approve a site located just outside your boundaries. Although the new facility is in the adjacent territory, its market area and time-distance contours overlap yours. The result? Your customer base is severely eroded.

Expectation 4 is also, in reality, not reasonable for the same reasons pertaining to selection. Even the most reputable and established franchisors cannot guarantee the demographics of a territory, even though they might have had the staff to make an original market survey. Populations change in character, and that is a risk that you must take when you select your site.

Overlapping market areas are of particular concern to those of you who are expanding by adding additional units. It may be more convenient to keep the units within a certain geographical area, but your entire system can be jeopardized if your units are competing for the same markets. On the reverse side of the coin, some of the most successful franchisees have deliberately overlapped their market areas because of the projected population growth. It is not unusual, in many parts of the country, to see communities double or even triple in less than a decade. We know of a planned community that went from a few hundred persons to 50,000 in three years. Granted, some franchises located in shopping centers during the early growth stages had some lean years, but when the adjacent community became mature, those that had done their marketing homework had, and still have, superior locations.

An Adequate Amount of
Architectural and Construction Aid

A franchisor whose trademark, logo, and image involve a certain architectural style will probably exceed your expectations to the point of allowing practically no flexibility in your own architectural style and construction ideas. Again, this is a matter of consistency. The franchisor wants the customer to recognize the building's exterior and be able to walk into familiar surroundings including the layout, furniture, and interior decor. Consequently, the franchisor will furnish complete building plans and specifications, along with either a list of approved equipment and fixture suppliers or at least strict specifications. Obviously, it will be very difficult for you to control costs.

High Potential Income

People are attracted to franchising for many reasons, but it is safe to say that two reasons top the list. One is the dream of being one's own boss, and the other is the chance to make a lot of money. Some of the newspaper and magazine stories about the amount of money made by franchisees in certain well-established and successful franchises have created a picture of franchise heaven with the streets paved in gold. Consequently, many people go into a franchise with high expectations about the income potential and assume that at least a decent profit is guaranteed. It is also fair to say that many franchise salespersons do not discourage these expectations and may in fact exaggerate the franchise's profit potential.

Is the expectation of high income and guaranteed profit reasonable? Probably not, according to the American Bar Association's Franchise Committee. Their estimates indicate that, within most franchise networks, one-third are making a decent profit, one-third are breaking even, and one-third are losing money. Some franchisees report that it was six months to two years before they saw their first penny of profit, and obviously many have given up after several years of operating in the red. The lack of significant or acceptable profits is one of the reasons for the trend toward multiunit ownership. Many franchisees earning, say, a $20,000 profit from one unit, expect that adding two or three more units will double or triple their overall income. This is an assumption that often proves to be true if the franchisee picks the additional locations carefully and has learned enough about managing the franchise from previous experience.

In general, franchisees recently interviewed had overestimated the amount of profits they expected to be making at this time. Although making a good living, they were still concerned about being able to sustain their current levels because of the general condition of the economy and an ever-increasing amount of competition.

A Comprehensive
Training Program

Most franchisees expect that the franchisor will train them in the operation of their franchise. Almost without exception, the franchisors listed in the *Franchise Opportunities Guide* of the International Franchise Association* provide some type of training. Most provide classes and hands-on experience in the production and/or sales of the product or service, together with information about marketing, purchasing, forms and reports, and other details about the relationship between the franchisee and the franchisor. However, franchisees tend to expect training in all aspects of managing a business, and most franchisors do not meet these expectations.

There are, essentially, two important questions to be answered about the training issue: First, is it reasonable for the franchisee to expect complete management training in addition to operational instruction? Second, are the promotional materials and sales presentations by the franchisors designed to create the impression that management training

*International Franchise Association, 1350 New York Avenue, N.W., Suite 900, Washington, DC 20005

is included? In our opinion, the answer to both questions is no and here's why:

A review of many promotional brochures and advertising pieces provided by franchisors shows that one of the qualifications emphasized as needed by potential franchisees was experience in business and/or management. Usually it was clearly stated that the franchisees are responsible for providing their own management expertise. Also, the training described in most of the franchisor's literature was clearly limited to training in specific operational areas. Since management is a very complex skill, we do not think that it is reasonable to expect it will be taught during the limited time frames of most franchise training programs.

Continuous Update on Markets and New Products

Franchisees' expectations in this area are usually based on their general knowledge of business dynamics and the emphasis that the franchise literature places on continuous market studies and new product or service research and development. Considering the amount of competition in today's business climate, it can be expected that any reputable franchisor will devote some resources to staying on top of market trends and developing new products and services to meet emerging consumer needs. Therefore, persons currently operating franchises have every right to expect this type of continuous support from their franchisors. In fact, many feel that this is a primary justification for the royalty fees.

Continuing Field Support

While franchisees in general feel that field support is one of the main attractions of franchising, there are considerable differences in how field support is defined. Some look at field support as an entitlement to information and help in every area of operations including legal and management consulting, while franchisees with an extreme opposite view look at field support representatives as spies for the franchisor. In fact, the issue of field support is currently one of the most litigated areas in the franchisor-franchisee relationship.

What is a reasonable amount of support to expect from a franchisor? Usually persons just beginning to look into the possibilities of buying a franchise have few advance expectations and their anticipations will be shaped largely by the franchisor's promotional literature and the sales presentation. Realistically, however, you as a franchisee should reasonably expect the amount and type of field support that is set forth in the franchise agreement. Often, if the amount of support promised in the literature is compared with the amount described in the disclosure statement and, again, with the amount and type set forth in the franchise agreement, substantial differences can be seen. Obviously, the only amount and type of support the franchisor is committed to furnish is that stated in the franchise agreement. An additional basis for a reasonable expectation of field support is the number of franchisor staff and field representatives who are capable of providing such support.

We might add, at this point, that most books written on selecting a franchise emphasize the importance of investigating field support and consulting capabilities before making a decision. A franchise that has only an owner, a salesperson, and a secretary/bookkeeper is hardly in a position to offer expert information, but an established, fully staffed franchisor with an effective field support network should be able to provide good advice on a variety of subjects.

Help in Advertising and Promotions

National or regional advertising and promotion is one of the primary appeals of franchising, and understandably a franchisee will expect considerable help in this area. Most franchisors charge, in addition to royalties, a fee based on a percentage of gross sales that is specifically designated for use in an advertising and promotional pool. Since the use of this pool has always been a source of controversy between the franchisor and its franchisees, many franchisors maintain these funds in a separate account, usually managed by a separate board or committee that includes franchisees.

Realistically, the effectiveness of this advertising pool will depend on several factors. First, if the franchise is small and has only a few franchisees, advertising through the mass media will be limited unless the locations of the franchisees are concentrated within a specific area. Second, the amount of advertising will be based on the amount of money available in the pool. Since mass media advertising is extremely expensive, efforts by a small franchise may be limited to providing each franchisee with logos, promotional material, and prepared advertising. Third, advertising created for national or regional markets may not be appropriate for some local areas.

Many franchisees also anticipate that the percentage paid to the pool will be the extent of their advertising or expense. Most franchising agreements, however, indicate that local advertising will be the responsibility of each franchisee, even though the franchisor retains the right of approval of all advertising and promotional material.

As a franchisee, you should expect to spend an additional amount for local advertising. The franchisor's pool advertising may enhance name and logo recognition, reinforcing the franchise's reputation, but it will not tell your potential customers the location of your facility. You also should expect that the advertising pool funds should be spent to support the existing franchisees. They should not be spent to advertise spin-off franchises or, depending on the circumstances, open new areas to sell additional franchises.

You also should expect help in planning and setting up your grand openings. Most franchisors will provide marketing help and promotional banners and materials. Some will assign, as part of the training program, field personnel to guide you through the first week or two after the opening. The amount of the help you can expect usually can be found in the disclosure statement.

Financing or Help in Finding Financing

Generally, it seems franchisees tend to expect some type of financing help from the franchisor but are not aware in advance of the many forms that financing can take. A brief look at the *Franchise Opportunity Guide*'s listing of IFA members will reveal that approximately 50 percent of those members either state that no financial help is available or give no information concerning the possibility. The remaining 50 percent offer help but in a variety of ways. For example:

"Help in obtaining SBA financing if qualified."

"Assistance in locating third party financing."

"Equipment financing available."

"Will assist franchisee in obtaining financing through banks or leasing companies."

"Will assist franchisee in preparation of business plan."

"Direct financing available to qualified franchisees." (Very few offer this last help.)

Knowing that only about half of all franchisors offer any kind of help, you probably would be wise to lower your expectations about this. It is also true that many current multiunit franchises recommend that, if possible, all financing and leases should be obtained outside the franchise network except when the franchisor offers to help with the business plan and loan applications but allows the franchisee to control the source. Their reasoning is that the franchisor will have enough control over your business through the franchise agreement without your giving additional leverage by getting involved with their financial programs.

Bookkeeping and Accounting Assistance

Most franchisors will offer some type of assistance in bookkeeping and accounting, but the type of assistance will range from supplying a few forms to requiring that you participate in a centralized accounting system. Many of these required systems produce statements that are useful to the franchisor because they identify the gross sales, which are the basis of the royalty payments, but they do not provide the type of management information helpful to you in operating your franchise.

All franchisees expect some type of gross sales reporting system that will substantiate royalty and advertising fees, but beyond those reports few franchisees expect any kind of accounting control by the franchisor. Consequently, many are astonished when they are asked to participate in some type of controlled accounting program offered by the franchisor.

Before enrolling in one of the programs, you should consider several points. First, an accounting package designed by your own accountant will fit your needs better than a boiler plate program offered by the franchisor. Second, an accounting program should do more for you than track income and expense, and provide periodic statements. It should produce analytical management data. Few stereotyped accounting packages do so. Third, financial information is only valuable when it is received in time to take corrective action if necessary. Financial statements received six months after the close of a fiscal period are useless. Yet this extreme tardiness is a common complaint among franchisees who have participated in franchisor programs.

Certainly, there are other areas in which franchisees expect support from their franchisors and these will depend on the type of franchise. It is important that these expectations be communicated to the franchisor so that both parties can clarify what reasonably can be expected from each other. This is particularly true in relationships involving the sale of products or services by the franchisor to the franchisee. A franchisee rightly should have strong feelings about the pricing of these products and services and about their possible availability to competitors.

Franchisor Expectations

Most franchisor expectations are outlined in the disclosure document and the franchise agreement in great detail. In some areas, however, words in a contract cannot express the true level of a franchisor's expectations. Some examples follow.

Trademark and Logo

Established and reputable franchisors usually have invested great effort and considerable money to create the images that are represented by their trademarks and logos. The trademark and logo are, in essence, franchisor's most important and effective marketing tools because they, in turn, create the expectation by the customer that the product and service will be consistently good regardless of location. When the franchisor empowers the franchisee by granting use of the highly prized emblem, the franchisor expects that the franchisee will respect what the mark represents. In fact, if you, as a franchisee, have allied with a franchisor who does not almost fanatically guard the image of the trademark and logo, you may have some cause to worry.

Quality Control

This is probably the most important issue in the franchisor-franchisee relationship because the ability of everyone in the system to deliver high-quality products and services that are fully consistent with the standards of the franchisor is what franchising is all about. Most franchises are critically dependent on repeat customers because of the nature of its products or services and its limited market areas; consequently, the franchisor needs to insist on very tight quality control procedures and standards. Yet often franchisees resent these efforts and see them as overbearing and excessive. This entire issue of quality control again centers around the role of franchisees and their ability and willingness to act as members of a team rather than maverick entrepreneurs.

The Operations Manual

Franchisors regard their operations manual as a blueprint for your success as one of their franchisees. Most consider the manual as a confidential document, and in fact many franchise agreements specifically state that the manual is only loaned to the franchisee and is to be returned if the agreement is terminated. Agreements also will state that disclosure of information in the operations manual is prohibited and such disclosure is grounds for terminating the agreement.

An effective manual will describe the policies and procedures stipulated by the franchisor to be used in operating the franchise. It may include such requirements as hours that the business is to remain open, dress standards, recipes, product specifications, and descriptions of the methods of providing various types of service. It sets forth the franchisor's definition of the quality and service standards to be maintained during the operation of the business and is the principal tool for ensuring that all franchisees deliver their products or services in a consistent manner. The operations manual is so crucial to the continued existence of a franchise that many franchisors will include it as part of the franchise agreement.

Franchisors expect the franchisees to strictly maintain the confidentiality aspects of the operations manual, as much for their good as for the franchisor's. If much of the information in the manual were to be disclosed to a competitor, the damage would be harmful to both franchisors and franchisees.

As noted by Marcia Bestor (one of the franchisees profiled in Chap. 1), the franchise relationship is like a recipe in which both the franchisor and franchisee must furnish some of the ingredients. If all the ingredients are not included, the recipe will fail. As she stressed, adequate communication between the two parties is one of those essential ingredients because seldom in a long-term relationship do conflicts not appear. Good faith in dealing with these conflicts is the only way to preserve a successful franchise.

In the following paragraphs we discuss some of the more common sources of conflict and dissatisfaction in the franchisor-franchisee relationship. By being aware of these you can strive to avoid these situations, either by modifying the original agreement before making a commitment or by negotiating changes in the existing documents.

Common Areas of Conflict Between Franchisees and Franchisors

The American Arbitration Association has noted a substantial increase in the number of disputes between franchisors and franchisees, and certainly there has been a corresponding increase in the number of similar disputes being decided in the courts. Although some of these increases can be attributed to a general increase in the size of the franchise industry and also to the general litigious trend in our society, there is little doubt that most of these cases involve the increased complexity of the franchise relationship and the effects of the economy on the financial status of both parties. Some of the most common causes of conflict follow.

Estimates of Income and Expense

Although claims of income or profit are prohibited by the FTC or UFOC regulations unless the claim is substantiated by disclosing the basis of such estimates, the estimates of typical expense are far more difficult to control. For example, an estimate of rental expense, even if expressed in ranges, may be appropriate for one section of the country but not for another. Labor cost estimates may also be similarly inaccurate, again because labor rates differ significantly from one labor market to another. The question always arises, when actual expenses are in excess of the projections, whether these estimates were made in an attempt to defraud or were made in good faith. It is incumbent on any franchisee to verify these estimates of expense for the area in which a franchise is to be located.

The Diversification of Products and Services

Franchisees commonly expect that the franchisor will continue to research consumer markets and develop products or services to meet emerging consumer needs. Conflict occurs when these new products and services are not compatible with the franchisee's current market profile or require additional expenses that the franchisee cannot hope to recoup through increased sales. The more sophisticated franchisors are attempting to avoid this type of problem by involving the franchisees or a franchisee association in product or service development.

Experimentation with Alternative Retailing Methods

Many franchisors will experiment with various retailing channels to increase product or service awareness and market presence. For example, an ice cream shop franchisor may begin to wholesale its product to supermarkets. Franchisees will probably view this as a threat to their sales when one of the supermarkets is within the franchisee's market area, and, if the franchise agreement grants an exclusive territory and prohibits the sale of additional franchises within that area, will consider use of alternative retail sales methods to be a breach of the franchise agreement. The franchisor's position will be that the exclusive territory agreement refers only to the individual shops and does not prohibit alternative retail distribution methods. Therefore, the limitations on both parties should be specifically set forth in the franchise agreement.

Advertising Strategies

The strategies used by the franchisor in advertising at the local regional and national levels are potentially a constant source of conflict between the two parties in a franchise agreement. Often, because of localized competition, the franchisor will spend a disproportionate amount of advertising dollars in a specific area or region. Franchisees outside that area will feel that such targeted spending is an improper use of their contributions to the pool. Also, as already noted, the same type of complaint may arise when the franchisor uses advertising pool funds to open new territories for the sale of their franchises. In addition, in numerous instances franchisors have diverted funds from the advertising pool to cover their own operational costs. Since such a move is clearly contrary to the expectations of the franchisees, these situations usually end up in arbitration or the courts.

Franchisor Rights to Modify
the Franchise System

It is not unusual for a franchisor to modify or fine-tune certain elements of a franchise system. In fact, efficient management of the franchise by the franchisor should be expected by the franchisees. However, the amount of discretion the franchisor has in modifying the system and whether this discretion is exercised in a proper way are often questioned by franchisees. This is particularly true if the modification substantially alters the procedures outlined in the operations manual and/or adversely affects the franchisee's costs or sales. If the operations manual is part of, or an addendum to, the franchise agreement, then the basis for contractual disputes may exist. Realistically, this issue involves the impact of the implied covenant of good faith and fair dealings and the standards of care imposed on a franchisor when making decisions affecting the franchise system.

Exclusive Territories

Because territorial boundaries have long been a source of conflict in franchise arrangements, many franchisors have increasingly changed their policies and currently do not grant exclusive territories. Franchisees, in turn, have become increasingly concerned about market saturation and are reluctant to depend on the franchisor's judgment about how many potential customers there are within a given area. If you, as a franchisee, have already signed a nonexclusive territory agreement, your next step may be to attempt to negotiate a separate agreement with the franchisor giving you first option on any franchise offered by them in or adjacent to your market area.

Promotional Sales

Often, particularly in the fast food industry, the franchisor will run promotional sales in which the prices of some items are substantially lowered. Although this may result in an increase in traffic and sales in some locations, the items on sale are less profitable or may even be loss leaders, and will affect sales of other items sold at normal gross profit margins. The overall increase in sales will benefit the franchisor because their income is royalty-based, but the franchisee's net profits may be substantially decreased. These promotions are usually run because of increased competition from other franchises or businesses, but in many instances certain franchisees do not have the same level of competition in their market. Consequently, they are forced to lower prices unnecessarily although their volume of traffic remains about the same. Sometimes, it is possible for franchisees to negotiate a letter of agreement with the franchisor allowing individual owners the choice of whether to offer merchandise or services at a discount. However, the chance of negotiating such an arrangement will be considerably lessened if the franchise is well established and very successful.

Fee Modifications

Most franchise agreements will provide for adjustments in the fees charged by franchisors. These adjustments most often involve contributions to the advertising pool or various charges for support services, such as consulting fees or accounting charges. Once the agreement is signed, these adjustments can only be negotiated when they occur. Some franchisors hold that these adjustments are nonnegotiable while others will negotiate on a case-by-case basis. Adjustment may be most readily made on optional services such as accounting or consulting fees. If these fees seem unreasonable, there may be alternative sources for advice, particularly if the problem is general in nature rather then one involving specific aspects of franchise operations. For example, an accounting question may be addressed to your own accountant rather than to a member of the franchisor's staff.

Buy-Back Clauses

Most franchise agreements outline the method and the basis for evaluating the worth of a franchise unit should the franchisor, because of a default in the agreement, be in a position to buy it back. If the agreement states that the sale price would be based on book value, there is a probability that there will be a serious conflict between the franchisee and the franchisor. Depending on the age of the franchisee's unit, much of the equipment could be completely depreciated on the books and yet still have considerable market value. Also, the book value would not allow for good will, nor would it take into consideration the value based on return on investment. The principal avenue open to the franchisee is to negotiate a more equitable method of determining the market value before the need for such an appraisal occurs.

The Role of the Franchisee Association

As the general knowledge, education, and net worth of franchisees continue to increase, franchisors are increasingly forced to either confront or deal with associations formed by the franchisees. Although a few of the more sophisticated franchisors have welcomed or even fostered the organization of a franchisee association, others have fought it every step of the way, and membership in the association has become a major source of conflict between the two parties. Franchisors who have sincerely welcomed the association of the franchisees have found that there are considerably fewer disputes and that the associations' input is a very valuable tool for evaluating new products, services, and marketing ideas. One major franchisor holds a monthly teleconference involving all their franchisees, region by region, to discuss common problems and successes. Several of these franchisees have said that the opportunity for them to get their minds together periodically is one of the most valuable elements of the franchisor's support.

Usually, franchise agreements do not specifically address the existence and role of a franchisee association. If you, as a franchisee, believe that such an association might benefit all of you, it is best to obtain an indication of the amount of cooperation you can expect from the franchisor. If the franchisor seems clearly opposed to the idea, it may be best to re-examine the reasons for organizing the association. If the organization is motivated by the desire to benefit everyone through closer cooperation, then it is worth the effort to try to sell the advantages to the franchisor. If the effort is motivated by the desire to obtain greater leverage against the franchisor, then perhaps it is best to explore other options. A continued adversarial relationship between franchisors and franchisees can do nothing but detract from the overall image and effectiveness of the franchise.

Lack of Continued Support

When a franchisee notices a significant decrease in the level of support from the franchisor, it is highly probable that either there are financial problems in the background or the franchisor is diverting attention to other matters. In either case, this is a portent of potential conflict and, under these circumstances, it is time for you and your advisory team to discuss your options should the franchisor fail or attempt to sell the franchise.

Sales Quotas

Some franchisors, particularly in the automotive aftermarket, set periodic sales quotas that must be met by the franchisee as a requirement to retain the franchise. Obviously, when a franchisee fails to make the quota, the possibility of a serious conflict arises. Since changes in the local economy or demographics could be the reason for a drop in sales, there should be an appeal process or some other mechanism to adjust sales quotas when conditions warrant this action. It is best if this adjustment mechanism is stated in the original franchise agreement; however, it may be possible to negotiate an addendum to an existing agreement clarifying the conditions under which the franchisor can cancel the agreement, and adding an appeals or optional process. The most important element of this modification of the agreement is the ability to avoid cancelation when the conditions causing the default are beyond the control of the franchisee.

Quality Control Issues

Despite the fact that the consistency of products or services and the condition of the facilities form the basic attractions of franchising, the extent to which a franchisor may control these products and services has always been a source of conflict between the two parties to the agreement. Federal courts have limited the franchisor's ability to require that the franchisee buy products, supplies, and equipment from them, but it is generally accepted that the franchisor may either provide a list of approved vendors or require that any products, supplies, or equipment purchased by the franchisee meet very tight specifications. Conflict usually arises when the franchisee locates a source that is less expensive than the one provided by the franchisor. A possible solution to this problem lies in a provision in the franchise agreement, or in a subsequent letter of agreement, that allows a franchisee to submit alternative sources of supply to the franchisor for quality checks. It is expected that, if the product meets the specifications, the franchisor will act in good faith and approve the purchase.

Sales Volume Versus Profits

Although it may appear that the franchisor and the franchisee have the same high sales volume goals, often the true goals are quite different. The franchisor wants high sales volume regardless of the selling price because royalty income is usually based on a percentage of gross sales. The franchisee is more concerned with net profit, and there are at least three circumstances in which a larger sales volume may not translate into a higher net. First, as stated in the discussion of break-even points (Chap. 11), higher sales often require an increase in semifixed costs (for example, labor), which in turn increases the break-even point. At some point in the sales curve the increase in the BEP is greater than the increase in gross profits, resulting in an actual decrease in net profits. Second, franchisor promotions that involve price discounts on certain products or services may increase traffic and sales volume, but the discounts may be so deep that they eliminate any margin for profit and also cut into the sales of other items with normal price margins. Third, promotions involving coupons that are not redeemable through the manufacturer may increase sales, but, since the franchisee must absorb the cost of the coupons, their use often decreases net profit. The franchisor, however, continues to collect royalties on the gross sales with no credit given for coupons.

Since none of us has a crystal ball, it is impossible to predict all the areas in which a potential conflict may develop between you and your franchisor. The possibility of conflicts can be greatly reduced, however, if the lines of communication are kept open and both of you are willing to negotiate in good faith. Often, the need for negotiation is caused by changing conditions in the marketplace or the economy, changes that are beyond the ability of either party to foresee or control. Survival then become a matter of being able to adapt to these changing conditions as rapidly as possible.

Some franchisors will be more disposed than others to flexibly cooperate with franchisees who are faced with changing conditions, emergencies, and crises. Therefore, it is advisable to make a patient comparison of this inclination before signing any franchise agreement.

5
Understand the UFOC and Franchise Agreement

During the 1960s and 1970s, franchising was often touted as the easy way to get rich. Numerous magazine and newspaper editors published glowing articles and stories about the success of franchisees who got in on the ground floor of some of the rapidly expanding franchises, and also about the accumulating wealth of the franchisors. These stories began to attract many business people who saw franchising as a way to expand their customer base without having to invest a tremendous amount of capital for new facilities and labor. Unfortunately, the stories also attracted con artists and others without business ethics who saw franchising as a way to make a quick buck, and soon editors were writing about the people who were cheated out of their life savings.

In response to the growing number of complaints from those who felt exploited, the federal government and some of the states drafted regulations concerning the offering and sale of franchises. In 1979 the Federal Trade Commission (FTC), after seven years of hearings and debate, adopted trade regulation Rule 436, a regulation to govern the amount of information that a franchisor must disclose to a potential franchisee before any sale can be consummated. At this writing, 15 states have also adopted more demanding regulations based generally on a format developed by the Midwest Securities Commissioners Association in 1975. Named the Uniform Franchise Offering Circular (UFOC), this format required a more detailed disclosure than the Rule 436.

The states that have adopted some variation of the UFOC are:

California	North Dakota
Hawaii	Oregon
Illinois	Rhode Island
Indiana	South Dakota
Maryland	Virginia
Michigan	Washington
Minnesota	Wisconsin
New York	

In addition, several other states have adopted some type of business opportunity laws designed to protect the purchasers of franchises and to regulate the offering of new franchise companies whose trademarks are not yet federally registered.

As was the case with the Fair Labor Standards Act and the Federal Unemployment Tax Act, Rule 436, as adopted by the Federal Trade Commission, allows states to establish their own rules as long as they are substantially equivalent to FTC Rule 436.

Basically, FTC Rule 436 requires that a franchisor offering a franchise in the United States must provide a prospective franchisee with a circular disclosing information about the franchisor and to do so within a certain time period before the franchisee is required to sign a franchise agreement. The circular must provide information concerning 20 areas of the franchise's ownership and operations. (A summary of Rule 436 can be found in the appendix at the end of the book.)

Rule 436 covers either of two types of continuing commercial relationships defined as a "Franchise."

The first type, called a *Package and Product Franchise,* has three characteristics:

1. The franchisee sells goods or services that meet the franchisor's quality standards (in cases where the franchisee operates under the franchisor's trademark, service mark, trade name, advertising, or other commercial symbol designating the franchisor or that are identified by the franchisor's mark).

2. The franchisor exercises significant control over, or gives the franchisee significant assistance in, the franchisee's method of operation.

3. The franchisee is required to make a payment of $500 or more to the franchisor or a person affiliated with the franchisor at any time before or within six months after the business opens.

The second type, called *A Business Opportunity Venture*, also has three characteristics:

1. The franchisee sells goods or services that are supplied by the franchisor or a person affiliated with the franchisor.

2. The franchisor assists the franchisee in any way with respect to securing accounts for the franchisee, or securing locations or sites for vending machines or rack displays, or providing the services of a person to do either.

3. The franchisee is required to make a payment of $500 or more to the franchisor at any time before or within six months after the business opens.

The Rule exempts (1) fractional franchises and (2) leased department arrangements, and purely verbal agreements. The Rule excludes (1) relationships between employer/employees and among general business partners, (2) membership in retailer-owned cooperatives, (3) certification and testing services, and (4) single trademark licenses.

Rule 436 also requires that:

> The information in the disclosure statement must be current as of the completion of the franchisor's most recent fiscal period. In addition, a revision of the document must be prepared quarterly whenever there has been a material change in the information contained in the document. The disclosure document must be given to a prospective franchisee at the earlier of either (1) the prospectives franchisee's first personal meeting with the franchisor or (2) ten days prior to the execution of a contract or payment of money relating to the franchise relationship. In addition to the document the franchisee must receive a copy of all agreements which he will be asked to sign.

The Federal Trade Commission, in Rule 436, specifically allows states to use the UFOC adopted by the Midwest Securities Commissioners Association plus any modifications thereof that do not diminish the protection accorded to the prospective franchisee, which may be made by a state in which such registration has been made effective. However, four provisions of the Rule must control even if the state has adopted the UFOC format: (1) the persons required to make disclosure, (2) the transactions requiring disclosure, (3) the timing of the disclosure, and (4) the types of documents to be given to the prospective franchisees.

Although franchisors in those states not requiring UFOCs may abide by the requirements of the FTC rule, which may be less stringent, most franchisors will use the UFOC format because, with minor variations, it is acceptable nationwide. We will limit our discussion about disclosure rules to the UFOC because it is more commonly used.

As a franchisee, or at least as a potential franchisee, you should make yourself thoroughly familiar with the offering circular provided by your franchisor. Even though much of the information contained in the circular is repeated or confirmed in the franchise agreement, there is considerable information that is not. If, however, material changes in the franchisor's operations change or contradict the original information furnished you, the franchisor is required to revise the document.

Knowledge about the UFOC requirements is also helpful to you because it is not uncommon for a franchisor to claim that a particular clause in the franchise agreement is required by the FTC and is therefore not negotiable. While it is true that Rule 436 or the UFOC may require that a certain issue must be addressed in the agreement, the rule does not necessarily establish the terms. Consequently, the terms are open to negotiations in many areas.

Be aware also that the information in the UFOC or the disclosure circular has not been checked for accuracy by the FTC or any other governmental agency. In fact, the FTC requires that a statement declaring that the information has not been verified must be included in the disclosure statement.

Since each state may have rules and regulations over and above the basic FTC rule or UFOC requirements, we strongly suggest that you ask an attorney, who is knowledgeable in your local franchise law, to provide you with the complete requirements for your area. Generally, the UFOC will require the following disclosures:

The Franchisor and any Predecessors. The background of the franchisor and any predecessors should be disclosed, including corporate and trade names, organizational structure, history of the corporation, prior business experience and affiliated businesses, dates of incorporation, and the address of the principal headquarters. This section should also include a description of the franchise to be operated by the franchisee.

Identity and Business Experience of Persons Affiliated with the Franchisor Including Franchise Brokers. The identity of each principal—that is, owner, director, trustee, general partner, officer, manager, and department head—having significant responsibilities in the operation of the franchisor's business or in support services provided to the franchisees must be disclosed. The employment or activity history of each for the past five years must also be disclosed. Generally, marketing representatives are included, as well as franchise brokers authorized to represent the franchise.

Litigation. Litigation, administrative hearings, or arbitration affecting or involving the franchisor, officers, directors, or marketing or sales representatives must be disclosed if the allegations or proceedings would concern the potential franchisee. Details of each action, including its current status, must be presented.

Bankruptcy. The franchisor must disclosure whether it or any of its officers, general partners, or predecessors have filed for bankruptcy or reorganized due to insolvency during the past 15 years. If so, details concerning each action must be disclosed.

Franchisee's Initial Franchise Fee and/or Other Initial Payment. The amount of the initial fees, any other initial payments, and the terms of such payments and fees must be disclosed. Generally, if the franchisor has any different fee or payment schedules for multiple-unit or addition unit purchases, such schedules must also be included. Also required is information concerning any deposits and whether the fees and/or payments are refundable in whole or in part. Often, this section will also include a time limitation within which the franchise must be utilized. If not, the franchisor should be questioned about this issue. The UFOC also requires that the franchisor disclose the disposition of these fees and payments.

Other Fees. All other fees must be disclosed including royalties, and those for advertising pools, fees audits, transfers, assignments, consulting, training, minimum insurance requirements, rent (if applicable), and mandatory or optional equipment leases. Details including amounts, estimates, and terms must also be disclosed.

Franchisee's Estimated Initial Investment. All other expenses that a franchisee may expect to incur must be either stated or estimated in this section. These expenses may include, but are not limited to, architectural and design costs, construction, real estate, equipment, fixtures, licensing and permits, working capital, and support service fees. The information should include to whom the payment is made, under what terms, and what portion, if any, is refundable.

Obligation of the Franchisee to Purchase or Lease from Designated Sources. Any contractual requirement by the franchisor that the franchisee is required to purchase goods, services, supplies, equipment, fixtures, or insurance relating to the opening or the operation of the franchise from a source designated by the franchisor must be fully disclosed. Also any requirement to lease facilities, fixtures, and/or equipment from a designated source. The disclosure must include terms of any such purchase or lease, along with any benefit or direct or indirect income derived by the franchisor from these required transactions.

Obligations of Franchisee to Purchase or Lease in Accordance with Specifications or from Approved Suppliers. The specifications for purchases do not have to be included in the disclosure statement, but the fact that the franchisor will require the franchisee to purchase or lease either from preapproved suppliers or according to franchisor specifications must be disclosed. Usually, other details such as pricing, discounts, and the procedures to have suppliers approved by the franchisor are also included in the statement. The actual specifications are usually described in the operating manual. Franchisors must also disclose if they receive income from the approved suppliers as the result of purchases by franchisees.

Financing Arrangement. A complete description of the terms and conditions of any financing programs offered either by the franchisor or by its designates or affiliates must be disclosed in this section. These arrangements may include, but are not limited to, lines of credit, equipment or facility leases, direct or indirect debt financing, or credit for inventory.

Obligations of the Franchisor; Other Supervision, Assistance or Services. This section describes the initial and continous services and support provided by the franchisor. Usually, the description of services offered is divided into two parts: first, those obligations outlined in the franchise agreement and, second, those obligations that may, at the discretion of the franchisor, be offered to the franchisee. Those obligations required by the franchise agreement must be referenced to the appropriate paragraph in the agreement. Examples of the types of services and support that may be offered are:

Help in site selection	Market research
Architectural plans	Engineering plans
Construction supervision	Permits
Training	Consulting services
Advertising materials	Operating manuals
Suppliers' names	Pool advertising
New product testing	Field supervision
Preopening promotion	Equipment specifications
Product specifications	Contract negotiations
Computer services	Inventory systems

If training is offered or required, the training program must be described in reasonable detail including location, duration, cirriculum, and the qualifications of the staff.

Territorial Rights. If the franchisee is granted exclusive territorial rights, the territory and the rights must be fully described in this section. Any conditions that must be met by the franchisee to retain these rights must be disclosed, along with the rights of the franchisor, if any, to adjust this territory after the franchisee has signed the agreement. If franchisor-owned stores are excluded from the granting of territorial rights, this fact must be disclosed. It should be noted that granting of territorial rights refers to the location of the franchise unit, not to the location of the customers.

Trademarks, Service Marks, Trade Names, Logotypes, and Commercial Symbols. The franchisor must disclose the extent of legal protection obtained for its trademarks, service marks, trade names, logotypes, and commercial symbols, including information concerning the registration of these marks with the United States Patent and Trademark Office and also including a list of states and countries in which the marks are registered. Any limitations imposed on the franchisee by the franchisor in the use of these marks must be disclosed.

Patents and Copyrights. The franchisor must disclose any patents and copyrights that are or may be involved in the operation of the franchise.

Obligation of the Franchisee to Participate in the Operation of the Franchise Business. The question as to whether the franchisor will require the active participation of the franchisee in the operation of the franchise must be answered in this section. If active participation is required, then the terms or conditions of such participation must be defined. Some franchisors will require that, if the franchisee hires managers, the managers must attend the franchisor training program. Such requirements must be disclosed.

Restrictions on Goods and Services Offered by the Franchisee. Any requirement that limits or establishes minimums on the amount of goods or services the franchisee may offer must be disclosed in this section. Typically, information concerning the introduction of new products or services is also disclosed.

Renewal, Termination, Repurchase, Modification and Assignment of the Franchise Agreement, and Related Information. This section is, by far, the longest and the most complex of the franchise disclosure statement. It outlines the franchisor's requirements and the franchisee's options when a franchise is to be renewed, terminated, repurchased, modified, or assigned. Because it usually addresses such potential problems as the rights of heirs on the death of a franchisee, and assignment of the rights of the franchisee under other circumstances, this part of the disclosure statement should be very carefully reviewed by an attorney familiar with the franchisee's personal status, particularly if the franchise is family-owned. The requirements of the franchisor can have considerable impact on the business structure of the franchisee and on his or her estate planning.

This section should cover the definitions of default, the time limitations, the conditions under which the franchisor may terminate the agreement and the posttermination obligations of the franchisee. The franchisor's right of first refusal to purchase the franchise and the limits or conditions imposed on the assignment or transfer, sale, lease, or sublease of the franchise by the franchisee must be disclosed. The franchisor must disclose the procedures involved in modification of the agreement by either the franchisor or the franchisee.

Arrangements with Public Figures. If the franchisor has provided any compensation or benefit to a public figure in return for an endorsement, the fact must be disclosed. If the public figure is involved in the ownership or the management of the franchise, this fact also must be included. If the franchisor limits or conditions the right of the franchisee to use endorsement from local public figures, this fact must be disclosed.

Actual, Average, Projected or Forecasted Franchise Sales, Profits, or Earnings. If the franchisor makes a claim or representation of sales, profits, or earnings, then the franchisor must provide a description of the factual basis for the claim and an overview of the material assumptions of the claim. Those franchisors who decline to provide actual, average, projected, or forecasted franchise sales, profits, or earning must include a statement or disclaimer about this fact.

Information Concerning Franchises of the Franchisor. The franchisor must provide a summary of franchises sold, the number actually operating, the number of agreements signed but not in operation, and the number of company-owned units. A list of the franchisees, including names, addresses, and telephone numbers, is required. Also required is information on the number of franchisees terminated or not renewed, and each cause for termination or nonrenewal for the past three years.

Financial Statements. A complete set of financial statements must be included as addenda or exhibits to the disclosure document. In most registration states, the statements must be audited and prepared within certain time limits before the documents are submitted to the state. In some states, new franchisors or those with weak financial statements may have to satisfy additional requirements.

Franchise Agreement and Related Documents. Copies of every document that the franchisee is required to sign must be enclosed as exhibits. This section is extremely important because most franchisors have a variety of agreements to be used under different ownership circumstances, or for optional services such as sign leases or inventory purchase arrangements. In most cases, these agreements will be far more detailed than described in the disclosure statement.

As already noted, even though the disclosure statement has been filed either with a state registration office or the FTC, neither of these agencies will check the statement for accuracy. Usually the statements are accepted at face value until complaints or evidence of irregularities prompt an investigation.

The Franchise Agreement and Related Documents

The franchise agreement is the basic contract governing the relationship between the franchisee and the franchisor. This agreement should confirm in detail the statements made in the disclosure document, and any differences should brought to the attention of your attorney and the franchisor before any ongoing commitment is made. The related documents are usually limited to clarifying the liability and security involved under various business structures, and the contracts or agreements concerning required or optional services such as accounting or equipment leases. Other related documents may be required if, during the course of future operations, circumstances change and the franchisee wishes to assign the agreement to another party or the territory is adjusted.

During the initial meetings between the franchisor and the franchisee, the question always arises as to what elements of the franchise agreement are negotiable. As noted, the representative of the franchisor would usually like the franchisee to believe that the agreement is nonnegotiable because of state or federal regulations. In some states, the possibility and the extent of possible negotiations are less than in other states, because the regulations require much more detailed disclosure statements, and consequently any material change negotiated by the franchisee may result in a required filing of a modified disclosure statement by the franchisor. In other states, the required elements of the disclosure statement and the material change rules may be sufficiently general to allow considerable latitude in negotiations. This fact alone reemphasizes the need to have an experienced franchise attorney on your side.

Realistically, negotiating a franchise agreement is like negotiating any other contract: It is largely a matter of who has more leverage. A new franchisee will be in a better position with a young franchise than one that is firmly established with a solid record of success. A franchisee who is currently operating one or more successful franchises and who wishes to obtain additional territory and units will also be in a better negotiating position. Under any circumstances, however, the franchisee should begin the relationship with a full understanding of the legal requirements of the state in which the franchise is to be located.

Although franchise agreements will differ in content and format from state to state and from industry to industry, most will contain the following elements.

The Recital. The recital establishes the purpose and some of the basic assumptions underlying the proposed relationship between the franchisor and the franchisee. Some examples of the issues that may be addressed are:

1. The type of business.
2. The intent of the franchisor in granting franchises.

3. The need for confidentiality.

4. The extent to which the franchisor plans to develop and grant franchises.

5. Assumptions about why the franchisee wishes to obtain franchise.

6. The consideration involved in obtaining a franchisee.

7. Acknowledgment by the franchisee of receipt of the franchisee agreement within the time specified by state regulation.

8. Disclaimer of projections of sales, income, or profits by any representative of the franchisor (if applicable).

9. A statement by the franchisee that he or she understands that the franchisor does not guarantee that the franchise will be profitable or will not fail.

10. A statement to the effect that the franchisee understands that he or she will operate the franchise in accordance with the business format and quality control requirements established by the franchisor.

Initial Fees. The initial fees are itemized, including payments, terms, and any variation in fees based on multiple-unit purchases. The conditions or limitations on refunds, if any, should be covered in detail. Usually, there is a statement indicating that the costs of transportation, lodging, and meals for franchisee personnel when attending training sessions and required seminars are the responsibility of the franchisee.

Ongoing Fees. Those fees charged on an ongoing basis, such as royalties, advertising fees, accounting, and other regularly assessed charges, should be fully described including the basis for such charges and the percentages. Any charges based on gross sales should be exclusive of sales or excise taxes and returns. The dates on which these fees are due are usually included in this section.

Grants by the Franchisor. The rights granted to the franchisee should be fully explained. These grants may include, but are not limited to, access to the franchisor's business format and methods, formulas, recipes, operational manuals, trademarks, new product information, market data, new developments and techniques, business forms, and knowledge. Renewal rights and fees may also be addressed in this section.

Term of the Agreement. The term of the initial agreement and renewal periods are described, together with the notice required if the franchisee wishes to renew. While the laws governing disclosure statements require that the term of the agreement be disclosed, they do not establish any minimum or maximum terms.

Services Furnished by the Franchisor. The services that the franchisor is obligated to furnish should be described in detail, including any conditions or limitations. These services may include training, operations consultation and field services, access to home office staff for advice, architectural and construction consultation, product and equipment specifications, and promotional and advertising assistance. This section may also list services that the franchisor may provide, but is not obligated to, under the terms of the agreement.

In some cases, this section will include the procedure to follow if, in the opinion of the franchisee, the franchisor has failed to meet its obligations. Such disputes may be required to go to arbitration.

Agreements by the Franchisee. This section of the agreement is usually lengthy and should be reviewed with great care by franchisees and their attorneys. The items usually contained in the franchisee agreement section are:

1. The time period allowed between the signing of the agreement and the opening of business and the procedures for requesting extensions.

2. The procedures for site selection, including the approval process by the franchisor. If applicable, this section will also outline architectural and construction requirements and specifications, including both external and internal design features.

3. An agreement by the franchisee to operate the business in accordance with federal, state, and local laws and ordinances and to arrange for all necessary fees and licenses, usually at the franchisee's expense. In many cases, the franchisor's operating manual is made an addendum to the agreement, and in this section, the franchisee agrees to abide by the manual and any subsequent changes.

4. Limitations or restrictions governing the sale of any product or service not authorized or approved by the franchisor.

5. Assigning to the franchisee all costs for constructing and operating the facility.

6. Limitations or requirements of product specifications, sources of supply for products and equipment, and methods for obtaining approval for alternative products and equipment, if any.

7. General operating procedures including hours or operation, dress or uniform requirements, sanitary and appearance standards for the facility, customer service standards, and credit practices, if applicable.

8. Insurance, records and financial reporting requirements, including the type and minimum amounts of insurance, the types of records to be kept, the minimum period of their retention, and the types of financial reports that must be submitted to the franchisor and by what dates. As noted, the minimum insurance requirements may be enough to cover the franchisor's interest but may not be enough to protect the franchisee or the financing institution.

9. Noncompetitive clauses, such as the limitation on operating other businesses in competition with the franchise line of business, unless it is another licensed unit in the same franchise.

10. Requirement to allow representatives of the franchisor to enter the franchisee's place of business during regular business hours to inspect and audit business operations. This usually includes the procedures and the time limits allowed the franchisee to cure defaults.

11. Options open to the franchisor in the event that royalties, advertising fees, and other charges based on gross sales are underpaid because of underreported gross sales figures. Usually, in this situation, the franchisee is responsible for the amount underpaid plus the costs of the investigation or audit that uncovered the fact.

12. Signage restrictions including advertising that the store is for sale, or advertising of other businesses that might conflict with the franchise, or selling any product or service that might damage the reputation or image of the franchise.

13. Procedure to be followed if the franchisee wishes to relocate the franchise.

Franchisor's Rights to Terminate the Franchise Agreement. This section usually outlines the circumstances or conditions under which the franchisor may terminate the agreement. These circumstances may include the loss of premises, nonperformance of the conditions and terms of the agreement, insolvency, failure to maintain required licenses and permits, failure to comply with the operations manual, and misrepresentation. These conditions and circumstances will vary according to the type of franchise and may also be subject to state laws governing terminations of franchise agreements. This section also usually defines the remedies and the time period allowed to cure defaults.

Obligations of the Franchisee on Termination. The agreement will usually address the responsibility of a terminated franchisee to discontinue use of trade names and trademarks and any other material or advertising that is indicative of the franchisor. It may also, where legal, impose a noncompetitive clause in terms of distance and time after termination and hold the exfranchisees liable for damages if they subsequently disclose any trade secrets.

Sale, Transfer, and Assignment. The condition and requirements under which the franchisor will allow the sale, transfer, or assignment of the franchise are described in this section. Usually the issue of approval in event the franchisee changes his or her business structure but still retains controlling interest is also addressed. Also defined is the right of the franchisee to pass interests on to heirs upon death or disability.

Miscellaneous Provisions. This section contains the usual legal references to terms, definitions, and notice requirements, and also addresses such issues as abandonment of the premises by the franchisee, arbitration of disputes, waivers, the impact of invalid provisions on the whole agreement, the franchisor's right to transfer or assign the franchise, trademark challenges, and purchase of equipment and inventory on termination.

Riders, Amendments, and Addenda. Often a franchise agreement may contain riders, amendments, or addenda because of the requirements of a particular state.

6

Know Your Market and Aim to Earn It

Whether you are buying into a franchise or expanding one you already own, one of the first questions you must ask is, Are there enough potential customers for my product or service in the location I have selected? The answer is not a matter of population density. Few products or services are appealing to all ages, sexes, and income groups. Most products and services have been designed to sell to a specific segment of the population—teenagers, older males or females, upscale professionals, and so on. For many new items, much of the design or formulation is based on guesswork and hope rather than on a detailed market study; consequently, the product or service fails. The same fate awaits many small business people who do not test or analyze their market and who therefore risk their life savings in a business that is in the wrong location. Large chain stores and manufacturers can hire marketing specialists to determine their potential customers in given locations, but obviously the cost of such a study is far beyond the financial resources of most franchisees. Fortunately, however, a basic market analysis can usually be performed by a franchisee because much of the data needed can be supplied by the franchisor.

A franchisor should, indeed, be able to furnish a great deal of information about what can be expected from customers of a franchise, including average check or sales size, high and low traffic periods, and sales volume norms for other franchise locations. But perhaps the most important customer information a franchisor can provide is a profile of your potential patrons. This includes such information as age range, average or median income, sex, cultural status, level of education, and in some places occupations. Accordingly, unlike the entrepreneur who is starting an entirely new business, you have the advantage of knowing in considerable detail to whom your product or service will appeal.

In most franchise arrangements, the franchisor has to approve any site that you have selected. That approval process will involve a review of this location to determine whether or not it meets the market area criteria established by the franchisor. The extent of this review, however, will differ widely among the various franchisors; some will be quite diligent while others may be no more than a cursory glance. Your need for a market analysis, in reality, is not based on the fact that the franchisor may inspect the proposed location. Your need is based on the fact that you want to succeed. Unless you enjoy throwing your money away, you must have a detailed market analysis to tell you whether there are enough potential customers in your market area to give your franchise a good chance of success.

This is vital whether you are about to buy a franchise, wish to add more units, or have a single or multiunit franchise that is undermarketed and for which current local advertising is ineffective. Realize that a proper market study is not something that can be done either casually or cheaply. You cannot merely get some data from the census bureau and make assumptions about the characteristic profile of the population. One of the reasons that good market studies are so expensive is the fact that a large amount of groundwork is necessary. The entire market area has to be physically surveyed to obtain an accurate picture of the population base and mix.

Defining Your Market Area

Generally, your market area will be determined by the type of business your franchise is engaged in. The three categories of businesses used in market studies are those involved in selling:

1. *Shopper's goods:* Hardware stores, department stores, automotive dealers, and home furnishings are examples of stores that appeal to a wide market because of the variety and type of their inventories and the fact that their items are not considered to be staples.

2. *Convenience goods:* Grocery stores, various types of specialty food stores, restaurants, fast food establishments, and drug stores are examples of businesses that sell items used on a daily or weekly basis.

3. *Services:* Automotive repair, recreation services, dry cleaning, laundries, and barber shops are examples.

According to Wayne Lemmon,* most customers will drive for as long as 20 minutes to go to a store that sells shopper's goods, up to 6 minutes to go to a store that sells convenience goods, and also up to 6 minutes for services, although some service franchises are highly specialized and will draw customers from a greater distance.

Once you have determined what category your franchise fits into, you will have enough information to begin to draw the boundaries of your market area. First, obtain a large detailed map of your area. This usually can be found in stationery, book, or map stores. This map will be used to define the time-distance contours and should be large enough to show individual streets and other characteristics of the area.

The *time-distance contour* is defined by the distance in all directions that you can travel within the allotted time. You might assume, therefore, that all you must do is calculate the number of miles you can go in the time allotted to your business category, traveling at the local speed limit and then just draw a circle around your location. This is simple but it won't work. The problem with this assumption is that it does not consider such conditions as the number of stop signs and stop lights, the way streets are laid out, the fact that freeways form barriers, and speed limits vary. The only way to accurately judge how far you can drive in the allotted time is to actually drive. For example, if you own a restaurant franchise that is considered to be in a convenience category, you should drive for 6 minutes in all directions and mark on your map the places at which you reach the time limit. You soon will find that, instead of a circle, you will have an area shaped more like an ink blot. The perimeter of this area is your time-distance contour. The contour will tend to bulge along major streets if they do not have an excessive number of stop lights or signs and you probably will find other areas that are restricted because of freeways, parks, or other obstacles.

The percentage of your potential customers who will reside within these contours will depend on the location of your franchise relative to major streets and thoroughfares. If, for example, your business is convenience goods or service-related but is located on a high traffic street, you probably will realize a significant amount of sales to people living outside your market area. Some market surveyors refer to this segment of a market as "destination traffic," traffic that habitually uses a street to get to a common destination or focus point. (A focus point is a facility to which people go repeatedly for a specific purpose: office buildings, factories, churches, schools, shopping malls, recreation areas, for example.)

*Wayne Lemmon, *The Owners and Managers Market Analysis Workbook* (New York: AMACOM, 1980).

Locate these focus points on your map, then look at their relationship to residential areas, freeway exits, and all major streets. If, for example, a large residential area is located to the east of your location, a major manufacturing facility is located to your west, and your street is the major route between the two, you know that a substantial amount of traffic on your street will be that of employees at the manufacturing facility. The fact that the residential area is beyond your time-distance contour does not mean that the area could not be an advertising target.

The time-distance contour may outline the perimeter of your market area, but it does not mean that everyone within that area is a potential customer. The contour does not take into consideration the population demographics of the area. Accordingly, the next question you must obtain the answer to is, How many people living in the area match the customer profile? If your customer profile is affluent males 20 to 30 years old, and your market area demographics show the population as largely blue collar workers and retirees, obviously you have a mismatch.

Many franchisors offer their franchisees a specific area and agree that they will not sell another franchise within the boundaries of that area. During market surveys, a frequent question is whether the protected area should be the geographic market or the one defined by time-distance contours. This issue must be judged on a case-by-case basis, but several factors must be considered:

1. *The basis for awarding a protected territory:* Is it population density or some type of geographic or governmental boundary?

2. *The definition of "protection":* Remember that a protected territory refers to the location of the franchise facility. The franchisor agrees not to sell another franchise that would be located within that area. This does not mean that all the people located within that area are your customers. Consequently, your customer base will still be defined only by the time-distance contours.

3. *The comparison of the protected territory boundaries with the time-distance contours:* If your territory is smaller—that is, if it lies completely within the contour—then it is likely that the franchisor will sell other franchises whose market area will overlap yours. If your territory is larger than the contour, you have a greater measure of protection but your customer base will still be governed by time and distance. Your decision to invest in the franchise or increase the number of franchise units you own must still be made on the basis of your potential market, not the demographics of the protected territory.

Determining Market Area Demographics

Obtaining market area demographics is not a simple task. So plan to devote enough time to become thoroughly familiar with your area. Some of the information you need can be obtained from town or city government departments such as Planning, Zoning or a Development Commission. If you live in a city with a population of more than 50,000, it is very possible that the area is designated as a Standard Metropolitan Statistical Area (SMSA). Generally, SMSAs are divided into small geographic units called Census Tracts. The data obtained during a census is reported for these tracts, as well as for the counties and cities, and is used by governments and marketing consultants in making estimates of population, income levels, cultural mix, and other data concerning the demographics of each area.

If you are not in an SMSA, these same municipal departments may still be of some help because they have researched the area themselves and have at least some demographic information about most parts of a town or city. The most important part of your demographic information, however, will come from your own legwork. Your franchisor should be able to give you a customer profile in terms of age range, income level, occupational group, life style, and in some cases cultural mix. With this in mind, drive through the areas within the time-distance contours, and do the following:

1. Visit supermarkets and department stores in each section of your market area several times and note the mix of their customers—age, sex, appearance, income range, cultural mix. Note the location of each store on your map using some type of code so that you can reference each location in your notes.

2. Locate and identify the various neighborhoods. Usually these are bounded by major streets or by some other type of topographic feature. Observe the houses, cars, the people on the streets, the amount of toys and play equipment in the yards. Also you can draw certain conclusions such as average age, whether the bulk of the population consists of families, older persons, or singles, and if there is majority of one ethnic group.

3. Visit one or two local real estate offices and obtain average housing values for each neighborhood. Generally, annual household income will be 25 to 30 percent of the housing value.

4. Visit the major apartment complexes. A chat with the manager should provide a wealth of information about the residents—ages,

marital or family status, cultural mix, and income levels. Remember that most apartment dwellers must have a monthly income of at least three to four times their rent to qualify as tenants.

5. Look at the various churches in your market area. Sometimes this will provide information about the ethnic mix.

Some market surveys will provide estimates of total personal income within a specific area, a figure that may not have much meaning to many franchises. Franchises in general are designed to cater to niche markets and do not have the broad appeal of a department store, supermarket, or auto dealership. Your goal, therefore, is to determine the market for your product or service in your area by estimating the number of people who fit your customer profile, not the total population or total disposable income. You also should recognize the fact that, in most areas, other franchises or independent businesses will be competing for the same customers. To get a sense of how strong the competition will be, mark the location of each competitor on your map and estimate their time-distance contours. Be certain that you include those outside your market area but whose time-distance contours will infringe on yours. You will not be able to draw these contours in detail, but if you use an area roughly the same size as yours for each competitor, you will get a picture of how much your markets overlap. If the area is highly competitive, then name recognition will be a significant factor in deciding whether you wish to go head to head with other businesses offering the same kind of product or service.

Another important factor you should consider is the projected future of your market area. After all, you will be committing yourself to 10 to 20 years when you sign that agreement. Here are some of the questions to be answered:

1. Is the area in a condition of population growth or decline? A comparison of census figures and annual population estimates by the local planning commission can give you some clues about this, but be aware that you are primarily interested in your market area and that may or may not follow the trend of the city or the state.

2. How much of your market area is in a state of transition. Granted, all neighborhoods and commercial areas change eventually, but certain types of change can significantly alter your market area. As commercial zones spread into residential areas, the neighborhoods immediately in front of the growth will be in a state of rapid transition, which not only can change the number of potential customers but also change the character of the neighborhoods. This in turn affects

the demographics and may be a negative or positive factor depending on the nature of your product or service.

3. What is the housing status of your market area? Usually, as the core of a city or town moves outward and commercial zones encroach on the former suburban areas, the housing status in the growth changes from home owners to renters. Commercial growth often stimulates the construction of multifamily housing, which in turn can actually increase population density and, depending on your customer profile, may add significantly to your customer base.

4. What are the projected changes in transportation and highway networks? A new limited access highway that will run diagonally across your market area could virtually eliminate a large segment of your customer base because it will act as a barrier to persons residing on the other side. One running adjacent to your market area could expand your base because the time-distance contours will change. A chat with the local highway department will provide you with information concerning highway expansion over the next 5 to 10 years.

5. What are the growth patterns of the local economy? You will be particularly interested in business and industrial growth in your area, but in extreme cases the economy of your state can have an impact on your market. When a major industry downsizes, relocates, or just goes out of business, the whole economy of a large area is affected. Disposable income decreases, people relocate, and neighborhoods decline. A check with the local Chamber of Commerce will tell you whether the local economy is diversified or is based on a single company or industry.

Conversations with local business groups, planning and zoning commissions, and real estate brokers should provide you with numerous opinions about the future of your area. No one has a magic eye, but applying their opinions to several different scenarios in terms of growth and the economy should give a sense of the direction of your market area.

Developing the Final Market Analysis

Putting all this information in the form of a written report will serve several purposes. First, if you are just applying for a franchise, a well prepared market analysis will help convince a franchisor that you are a responsible person. Even though they may do an analysis of their own to confirm yours, you will be in a better position to discuss any differences.

Second, any financing proposal generally will include a market analysis as the basis for a marketing plan. Third, although most franchisors will have an advertising program on a national or regional basis, you will be responsible for local advertising and promotion. Your marketing analysis will tell you where most of your potential customers are located.

As noted, total personal income calculations for a specific area are not really applicable in a franchise or niche marketing situation. What is important is a guesstimate of people in the area that meet the customer profile. For example, if your customer profile involves lower- and middle-income families, then your notes on the various neighborhoods, plus the inhabitant data from real estate offices and the planning and zoning commissions, should provide you with a reasonably accurate number of potential customers living in the target areas. That number should be supplemented by multifamily housing numbers obtained from the various apartment managers. If you are located on a street where there is considerable destination traffic, this may be added if the traffic profile matches the customer profile. For example, traffic consisting largely of people going back and forth to work may substantially contribute to a fast food or a convenience store franchise but would be of little help to a children's clothing franchisee.

Thus, intelligence should guide both you and a franchisor in deciding whether you should get together at all, and if you do so should guide you in your advertising and selling. From the outset, the market analysis is the basis for targeting local advertising and for beginning to become familiar with your local patrons. It makes little sense, for example, to send direct mailings to an area populated mostly by retirees if your customer profile is that of people in their late teens to early thirties. The definition of the market also affects the cost-effectiveness of newspaper, television, and radio advertising.

Advertising

Most franchising networks require that each franchisee contribute a certain percentage of sales income to an advertising fund to be used to promote the name recognition of the service or product throughout the areas in which the franchisor has operating units. The allocation of the fund is usually at the discretion of the franchisor, but often there is an advertising or promotional committee whose primary responsibility is to ensure that the funds are used to the advantage of all franchisees. Advertising and promotion in local areas, however, are usually the responsibility of the individual franchisee. The extent of local advertising and promotion by a franchisee is, in reality, a matter of name and logo recognition and traffic patterns. A Pizza Hut franchise owner may do little or no local advertising because of widespread media saturation, while an owner of a new or lesser known franchise may have to advertise locally as much as an independently owned business.

How much advertising is enough? We don't think anyone has an accurate answer to that question, but it is safe to say that some local advertising is necessary for all but the largest national franchises. Even if your franchiser has a well known name and logo, it seldom is enough to depend only on traffic to let people know where you are. This is particularly so if you are in a stand-alone building that is not on a main thoroughfare.

Radio and Television Advertising

The cost of radio and TV advertising usually is well beyond the resources of single franchise unit owners. Also, these types of media generally reach much further than their market areas and are therefore not cost-effective. Radio and TV advertising should be the responsibility of the franchisor and should used to benefit a number of existing franchisees. Often, however, when franchisors wish to expand into a new territory, they will blanket the area with media ads that are really aimed at selling franchises. Using existing advertising pool funds for this purpose is questionable.

Radio and TV may be cost-effective if there are several owners in the same franchise network served in a specific geographic area by one or more stations. Often, under these circumstances, the owners can advisedly share the cost of a commercial that advertises not only the franchise but also the locations of the various units. In some franchises, the franchisor advertising pool will contribute to the cost of regional advertising.

Newspaper and Regional Magazine Advertising

The same rules that apply to TV and radio also apply to newspaper and magazine ads. There is little sense in advertising outside your market area. But newspaper ads may be appropriate for grand openings and special promotions, particularly if the ads contain coupons. In addition to stimulating business, coupons also can be valuable for estimating market penetration if they require the user to furnish address information. Service franchises are more dependent on newspaper advertising than most product franchises because they often are in office locations rather than high-traffic retail areas. Their market is usually highly specialized, and consequently their target area must be much larger.

Most franchisors will have advertising formats and logos that you will be required to use in all types of advertising.

Direct Mail

Direct mail is also very expensive unless you can develop mailing lists that correspond approximately to your market area. It is very effective, however, if your franchise thrives on repeat business and you are able to obtain the names and addresses of your customers. Although, again, you must use the name and logo of the franchise, the primary purpose of the direct mail piece is to advertise your particular location, not to advertise the entire franchise.

The *Yellow Pages*

Advertising in the *Yellow Pages,* for some franchises, is strongly recommended, and for others is absolutely necessary. In fact, newspaper and *Yellow Pages* advertising may be the only way that some service franchises can reach their markets. Check with your franchisor, because many have *Yellow Pages* programs in which all the franchisees in an area are listed under the name of the franchise in the appropriate product or service section.

Handouts and Drops

An increasingly popular and effective way of advertising is the use of handout coupons, usually delivered door to door by employees not associated with the post office. In densely populated urban areas, the distribution is more cost-effective than direct mail because the areas can be more closely targeted, and a good delivery person may distribute advertising and coupons at a rate of 120 to 140 an hour. Brochure type advertising can also be delivered in bulk to apartment complex offices (with their permission) and other public areas.

Coupons are also a highly effective way of measuring the productivity of the advertising program, as well as the comparative strength of various market areas. By coding the coupons according to areas, you can measure both relative effectiveness and market strength by monitoring the number of coupons cashed in from each area. Compare the number of coupons returned with the number distributed in each area, and you have a very accurate measurement of cost-effectiveness.

Signage

The use of signs is more closely controlled than most other types of advertising. First, the franchisor will dictate the design and use of the signs. Second, if the franchise is located in a shopping mall or strip center, the developer also will have some requirements. Third, most municipalities have sign and advertising regulations. For example, as McDonalds discovered when they opened their first unit in Scottsdale, Arizona, their traditional arches did not meet the town regulations. They and the town finally agreed on golden arches that were about 4 feet high. Obviously, signage will be a part of your marketing plan but be certain that you have touched all the necessary bases before committing to a design and size.

Customer Relations in Franchising

Your marketing plan may cover all the aspects of marketing your franchise and include various methods of stimulating sales. But one aspect of running a successful business cannot be adequately covered by any written document: selling and customer relations. The quality of customer relations can make or break your franchise.

There can be little doubt that the American consumer is becoming more quality and service conscious. For years, the Detroit auto manufacturers tried to ignore this fact and consequently watched their bottom line go from black to red. Electronics manufacturers went through the same experience of having problems with the quality not only of their products but also of their services. At first these companies concentrated on improving the quality of their products but foreign competition continued to gain in sales. Slowly, these companies began to realize that we, as consumers, want to be treated like valued customers and, although product quality is important, we want to do business with someone who expresses decent respect while taking our money. Detroit then began to train their dealers in customer service. Department store chains changed many of their policies to improve customer relations, and business in general is realizing again that, in most respects, it is always a buyer's market.

Today, companies are spending billions to recreate their image. The dominant theme is that of a company who cares about both product quality and their customer satisfaction.

The creation of an image of a high-quality product and good service is a basic reason why franchising exists today. The successful franchisors jealously guard their reputations and constantly work to improve their image because the image created by a logo or trademark is the most important kind of sales tool. Yet that image could be destroyed by a few franchisees within the system who are not fully committed to quality and service. Customers expect consistency from a franchise. They want to feel safe in the belief that they will get the same product and quality wherever they see that sign and logo. This sign and logo will get them through your front door the first time, but only the service they receive from you and your employees will get them back again and again. And, in almost every franchise, the key to success is repeat business.

As the owner of the franchise you are the head salesperson. It is your attitude and behavior toward your customers that will set the standard for your employees. You need to work sincerely to give your customers the best break you can. It pays to cultivate throughout your organization the old-fashioned virtue of doing things *for* people, not *to* them. Nothing makes selling any easier than a genuine good-natured concern for people. But don't expect that it will be simple to keep this attitude. Sometimes customers can be unreasonable, overdemanding, and difficult to deal with. In fact, how many times have you heard someone say, "This would be a wonderful business if it weren't for the customers." However, dealing with a difficult customer is a highly developed skill—a skill that, once learned, should be a source of pride and accomplishment. Teaching that skill should be a primary purpose during your employee training program. If you can get your people to feel good about themselves after dealing with an overdemanding or complaining customer, you will help them to have the confidence and composure to effectively deal with the next one. Handling this type of a customer requires a calm voice, an air of confidence and respect, and a willingness to listen to a complaint or problem and do something to solve it. Most people like to be reasonable, and when they complain they usually have something to complain about. Instead of treating them suspiciously, a quick resolution of their problem will calm them down and help them go away satisfied that you and your employees really care. Besides, in most cases, they are voicing their complaint in front of other customers, and you have the opportunity to either impress these others with your sincerity or convince them that they also should never come back.

Building Up Your Image

As noted, one of the advantages to franchise ownership is the fact that much of the work in image building and customer relations has already been accomplished. Most franchisees, however, are in competition with other franchisees in the same line of business even though they are in different franchises. For example, a Dairy Queen franchisee may be competing with a BurgerKing, a Wendys, and a Whataburger, all within the same market area. Consequently, image building is a continuous and never ending process that in most retail franchises depends on the continuing relationship between your employees and the customers. At the risk of seeming elementary, we must stress this creed: *Every employee is a salesperson.* Every contact that one of your employees has with a customer either reinforces or detracts from your image and the image of the franchise. We all have heard a friend say, "Don't do business with them, they are no good." That statement projects the image of a company or franchise as being heedless, untrustworthy, or in some other way an undesirable place to shop or do business with. Granted, the franchise or business under discussion may have rightfully gained that reputation because of inferior merchandise or poor service, but in far more cases the reputation was caused by the actions of a nonsales employee such as an uncooperative deliveryperson or an obnoxious bookkeeper. Another very common example is a restaurant in which you are greeted very warmly by a friendly, gracious hostess giving you a very positive image until the waiter comes. The waiter's behavior and unprofessionalism quickly turns a positive image into an extremely negative one, and the restaurant has lost another repeat customer.

The answer to this critical problem is essentially simple to see, but painstaking in execution. Appoint everyone to be responsible for sales. Explain that all your employees are customer relations specialists first and busboys or copy machine operators second. Build this attitude into your recruiting and training. Precisely how is something you must spell out for yourself, keeping in mind the kind of franchise you have, the people you have identified as potential customers, and the available employment pool. You must focus always, down to the smallest detail, on what you can do to please, and thereby deserve and earn the business of, that all-important person, the customer.

7

Guard Yourself and Your Franchise with the Right Lawyers

Whether you are just starting in a franchise, already have one, or are an expanding franchise owner planning to buy additional units, you need at least three kinds of professional allies: legal, accounting, and financial. You need lawyers to guard you against the dangers of this complex world. You need an accountant who will make certain your financial management systems are sound. And you will need a financial advisor to provide counsel on important money matters, such as working capital, inventory handling, and expansion funding. Since nearly everything today has legal requirements or implications, let's begin by considering how to have the right lawyer.

We live in a society that has become not only very complicated but also very litigious. Furthermore, lawmakers and government agencies are continually adding to an already bewildering labyrinth of laws and regulations. To guard you from mistakes and from the actions of others, you need to have at your side a lawyer who is competent, principled, compatible, and amply qualified to handle your particular needs or problems. But to find this kind of person, you should have some familiarity with the basic types of law and its specialized branches, and with the various ways lawyers serve their clients and set their fees. You should also understand how to locate and interview suitable candidates, and finally how to arrive at a satisfactory relationship.

You should know about the basics or fundamentals of business law, but we certainly are not suggesting that you should try to be your own lawyer.

Judges have an old saying on this subject: "The man who is his own law-yer has a fool for a client." This saying is very much to the point in today's society. Nevertheless, franchise owners can best help both themselves and their lawyers if they have at least some fundamental legal knowledge. If you do not have this knowledge, some excellent books are available on the subject, and colleges and universities offer seminars or evening courses on the fundamentals of law for the business person.

When to Seek a Specialist

Among lawyers, as among physicians, there are general practitioners and there are specialists. Even those who maintain a general practice tend to specialize or gravitate to certain areas of the law. No one lawyer, however, will have the expertise necessary to solve all your problems. Conse-quently, there will be times when you will find it necessary to obtain a spe-cialist; then how to locate the right lawyer at the right time will depend largely on your circumstances. If you have a trusted and experienced gen-eral lawyer who is well acquainted with the legal talent in your local area, it is usually safe to rely on his or her advice on the selection of a specialist for the particular problem. This approach depends on your faith in your general counselor to recognize the areas in which he or she is not expert and who will unhesitatingly admit to this fact.

An all-too-common problem is the reluctance of lawyers to admit they do not know it all and consequently to provide advice that does nothing but further complicate a situation.

Some of the specialized problems for which you might require special counsel, either as the head of your business or as a private individual, are those relating to the following matters.

The Disclosure Statement
and the Franchise Agreement

In most cases, these two documents are extremely complex and are regu-lated to some extent by the Federal Trade Commission and state laws. Many of the provisions of the franchise agreement may be negotiable despite the fact that some franchisors may claim that all the provisions are rigidly set. For example, while the FTC or state laws may require that the length or term of the agreement be included, the actual length may be negotiated.

Franchise agreements are a special type of contract, and few generalists are sufficiently knowledgeable about franchising to adequately protect your interests. Unfortunately, however, most lawyers with expertise in franchising represent franchisors, and you may experience some difficulty in locating one who will be willing to represent you as a franchisee.

Leases and Other Contracts

Most generalists are competent in the area of contract law even though they are not familiar with franchise agreements. This area will include facility and equipment leases and service contracts.

Wage and Hour and Fair Labor Standards

Wage and hour regulations are responsible for most of the actions filed today against franchisees and other small businesses. Because few franchise owners are large enough to have a full-time personnel manager or department, most of them operate without a knowledge of minimum wage and overtime regulations; this also is an area that few legal generalists know much about. Having a knowledgeable lawyer who specializes in labor law available to review your personnel policy and practices for compliance with the regulations can save you thousands in potential back pay awards.

Employment Discrimination

This is an increasingly active area of the law. Because more and more employees are coming from the ranks of minorities and culturally diverse populations, employment discrimination will continue to be news as Congress wrestles with new legislation. This is a highly specialized area and, should you become involved as a defendant, you will quickly need the services of someone amply familiar with Equal Employment Opportunity issues.

Liability for Negligence, Products, Services, and Hiring Practices

Unfortunately, this area of the law is the one that most often reflects the increasing trend towards litigation within our society and probably represents the greatest potential expense to franchisees. Generally speaking, those franchises whose employees have opportunity to invade the privacy of individuals (such as hotels, motels, carpet cleaning, and janitorial services) are most exposed to suits involving negligent hiring practices; those franchises dealing in products are most exposed to unsafe product or negligence liability. In either case, defense against a liability suit is not the domain of most generalists and will require the services of a specialist.

Taxes

Although most tax matters can be handled by a competent accountant, there will be times when the advice of a qualified tax lawyer will be needed. A word of caution: the last person you need is a daredevil tax attorney who attempts to dodge through every conceivable tax loophole. In essence, he or she may be gambling with your money and getting paid handsomely to do so.

Some Other Areas of Possible Legal Needs

Depending on the type of your franchise activities, you may need legal services in other areas, such as:

Acquisitions.

Bankruptcy of debtor.

Company legal forms.

Consumer protection.

Copyrights and patents.

Credit and collection.

Environmental policy.

Insurance claims.

Issuance of stock.

Labor relations.

Malpractice.

Partnership agreements.

Property damage.

Real estate.

Many of these areas can be handled by a generalist, but, again, you should make certain that this person is genuinely qualified.

Individual Lawyer or Law Firm?

About half of the independent lawyers (those not employed by corporations or the government) operate as individual practitioners, while the other half practice as members of law firms of various sizes. Which is better for you? It is mostly a matter of individual preference and often the answer can be, "Both." Either can have advantages, depending on the particular matter at hand. In theory, it should cost no more to use different attorneys or firms for specialized cases; in fact, it should cost less and produce better results since presumably you will hire the most efficient specialist in each case. On the other hand, a general attorney who has accumulated much information about you and your business may be more efficient and economical because he or she does not have to spend long hours gathering information.

Advantages of an Individual Lawyer

Generally, lawyers who operate on their own handle a broader range of legal matters than lawyers in a large firm, and are well qualified to handle much of the business and personal legal needs of the average franchise owner. Too, individual lawyers may be harder working and more aggressive on behalf of clients because of the need to obtain and hold clients single-handedly, whereas a lawyer with a large firm representing corporate clients may not feel as strong an incentive to serve the smaller clients. Also, a lone attorney may cost less because of lower overhead.

The individual lawyer may be more readily available to give personal attention to the work of clients and to push jobs to a quicker conclusion, especially if the lawyer-client relationship has been a lengthy one. By comparison, the small franchisee who retains a large firm may seldom, if ever, see the principal partners. The work is more often delegated to a junior member and a clerk to grind through the mill.

Some of the very best lawyers prefer to practice as individuals, but there also are some who practice as individuals because their incompetence or dispositions make them unwanted by larger firms. By investigating patiently and thoroughly, you should be able to decide what is true about the lawyer you are considering.

In size, there are two types of law firms: the small local firm and the large one, which may have numerous branches, perhaps in several states. Sometimes it is difficult to say to which group a particular firm belongs, but as a general guide it may be said that a firm with two to ten lawyers is classified as small. As the firm grows beyond ten members, it is getting more and more into the large category.

Advantages of the Small Firm

Often a small law firm can provide a franchise owner with the advantages of competent individual attention plus additional skills and resources available through other members of the firm. However, in some small firms, members occupy the same facilities for convenience and expense sharing but offer no significant additional benefits beyond those of an individual practitioner.

Advantages of a Large Firm

A large firm is likely to wield the most influence in political circles, in the courts, and even with opposing attorneys. Partners in large firms usually include active members in both political parties. Generally, the partners are also active in civic matters and charitable endeavors which provides them with a wide range of contacts and influence. The reputation and the clout of a large firm can be of great advantage in negotiating out-of-court settlements because of the pressure that can be exerted on opposing parties.

Large firms get many of the top graduates from the leading law schools and provide them with the opportunity to gain experience in one or more of the highly specialized legal areas. Many specialties may be represented in one office. In a large firm responsibility is centralized, services are coordinated, and, because of a large resource base, problems may be handled more efficiently. It also is safe to say that a lawyer is more apt to refer a matter to someone within his or her own firm rather than to an outsider. Consequently, if your primary contact does not feel comfortable with your particular problem because of a lack of experience in a specialty, the chances are much better in a large firm that the matter can be referred to someone else in the same office who does have the necessary expertise. Usually, then, there will be no forwarding fee.

How Lawyers Charge

A cartoon in *The New Yorker* magazine shows a lawyer talking to a prospective client and asking, "How much justice can you afford?" Apparently, Americans can afford a lot because they spend many billions each year for legal and related services. Some of these billions are wasted by clients who tie up the courts with vengeful or frivolous litigation, but much of this expense is also the result of unnecessary procedures and overcharges by unprincipled attorneys.

If a law firm is thoroughly honest, charges are usually based on the total number of hours spent by the attorneys and staff to complete the job. An attorney's hourly rate may vary today from $75 to $500 depending on his or her education, degree of specialization, years of experience, amount of success in court, seniority in the firm, the degree of difficulty involved, and the financial stakes. Rates are also affected by the amount of competition in the area and by the size and prestige of the firm and its clients.

An attorney may require an advance retainer to handle a particular job, against which subsequent hourly charges will be made. On protracted projects, the lawyer or firm will usually render monthly progress billings for work done to date. Whatever your arrangement, you should request a detailed statement of hours worked, by whom, and the applicable rates or fees. Never accept a lump-sum bill for "Services Rendered."

Types of Fees

Make certain that you understand and agree with the attorney's method of charging before making a commitment to have work done. Some of the more common methods of charging are:

Hourly fee: The sum of the actual hours of work performed by the principals and their assistants, paralegals, clerks, and others, multiplied by their respective rates plus incidental expenses.

Fixed fee: A flat amount quoted in advance for certain standard jobs such as an ordinary sales contract, property purchase documents, copyright registrations, or wills.

Fixed percentage: A prestated percentage of all moneys involved regardless of the amount—usually an unsatisfactory arrangement. The fee can come to ten to twenty times that charged by a highly principled lawyer.

Contingency fee: In this arrangement the client pays the lawyer an agreed-on percentage of the award only if the case is won. The fee can range as high as 50 percent on awards of small amounts but is usually based on a sliding percentage that decreases to an average of about 33 percent as the award amount increases to the tens of thousands and more. This method is used by people of limited means seeking recovery of expenses in cases of negligence and personal injury, or in complex litigation involving medical malpractice or stockholder derivative actions.

Debt collection: Usually one-quarter to one-half, or a graduated percentage of the amount collected. Most states place a legal limit on the percentage or dollar amount of this type of fee.

Obtaining Estimates

Before authorizing an assignment, ask for an itemized projection of costs for the entire undertaking, broken down by types of work and rates for all members of the firm who might be involved. Also ask for estimates of the cost of related or referred work involving questions that often arise. Some clients will set a dollar limit on expenditures and require that the attorney obtain their permission before exceeding that amount.

It is very important that you know in advance who does what. Although much of your contact may be with the attorney, much of the work may be turned over to assistants. Be very sure that you are not paying principal's rates for work done by junior apprentices, interns, paralegals, secretaries, and clerks. Also know how much of your billing will be for filing fees, court costs, documents, depositions, field investigations, research, typing, photocopying, faxing, and phone calls.

Where to Look
for the Right Lawyer

How do you find a lawyer who will fully earn his or her fees—the right lawyer, one who does not overcomplicate matters to build up billing time? First, never hire a lawyer in a hurry or solely because a friend recommends one to you (although the recommendation of a trusted friend often leads to the best choice). Select your lawyers before you are forced by circumstances to act quickly. The larger the number of reputable candidates you have to choose from, the better your final choice is likely to be.

Assemble a list of prospects from a number of sources. Some of these might be:

Noncompetitive people in your field or business.

Owners of other businesses in your area.

Civic officials and department heads.

Judges and other court personnel.

Leaders of political organizations.

Congressional representatives and state assemblypersons.

Other professionals in your area, such as accountants, tax and financial advisors, investment counselors, bankers, trust officers, and business executives.

Faculty members of nearby law schools and business administration schools.

The American Bar Association, state bar association, and legal referral agencies.

Telephone book *Yellow Pages* listings by specialty.

The *Martindale-Hubbel Law Directory* lists U.S. lawyers by states and cities, rates them, and indicates their firm affiliations. It also provides educational and biographical data. The directory provides lists of firms, their partners, and areas of specialization. This reference book usually can be found in public and courthouse libraries and the libraries of large law firms. It is an excellent source, especially for comparative purposes.

Interviewing Candidates

After you have decided which lawyers you would like to interview, telephone them and give each one a brief synopsis of your business operations and legal requirements. If they are interested in having you as a client, then find out if they or their firm services any of your competitors or whether the firm has any actual or potential conflicts of interest that might impair a candidate's ability to exercise professional skill and judgment in your behalf. Also ask if you can meet the firm's associates or partners. If you feel comfortable with this discussion, then set up an appointment.

Before you meet, outline the legal services that you have received during the past year or two, plus those that you might anticipate. This information will provide the prospect with an idea of your past, current, and future needs. Also include any problems peculiar to your type of a franchise. Make a list of all the questions that you wish to ask at the interviews to ensure that you receive all the information you need. Note down the answers so that you can make accurate comparisons once the interviews are completed. Try to bring your accountant or principal advisor with you. This will give you an edge because he or she will undoubtedly think of additional questions and also be able to provide a second opinion of the candidates.

Some people feel shy in the presence of a lawyer. There is really no reason to do so. When you interview candidates, do not hesitate to ask the most searching questions and insist on specific answers. You are the customer and your money is at stake. Candidates would not have agreed to the appointment unless they wanted your business.

Important Questions

Be certain at the outset that you are interviewing the person who will be personally and regularly handling your work; otherwise you will be wasting your time. Law firms often have a personable senior member contact the client at first and then gradually shift the client's work over to a lower-paid, less experienced junior member.

Investigate prospective lawyers as thoroughly as you would an applicant for a top position in your franchise. Ask about their educational background, previous positions, clients, business and community positions, political affiliations, and club memberships. Ask similar questions about the firm's senior partners.

Request specific information concerning the firm's experience in representing clients whose legal needs are similar to yours. In what areas of the law does the firm specialize? Check with some of the firm's clients about quality of service, efficiency, fairness of charges, general integrity, compatibility, and any areas of dissatisfaction they may have.

Ask for a detailed fee schedule indicating hourly rates for various types of work. Inquire if your billing will define each item by the nature of the job performed, name of the employee, and the number of hours worked to the quarter hour. Will a job estimate of time and cost be supplied in advance? Will the lawyer charge a fee for referring all or a part of your work to another lawyer?

Because of the complexities of the law, clients have little choice but to entrust most of their legal affairs to an attorney. These matters often concern personal or business affairs that are confidential and involve large sums of money. Therefore, in choosing legal counsel you should exercise extreme care to hire a person of the utmost integrity. In fact, you should always be watchful of your own interests where legal matters are concerned. The American Bar Association and its many affiliated legal societies, all of which are self-policed, are owned and governed by the lawyers themselves. Their "oaths" and codes of ethics mainly guard the rights and the privileges of the law profession. It was Chief Justice Charles Evans Hughes who observed that, "Institutions are noble; their members but mortal."

The Value of Practical Experience

It requires many years of schooling and on-the-job training to acquire a basic working knowledge of the law and still more years to become expert in a specialized branch. Authorities say that it takes seven to ten years of working experience, after being admitted to the bar, to become a seasoned professional. At the other end of the profession are the older attorneys who have arrived—the established independents, specialists, and senior partners of firms. Senior partners customarily devote their attention to their firm's largest and most lucrative corporate clients. As a franchise owner, you should be looking for a lawyer who is old enough to be seasoned and young enough to be still hungry. As a general rule, this would indicate someone who is in midcareer, roughly between 35 and 50 years old.

Making the Choice

Give a prospective attorney the opportunity to ask questions, too, about your company and your personal needs. Do not, however, at this point give out confidential information about your franchise or personal financial affairs. Until a formal attorney-client relationship has been established, the confidentiality of your communications with the attorney may not be entitled to the protection accorded to a client by the legal profession's code of ethics and the law. Make no commitments of any kind until you have reached an agreement with the lawyer or lawyers of your choice.

If the size of your franchise or the number of your units warrants it, there is no reason why you cannot have more than one general lawyer: a bright young less expensive one to handle routine documents or transactions and a large influential firm to handle the more complicated issues and litigation.

The Attorney-Client Relationship

When you select an attorney, it is prudent to have him or her prepare a brief memorandum generally outlining the essential elements of your new attorney-client relationship. This memorandum or letter should, at the very least, contain a description of the legal services to be performed, the anticipated professional fees for those services, the basis for computation of the fees, a description of expenses considered to be outside the scope of the agreement, and the billing procedures to be used.

Remember also that client-attorney relationships are not cast in concrete. The memorandum should allow for instant termination if you are dissatisfied. In fact, you need not make a continuing agreement the first time you use a lawyer. You can try him or her out on a single job. It is an excellent way to get better acquainted and to evaluate the way the work is done.

The Value of Communicating

In the final analysis, the success of your relationship with your lawyer and his or her effectiveness on your behalf depends on the amount of free and open communication between the two of you. Just as you may not immediately grasp the nature and the complexity of the law, your lawyer may not immediately grasp the nature and complexity of the regular or special problems in your business or personal affairs.

Educate and inform your lawyer. Communicate your problems and needs. Similarly, to enable you to understand the efforts your lawyer undertakes on your behalf, request that you be regularly supplied with copies of correspondence or documents he or she has prepared. When necessary, request any further explanation of the nature, effect, or impact of each of the legal services and procedures involved.

Your need for a knowledgeable lawyer or lawyers as members of your advisory team cannot be overemphasized. Few areas of owning a franchise are not affected by the law; and the fact that you are operating within a franchise network imposes an additional contractual burden on you. The franchise agreements, as well as the laws concerning franchising, are extremely complex and are far beyond the understanding of not only a layman but also many generalists in the legal profession.

8

Guide Yourself with the Right Accountant

Determining the Type of Accounting System You Need

Finding the right accountant for your business is much like finding the right architect to build your building. You can't decide on an architect until you know what type of building you want, and you can't decide on an accountant until you know what type of accounting system you need. Although most franchisors will provide you with guidelines concerning the information your system should produce, remember that the franchisor's goal is have an accurate gross sales total on which to base the royalty charges, while your goal, as the owner, is to have the information essential for profitably managing your business.

A few franchisors will require that you accept their accounting package as a condition of signing the franchise agreement. Most, however, will have some reporting requirements but let the actual design of the system be your responsibility. The financial reporting requirements also will differ among franchisors. Some will require only weekly or monthly gross sales figures. Others may request various income and expense totals, and will provide you with reports that compare your performance with the averages of other franchisees in your size and volume category.

Before beginning to search for the right accountant for your franchise, you should be prepared to give the candidates a general description of the type of system you desire and the information you want the system to generate. We will discuss financial statements, ratios, and fiscal policy in greater detail in Chap. 11, but at this point you should become familiar with certain essential elements of an effective accounting system for franchisees. The five basic requirements are to:

1. *Maintain the integrity of all assets within the franchisee's control.* Assets, in this instance, mean cash, accounts receivable, inventory, real property, securities, and anything else of value that is owned by or due to you as the franchisee. The system should have the capability of identifying and recording changes in the value of any asset as soon as possible after a transaction.

2. *Provide a system of checks and balances.* The system should be designed to provide a method of verifying or tracking every transaction. For example, daily sales totals should be instantly verified by checking cash plus increases in receivables (cash plus credit sales). Physical inventory decreases should be verified by sales and increases by the receipt of new shipments of products. An effective verification and tracking system will also discourage employee theft and embezzlement. Your expenses will be high enough without letting someone loot you.

3. *Provide the required data for financial and regulatory reports.* Every franchise must generate various financial reports for the franchisor, your lenders, the IRS and any number of other interested parties. Usually these reports must be prepared according to guidelines furnished by these parties. The system must be capable of producing income and expense information in a format that conforms to these guidelines.

4. *Provide information to help you manage the franchise and evaluate your financial condition and performance.* The system should distribute income and expense among your cost or profit centers so that you can evaluate the performance of each.

5. *Enable you to defend yourself successfully against claims by the IRS, the U.S. Department of Labor, and other regulatory agencies.* Each agency will require that certain types of records be maintained according to their standards. You must meet these differing requirements.

Perhaps the most important first decision you make will involve the choice between cash and accrual accounting systems.

In a *cash* system, income and expenses are reported when the money is actually received or expended. Sales income is reported when the customer actually pays the bill, not when the sale is made. The expense for merchandise is recorded when an invoice is paid, not when the order is booked or the merchandise received. This system may be adequate for a very small operation in which 95 percent more of the sales are by cash or credit card because it is simple to set up and maintain, but it is woefully inadequate for the production of useful management information.

The accrual method of accounting reports sales when they occur, regardless of whether they are cash, credit card, or charge account, and reports expenses when they are incurred, not when you get around to paying the bills. The accrual system is more complex to install and maintain, but it is truly the only system that will accurately measure and report financial performance, particularly if the income and expense information is being compared to some type of standard as a management evaluation tool.

When a system produces inaccurate information, you can be misled into thinking that your business is performing better than it actually is. For example, if you are operating on a cash accounting system and 99 percent of your sales are in cash, your records will report your sales income very accurately at the end of any one period (daily, weekly, or monthly). Since, however, your expenses are not reported until they are paid, your system will always underreport your costs. At the end of any month, your sales income reports will be reasonably accurate, but your expenses, especially for merchandise and services, will be understated by 15 to 60 days depending on how often you pay your invoices. In an accrual system, all the products and services you purchased during that month will be included as expenses even though you have not yet paid for them. Consequently you will have a much more accurate picture of your financial position. As a rule of thumb, if your annual volume exceeds $120,000 per year, you should be using an accrual system.

The most important management information an accounting system produces is the accurate comparison of actual income and expense to last month's total, to the same month last year, or to a predetermined goal. Comparing your actual totals to some type of measurement enables you to readily evaluate your performance and be alerted if problems are developing. For example, from comparisons, you may find that, although sales are increasing, certain expenses are rising far more than anticipated.

A well-known West Coast accountant, who specializes in designing franchisee accounting systems, states that in his opinion the area in which most franchisees fail is financial management. They do not understand the fundamentals of cash flow, inventory or receivables management, and in most cases they do not go to an accountant for help. Yet the majority of accountants are qualified to design a proper system and help them in understanding the importance of controlling the financial aspects of their businesses.

For help in designing a system and choosing an accountant, you might first want to obtain an unbiased and confidential opinion from an expert consultant or firm that specializes in accountancy for your particular line of business. This would be a one-time analysis of your needs plus recommendations. It should be understood from the beginning that the consultant will not be retained by you for regular services, so the opinions you receive will be independent of any future considerations. Usually a banker, lawyer, or other respected business person will be able to suggest someone for this purpose. This approach is also recommended if you already have a system in place. An independent review will ascertain whether you are receiving full and expert advice at a cost fair to both parties.

Choosing the Right Accountant

Once you have decided on what information you want your accounting system to produce, it is then time to actually begin the search for the right accountant. Generally accountants fall into three classes:

1. *Those who are qualified to handle bookkeeping systems and prepare routine tax returns and other simple government reports.* Such accountants may or may not be competent in computerized systems.

2. *Those who are tax specialists and can give money-saving advice.*

3. *Those who have the knowledge and experience to be valuable counselors in accounting, taxes, and general business and financial planning.* They also are knowledgeable about various types of computer hardware and financial software packages.

It is up to you to decide what you are willing to pay for. But bear in mind that it is not wise to look for the cheapest person available. The financial aspects of operating your franchise are too important for you to attempt to cut corners. If you expect an accountant to take the time and interest to work earnestly on your behalf, you also should expect to pay him or her adequately and gratefully. In your own interest, you should at the outset make it clear that you are will to pay an accountant well, but at the same time make it equally clear that you will be stern in judging performance.

To decide on an accountant use much the same procedure you would before hiring a key person. Give thought to the kind of person you want, the developments you expect to take place within the next few years, and what you will expect from the relationship. Write these thoughts down because they will:

Give you a clearer idea of what you are looking for.

Enable you to more effectively rate prospective accountants.

Give interviewees a more exact idea of your needs and enable them to quote a fee more accurately.

Serve as the basis for a letter of agreement (or intent) outlining the services that you expect to receive and that the accountant agrees to supply. A formal contract may not be feasible but a letter can help avert later misunderstandings.

Credentials

Ascertain the professional expertise of the person or firm you are considering, as well as its ability to prepare a system of procedures and to provide tax advice and financial guidance. What is its reputation with lawyers and bankers in your area? Does it have business or political connections that may be helpful to you?

If it is an accounting firm, how many employees does it have? How many are CPAs? What national and state societies does it belong to? Does it have branch offices? How many years has it been in business? Get a credit report on the firm. Drop in at the firm's offices unexpectedly and observe the amount of activity and the facilities.

Has the firm been growing rapidly, perhaps too rapidly? How many clients does it have? Is a list of clients available? What types of business are they in? How many are involved with products or services similar to yours? Contact a few of these clients for references.

Systems Knowledge

What records does the accountant recommend that your bookkeeper maintain? What records should your various departments supply? What reports are required for financial management, for tax purposes, for departmental administration, and for regulatory agencies?

How much does the accountant know about computer accounting and software packages? A qualified, modern accountant should be able to advise on various types of computers, their software, and peripheral equipment.

The accountant also should know how to integrate manual accounting systems with computer programs—what records should be entered into file and what reports should be quickly retrievable. Software is expensive and only essential programs should be installed. Tons of printouts are costly in terms of both money and time. Hard copy should be produced only when it is certain to be used.

Knowledge of Tax Issues

Any accountant can fill out tax forms. A good accountant will search for every possible credit and deduction. An excellent accountant—the one you want—will *plan ahead* to reduce taxes. He or she will:

Set up accounting procedures, or change them, to take advantage of the regulations.

Recommend changes in policy and actions on your part to gain benefits from new provisions or court decisions in tax law.

Keep you aware that tax evasion is fraud but that tax avoidance is absolutely legal.

Many franchise owners have their business accountants handle their personal taxes also. This can be valuable. Your personal accountant needs to know your company's type of legal entity, your salary, profits or dividends, deferred compensation, insurance, real estate holdings, tax shelters, capital gains, estate and gift planning, special allowances, together with the tax law and its effect on your situation.

Management Knowledge

It is one thing to have a good accounting system, but another to be able to analyze the contents of financial reports and know what actions should be taken. Your accountant ought to be able and willing to act as a financial management consultant to you and the heads of your profit or cost centers. He or she should be able to point out trouble spots and their causes, such as insufficient working capital, sales declines, inadequate pricing, low productivity, or whatever the menace may be. It is helpful if the accountant can go even further by suggesting changes in management policy or operational procedures.

Every financial problem has a cause for which there is the right corrective action. It may not be the answer you prefer, but it may be the best solution possible. Sometimes it is necessary to forget your ego and follow the path that is best for your franchise. Have an accountant who will help you do this.

Knowledge of Your Business and the Franchise Industry

Although accounting fundamentals are similar for most businesses, operating within the requirements of a franchise agreement often imposes additional accounting or bookkeeping requirements. Also, financial and operating ratios, state and federal regulations, reporting formats, and tax laws vary considerably. Therefore, it is crucial to have an accountant who understands your type of business, the nature of the franchisee-franchisor relationship and all applicable government regulations.

Location

While it is desirable for your accountant to understand your kind of business—perhaps even to handle other clients in the same field—you surely do not want one who is working for one of your competitors. Therefore, you may prefer to select an out-of-town accountant who has no affiliations that could cause conflict. On the other hand, you and your accountant should be within a reasonable distance of each other because of the need to confer on a regular basis. A city or town within or not too far from your business area should be a good place to look for prospective accountants.

Optimum Size

Accounting firms range in size from a single accountant to international organizations with thousands of accountant and staff members. The biggest firms maintain offices in most large and medium-sized U.S. cities. How big should your accounting service be? As with law firms, accounting firms usually assign their best qualified personnel to their largest clients. Therefore, the average franchise owner is likely to receive more personal attention from an individual or a smaller firm than from one that principally handles nationwide corporations. Also, an accountant who is an independent business person may be more understanding of you and your needs.

The larger accounting firm, however, should have sufficient manpower and expertise to provide thorough, high-quality services in all circumstances:

In the event your assigned accountant should be absent for a prolonged period of time.

During peak accounting demand periods, especially before year-end and April 15.

In event of a major tax audit.

In case of a critical development, such as an expansion, setting up a new corporation, going into a new venture, or making a change in ownership.

When you need specialized advice, as in the tax implications of profit sharing, employee benefit plans, or the installation of special equipment.

If you do decide to hire an individual accountant or a very small firm, be certain that your choice is mindful of its limitations and will not hesitate to refer you to a specialist if circumstances require such an action.

Who Will Really Handle Your Accounting?

Who actually will be your accountant? The one who contacts you regularly and does your work? Larger firms usually assign a CPA to a client under the supervision of one of the principals of the firm and the CPA, in turn, may assign the routine work to an assistant. Therefore, you should have it clearly understood from the outset exactly what person is going to work on your account permanently. In order to hold down costs, some firms will ease in a lower-paid, less-experienced trainee to assist. If you do not protest, he or she may become your regular contact.

Make sure that a major partner will be accessible if you urgently need advice. Some principals always seem to be "in conference" or "out of town."

A Cordial and Cooperative Relationship

Accountants should be loyal. They should keep your affairs strictly confidential. They should concern themselves with the financial well-being of you and your company, rather than ingratiating themselves with the tax collectors.

Some accountants are too conservative, preferring to do everything the easy, noncontroversial way—perhaps at your expense—rather than being willing to fight for your best interests. Others are too adventuresome, always wanting to test the system. Unfortunately, however, they are risking your money.

Accountants always should maintain a cooperative relationship with your employees and not assert unwarranted authority. They also should be eager to attend seminars and workshops that will help them be more knowledgeable financial officers for you.

In turn, you and your staff will benefit by *thoroughly* cooperating with the accountant, by supplying all the information and records needed, and by following any advice given. The more the accountant is made to feel a part of the organization, the better job he or she will do. Altogether, it is important that you feel a comforting rapport with your accountant.

Cost

Accounting firms usually charge a basic retainer fee, specifying the services included within this fee, plus an hourly or per diem rate for extra work. Large firms often charge more than small ones—as much as double. This may be so because of their highly specialized knowledge and breadth of services, or perhaps because of their prominence. Let the accountants you interview know you are definitely interested in holding down costs; otherwise you may be sure they will be higher. Candidates will be feeling you out on this, so don't suggest a figure or reveal what you have been paying.

A Dynamic System

An accountant's first priority should be to design or make certain of a purposeful accounting system for his or her client. If your franchise already has a system, this should be reviewed and restructured as necessary to provide you with the means for better analysis, closer control, and faster action.

Many accounting systems are no more than a dead history of what has already happened. Past records are necessary, but more important they should form a basis for goals and controls that will lead to improvements in performance, profits, and growth. Reports show you where you have been and where you currently stand. You also need indicators for the future.

If you currently are a franchisee and are adding one or more units, your current accounting system may become obsolete or ineffective. A common fault of multiunit accounting systems is that they fail to distribute income and expense properly. It is relatively simple to track sales income through each unit but expenses may be much more difficult to allocate. The more units you add, the more you will incur expenses that will be general in nature—i.e., expenses of the total franchise, not a particular unit. Fees that regularly fall into the general category include insurance, legal and accounting fees, local permits, and advertising and promotional costs. If you have only a few units and no central or corporate office, your accounting system can be designed to allocate these costs among the units. If, however, you are large enough to have a corporate office, then these general expenses can be charged to central administration and distributed or allocated among the units at the end of every accounting period. It is crucial that this distribution be made because central or corporate offices do not make money—they cost money. So it is important that the unit managers are aware that each unit must carry its share of corporate administrative expense.

Tax Considerations

In businesses both large and small, one of the most important functions of the accounting system is to generate information for use in calculating various types of taxes. Since your product and/or services can be subject to taxation by several levels of government in the form of sales, income, excise, or head taxes, and your payroll is the basis for social security and federal and state unemployment taxes, the recording and preservation of sales and payroll information is crucial. All these records are subject to audit by various government agencies, and complete and accurate information is not only your best defense, but your only one.

During years of working with franchisees and dealers, we have noticed that far too many business owners fall into either one of two extremes: those that do not give enough attention to allowable tax deductions and those who are obsessed with tax avoidance. Unfortunately, either extreme can cost the business considerable money in unnecessary tax expense and loss of profits. Lack of a proper bookkeeping system or professional advice will cause a careless person to pay too much in taxes. On the other extreme, the obsessed person will spend hours and days calculating against or arguing with tax authorities when this time and expense could be more profitably spent on the business. It is better to work to make money by tending the store than trying to beat the tax collector.

For most tax purposes a competent accountant, accustomed to handling taxes, can be the only tax adviser you need. But if you have, or should encounter, a complex problem, then it can be advisable to bring in a tax attorney to confer with you and your accountant. Tax laws frequently change, and a tax attorney is in a better position than most to monitor the changes.

As you and your accountant discuss the tax implications of your business, be certain you ask about the following:

1. What form of business structure is most appropriate for you at this time? Review the tax status differences between a sole proprietorship, a general or limited partnership, a private or S corporation or public corporation.

2. Should you elect a fiscal year other than a calendar year? If you are subject to an irregular or seasonal cash flow, you may find that a change in fiscal year may be advantageous.

3. What method should you use to value your inventory? Keep in mind that whatever method is chosen it must be used consistently.

4. What are the current tax implications involved in lease-buy decisions for equipment and vehicles?

5. Are you taking advantage of available favorable tax treatment of fringe benefits for yourself? Franchise owners can arrange tax deductions for insurance and pension plans in a number of ways.

6. What are the current tax possibilities if you want to borrow money from the business? When a company loans money to the owner or to a member of the family of an owner, the IRS becomes very interested. Check out all the implications before you fall into a trap.

7. Will your system have a method of checking or reviewing federal and state unemployment tax rates? These rates can vary by several percentage points depending on your claims experience. States are often lax in making adjustments that could reduce your rates.

8. What records does the accountant advise you to retain? Current and past records must show and *substantiate* all income and expense. Please note the word "substantiate." Many owners have been caught in the trap of showing expenses but having no records to prove that the expenses were related to business.

9. What documentation is necessary for travel, entertainment, and gifts for business purposes? The IRS usually demands extensive documentation for these types of expense.

10. What role would your accountant play if you were selected for a tax audit by a federal, state, or municipal tax authority? Reach an understanding as to who pays if the accountant is at fault. Agree in advance about the accountant's role in event of an appeal either at the appellate division of the IRS or a tax court.

9

Always Have
the Right
Business Structure

Are you a multiunit owner, already with a sizable spread of locations? Or are you a person only beginning to think about a franchise? Either way, you want success, and you can help yourself to get it if you have the most suitable kind of business structure. Of the numerous kinds of business structure, simple and complex, there is always the best kind.

Does this mean you should change your structure from time to time? Perhaps. There are so many ways to structure your business operations, that you can, if need be, make appropriate changes. The important point is to be aware of the forms available to you and from time to time review your situation. Do so, of course, always in close study with your lawyer and accountant.

And with full consideration of the franchisor. The franchisor will understand your desire to have a structure that enables you to best anticipate costs, liabilities, taxes, profits, and growth. But you, for your part, must realize that the franchisor is concerned, both sensitively and profoundly, with being certain the investment in you is well secured, especially if the franchisor is providing some of your financing or leases. Most franchise agreements will stipulate that, if you change your business structure, the agreement must be modified to make sure you still are personally responsible. The franchisor always will demand that you pledge your personal assets as collateral. The most common example of change occurs when a franchisee goes from sole proprietorship or simple partnership to a corporation.

There can be many good reasons over the years for wanting to change your business structure. During your lifetime you may want to do it several times. Keep open the possibilities in the forms described in this chapter. But first give yourself answers to the following questions.

Ownership

1. Are you the sole owner of the franchise?

2. Do you plan to divide ownership and involve your spouse and/or children in the future?

3. Do you wish to retain control even after ownership is distributed?

4. Do you plan to bring family or investors into the franchise?

5. Are you planning to acquire, expand, or merge?

6. Do you plan on going public?

7. Do you have loans that are secured by your personal assets?

8. Do you want the franchise or income from the franchise to go to your family in event of your death?

9. Do you have several children with varying degrees of interest in the franchise?

10. Do you anticipate sale of the franchise before your retirement?

Financial

1. Do you have sources of income other than the franchise?

2. Does your spouse's employment provide pension and medical benefits?

3. Are you able to shelter income to the maximum allowed by current IRS regulations?

4. Do you anticipate the need for substantial financing in the near future?

5. Do you have substantial personal assets that are not currently pledged as loan collateral?

6. Would incorporating offer you substantial tax breaks?

7. Do you have access to private investment capital?

8. Do you plan to expand into other states?

Miscellaneous

1. Are you concerned about details of your business operations becoming public information?

2. Are you able to expand your accounting capabilities to meet additional state, municipal, and federal requirements?

3. Would you be willing to relinquish total or partial control of your franchise to a board of directors?

4. Do you anticipate trying to raise venture capital?

Sole Proprietorship

In a proprietorship one person is the sole owner of a business or franchise. In theory, and largely in fact, you simply start doing business either under your name or some other that you choose. Commonly, the latter is called a DBA (doing business as). Although you will have to apply for a federal ID number and in many states obtain a state and/or municipal sales tax number, you will be less regulated than in any other form of business. You should be cautioned, however, that regulation of proprietorships is on the increase. Many states now require that all businesses be registered, and obviously there may be numerous local ordinances that will affect your operations. Still, the records you will have to keep and the reports you will have to file are the fewest possible in this bureaucratic age. You won't have to file a separate business income tax form because all franchise income, expense, profit, and loss are included in your personal tax return.

In a sole proprietorship, you are personally liable for all debts and liabilities of your business or franchise. So if someone sued the business and received an award not covered by insurance, your personal assets are then vulnerable and you could be bankrupted.

You will personally have to come up with all the capital needed for the franchise. Equity financing is, by definition, impossible with a proprietorship. You also will have to pay for all your personal medical and other benefits with after-tax dollars as the IRS will not regard these as business expenses. You are entitled, however, to establish a tax-deferred retirement plan.

If you have employees, social security and unemployment taxes must be paid and you will have to deduct, report, and pay withholding taxes.

Questions of differing legal control are virtually nonexistent in a sole proprietorship, although most franchise agreements do have stipulations about who has responsibility under a variety of circumstances. Future control and ownership of the franchise if the owner dies becomes a matter concerning the estate and the probate courts because a sole proprietorship has no true continuity of management and title of ownership.

Being the sole owner of a franchise can bring a person a very valuable emotional reward: the feeling of being, as much as possible, a free and independent person whose obligations to others are mainly voluntary. But this individualism, as magnificent as it may appear, can be risky, particularly when family members are involved.

General Partnership

Like a marriage, a partnership can be very satisfying, but, also like a marriage, it can cause many discontents and even misery. When these occur in a marriage, the union may still hold together because the parties love one another or have children but a business partnership is different. Altogether, a business partnership is a very fragile and hazardous arrangement. During the early and middle 1980s, the use of both general and limited partnerships increased dramatically because of tax law changes. Then losses incurred by the partnership could be used by passive investors to offset other income. When that law was changed in 1986, the use of partnerships as a method of doing business declined and at this writing is not nearly as popular as in the past. Still, a partnership can sometimes be the best form in which to conduct a franchise; therefore do not close your mind completely to the idea.

At the same time, keep in mind that the two principal reasons for forming partnerships are likely to be illusions. One of these is the belief that a partnership is easier and less expensive to form than a corporation. The fact is that a corporation can be much easier to form (some states have procedures and forms for doing it yourself, although we would not recommend it), and forming a corporation is likely to cost much less than drawing a prudent partnership agreement. This is especially true in states that have adopted various restrictive laws governing partnerships.

The other reason is a belief that a partnership saves taxes, a belief that is not necessarily so. Depending on the size, in many corporations you can minimize the corporate income tax by paying most of the profits as salaries to the owners who would not have to pay any more in taxes than if they got the money from a partnership. While a partnership does not have to pay income taxes as a business, it does have to keep impeccable records and file detailed comprehensive reports. The IRS is very demanding of partnership arrangements.

To be a partnership, a franchise must be owned by two or more persons who have a financial interest in the business. The "persons" may be individuals, corporations, estates, or trusts and the partnership agreement can be oral or written. Because oral agreements can be an invitation to disaster, we strongly advise against such an arrangement. In fact, a partnership agreement should be one of the most meticulously prepared of all business documents.

Nevertheless, a partnership is an extremely adaptable arrangement. Shares, duties, amount and type of investment, distribution of profits, and transfer of interest and control can all be stipulated in various ways. A partnership can subsequently evolve into a corporation without a significant tax problem and a partnership can be dissolved easily, especially if the provisions for doing so are set forth in the partnership agreement. In fact, partnerships are usually designed for relatively short-term projects or purposes. The agreement should contain explicit provisions for adjusting to the death of any of the partners, otherwise the continuity of operations after a death can be very complicated. Life insurance, incidentally, can be a great benefit.

A partnership is intrinsically a perilous venture because any one of the partners can be held liable for the acts of any one of the others; every partner is the agent of all. Furthermore, no partner can conduct outside transactions that could be interpreted as a conflict of interest. Partners must divide in agreed-on ways both the income and the expenses of the partnership and directly deduct losses as they occur. At best, a partnership can be no more stable than its least stable member. The so-called silent or secret partnership can be especially unstable because of its covert nature. If the state law requires that all members of a partnership be a matter of public record, such a hidden arrangement is manifestly illegal and subject to severe penalties.

A partnership arrangement should never be attempted without the counsel and the help of an especially competent attorney. It is a complex arrangement with many potential traps and should be approached cautiously by any franchisee.

Limited Partnerships

A limited partnership is an enterprise run by a person or a group of persons who are explicitly assigned the full responsibility for operating the business. All the rest of the so-called partners are actually persons who have invested in the venture but do not control, influence, or become involved in management. This is why they are called limited partners. A limited partner has no liability for the debts of the partnership but can profit from its activities. The 1986 Tax Act severely curtailed the benefits of passive limited partners.

Also, in most states, limited partnerships are subject to strict regulation. This type of a partnership is not particularly suitable for most franchise operations.

Syndicates

Essentially a syndicate is nothing more than a limited partnership, but the term is being used more and more, particularly in real estate ventures. In general, the principal distinction between a limited partnership and a syndicate is the fact that in a syndicate the word "person" is legally interpreted to allow business entities such as corporation to become limited partners. Again, this is not a format generally used by franchisees.

The Corporation

A corporation is one of the most ingenious devices ever conceived by man. Legally it is virtually a person in itself; its existence is distinct from that of its owners or stockholders. As a legal entity, it can, in its own name, buy, sell, negotiate, own property, sue and be sued without, in most cases, involving the personal property of the stockholders. It is largely this limit on liability on the part of the stockholders that makes the corporation such an attractive method of doing business. It should be noted, however, that the limits of liability do not apply if the personal assets of the stockholder have been pledged or if the stockholder has acted as a cosigner for debts of the corporation, a common situation when a franchisee buys a franchise. Another major advantage of the corporation is that it is assumed to be immortal and therefore can continue in perpetuity, unaffected by the death of a stockholder. However, the transfer or inheritance of stock can certainly affect the ownership and control of the corporation.

Before taking the step to incorporate, consider several important issues. The creation of a separate entity will affect your control position unless you thoroughly understand the duties and the rights of the directors. Your tax treatment of income will be altered, and reporting requirements by the state and federal government will increase considerably. In most cases, your accounting system will have to be modified.

The person who owns or controls a majority of outstanding shares can have absolute control in electing the board of directors and running the franchise unless the business is chartered in a state that requires cumulative voting of shares. Usually, this person is called the *majority stockholder*.

The person who can vote the largest number of shares can control the corporation even though the total number of shares voted is not the majority of all the stock issued. Called the plurality stockholder, this person can control if there is no concerted action taken by the other stockholders.

Partner stockholders are two or more persons who own equal interests. Unless they are harmonious, they can be very disruptive to a corporation as they bargain politically for control.

A *minority stockholder,* by combining with other minority stockholders, can often achieve substantial influence in the corporation.

If you incorporate in a state that requires cumulative voting, you must have proportionate representation of the minority stockholders on the board of directors.

In most states, the charter of a closely held corporation can enable the shareholders to act directly as the board of directors, an arrangement that can simplify control when a business is small but can cause complications as a business grows.

You can control a corporation even if you are a minority investor by using various classes of stock. Some of the classes available are common, common nonvoting, and several classes of preferred stock.

The laws and regulations concerning corporate taxation are continually being changed by legislators, regulators, new IRS interpretations, and the courts. Good up-to-date tax guidance is therefore an absolute necessity.

When forming a corporation, the owners generally exchange money, property, or other assets for stock. Usually this can be done without immediate gain or loss, but the IRS has some restrictive regulations concerning this matter.

The way you operate your corporation can affect your taxes in many ways. You should confer with your tax adviser about the dates of your fiscal year, accounting methods, valuation of inventory, investment tax credits, the methods of depreciation, and other business practices.

Understand from the outset that a corporation must do more record keeping and submit more complex reports than a proprietorship or partnership. However, if your system is properly designed and maintained or supervised by a competent accountant, the requirements should not too burdensome. You also may find that the reports will cause some loss of privacy and confidentiality. If this kind of loss is an important issue, explore this area carefully with your attorney.

S Corporation

An S corporation is a hybrid entity that combines several of the advantages of both a partnership and a corporation. The principal advantage is that business profits are not taxed at the corporate level because they are passed directly to the shareholders, much as in a partnership. Each shareholder must, however, report and pay taxes on this income whether it is distributed or not. Conversely, stockholders can deduct business losses from personal income. A stockholder may also enjoy certain tax-free fringe benefits not available in the partnership format. A competent tax adviser should be knowledgeable and up-to-date on S corporation tax law.

Joint Venture

The joint venture arrangement can be advantageous to a franchisee who must construct a facility according to franchisor specifications. A joint venture is an enterprise set up to accomplish a specific purpose or goals related to it. These objectives could involve the buying or selling of a certain property or business, constructing a building, or sharing a securities account for a short period. A joint venture, however, cannot be a business that is set up to continue indefinitely. It must be planned so that, when the goal is achieved, it will terminate. No particular termination date has to be specified.

To qualify as a joint venture, all the members must have an interest in the capital assets, have joint control over operations and profits, and share in any losses. Various duties and responsibilities can be divided among the members. For example, one member might furnish the land, another construct the buildings, and yet another bring management resources and know-how. Usually, when this format is used by a franchisee to construct a facility, the venture is terminated after the facility is completed and the property is then transferred to the business entity operating the franchise. In some cases, the property may be transferred to still another business entity that will, in turn, lease it to the franchisee.

Jointly Owned Business

Any business with two stockholders or partners can be called a jointly owned business. More specifically, however, a jointly owned business is one that has been specifically set up to be owned by two or more parties, especially if it assumes or performs certain functions for other businesses of the partners. Examples of such functions are doing the buying or selling, managing a mutually owned warehouse, combining deliveries, and sharing a computer system.

Going Public with Your Corporation

Often, multiunit franchisees consider going public to gain better access to the capital market but are uncertain whether their overall business is large enough to warrant such a move. At this writing, investment bankers recommend that sales be in the neighborhood of $10 million to $20 million annually and that the after-tax profit to equity ratio be in the 10-to 15-percent range. Bankers will also look at the growth rate over the past five years, expecting to see 10 to 12 percent per year.

Although there may be some advantages to going public, such as greater name recognition, the move involves a dilution of ownership, loss of control, and an increased amount of reporting to regulatory agencies.

The Corporate Board of Directors

The role of the board of directors of a corporation deserves special consideration and discussion. Most states require that a corporation must have a minimum of three people who will serve on the board of directors, although the articles of incorporation may stipulate that more than three can serve. In a family-owned corporation, the board of directors is usually composed of family members, a condition that can become very troublesome if the family cannot act in harmony. The bylaws of the corporation will identify the corporate officer positions, and, again, these positions are usually occupied by the family members who own the corporation. In most states the board of directors is charged with the responsibility of managing the corporation within the laws of the state.

The board of directors of a small corporation may play an important role, particular if the business is family-owned. Even though usually the board meets periodically only to comply with the requirements of the corporate charter, at some point circumstances will force the members to take a more active part in planning the future of the corporation. Children grow older, spouses die or divorce, and relatives change their interests and their needs—all events that can change both the function and the direction of the corporation. Those incorporators who have limited the board membership to family members may then realize that normal changes in family relationships can be severely disruptive to business operations, or that bickering and tension are affecting the performance of nonfamily employees. Often, when older children are involved in the ownership, their diverging interests cause them to place greater emphasis on short-term profits and less on the long-term health and stability of the company.

If you are setting up a corporation to operate your franchise and plan to include persons in your family as shareholders and members of the board of directors, give careful thought to the long-term future. Perhaps the most effective way you can insulate your business from the adverse affects of family strife is to provide, in the articles of incorporation, for nonfamily positions on the board. These additional board members should be people that you can trust to act in the best interests of the franchise and who have areas of expertise that will be helpful in long-term planning. Their primary function is, however, to provide balance and objectivity and to mitigate the influence of family prejudices on the operation of the franchise.

A balanced board of directors should be particularly able to fulfill the corporation's responsibilities as stipulated by the law and its charter, and also to fairly represent the interests of the shareholders and exert itself to make certain that the business is operated soundly and profitably for both the short and long range. It will not hesitate to act in important matters such as hiring, directing, and firing the manager. A balanced board can provide you, as the franchise owner, the opportunity to partially divest yourself of some elements of responsibility and consequently to avoid some of the pressure from members of your family.

The Advisory Board

If you are comfortable with your management situation and your ownership is not complicated by family shareholders, then the use of an advisory board may be very helpful. Very few franchises cannot profit from an outside group of specialists in diverse business disciplines, who can review the companies policies and performance and make recommendations for improvement.

No owner or manager can know it all or be always completely objective about all aspects of the business. An advisory board can provide you, as the owner, with valuable advice in any or all of the following areas:

1. Recommendations on current operating procedures: organizational structure, current marketing practices, personnel policies, purchasing and receiving, inventory control, sales, and secondary product merchandising.

2. Recommendations on current financial practices: accounts payable and receivable, cash flow, earnings and capital ratios, labor costs, potential sources of additional capital and overall profitability.

3. Review of operations with recommendations on plans to expand or to acquire additional franchise units.

4. Evaluation of proposed market strategies, preparation of long-term projections, and development of other elements of strategic planning.

An advisory board assumes none of the liability of the corporate board of directors and does not have any actual authority. Usually, it does not have to be created by the articles of incorporation or the bylaws since, in most states, a basic letter of agreement prepared by your attorney will suffice to establish membership on the board. The agreement should be very specific about the advisory role and the limits of both liability and authority of the members of the board. The members should be compensated in much the manner as the conventional board but, because of the lack of liability, the retainer and meeting fee can be less.

Meetings of an advisory board should be held at least quarterly, and the agenda should be in the hands of the members at least two weeks prior to the meeting. The chairperson of the board should be elected by the members, and under no circumstances should you as the owner assume that post. You, however, should regularly report on the implementation or the status of the board's recommendations. Its members will be neither effective nor diligent if they feel their recommendations are ignored or neglected.

One of the major advantages of the advisory board is the ability to focus objectively on corporate strategy without undue influence or pressure from stockholders to produce short-term profits. A well selected board is impersonal and impartial.

You, as a franchisee, have the opportunity to choose a board that best suits your situation and needs. Your emphasis can be on strategy, control, authority, or advice. Many of the issues in operating a franchise are best resolved by boardroom debate.

Corporate Reorganization

The simplest form of a corporation is one with just a single class of common stock. This may be quite sufficient especially during the early days of the business. Later, however, it may be very advantageous to reorganize the corporation and issue more than one class of stock. This mechanism is becoming increasingly popular for those persons who wish to pass their business ownership on to family members without losing control or an adequate income from it.

For example, the corporation is reorganized to create one or more classes of common stock and one or more classes of preferred stock. The preferred stock is structured so that it represents most or all of the value of the franchise at the time of reorganization. This stock is retained by the owner so that he or she can continue to own the equity that has been built up over the years and, at the same time, freeze its value for estate purposes.

The common stock can then be issued to the upcoming owners with little or no tax to pay, because the common stock will have little value at the time of initial issue. But, as the business or the franchise grows in value afterwards, this value accrues to the common stockholders. Furthermore, voting rights and other characteristics can be assigned among the various classes of stock to accommodate the long-term intentions of both stockholders and the board of directors.

Discuss this question of the right business structure carefully with your advisers. The correct choice can have far-reaching implications for you, your franchise, and your family.

10

Know the Ways to Raise Money for Start-Up and/or Expansion

The collapse of the real estate market in most parts of the nation during the late 1980s and early 1990s had a devastating affect on the banking industry and other capital sources. Scores of savings and loans and other banking institutions failed, and their assets were seized by the regulatory agencies. As the recession deepened in the early nineties, the remaining banking institutions and other lending sources stiffened their criteria for granting loans, and both independent small businesses and franchisees found it more difficult to obtain funding.

Banking sources and other lenders, however, insist that money is still available if the potential borrower knows where to look and is willing to satisfy the lender's requirements. Generally, most lender's will look more favorably at an applicant wanting to invest in a franchised operation than at one wanting to start an independent business, if the franchisor is reputable and has a record of successful franchises. This is not to say, however, that someone wishing to start or expand a franchise can walk into any lender and get a loan. A franchisee is subject to the same careful scrutiny and requirements that any applicant must satisfy. But being involved with a successful franchise will be a plus.

Typically, franchisees who are purchasing a first franchise or who are in the initial stages of expansion do not have access to major capital markets or public equity. Initial capital is usually obtained from personal savings and collateral and from loans from family and friends, sometimes combined with franchisor financing. Often, bank loans are also used, but these loans are secured by personal assets rather than business assets. As the franchise becomes established, some of the capital markets become more accessible, especially if the amount of the loan exceeds $500,000. Many banks, for example, are seldom interested in business-type loans that are under the half million mark.

Sources of Capital

Generally, the sources of capital available to you may be:

1. Common stock.
2. Preferred stock.
3. Debt financing.

Whether these three sources will be available to you will depend on your business structure. If you are a sole proprietor, the only source will be debt financing. If you are incorporated, you have the option of selling and distributing common and preferred stock. Generally in franchising most of the stock is held by the owner and minority interests are held by friends and family. Seldom is a franchisee large enough to make public offerings, and, in fact, most franchisors have clauses in the franchise agreement that prohibit such offerings without certain limitations or obtaining approval. Because of the limits of liability and other advantages offered by the corporate structure, many franchisees do incorporate and often will distribute shares to family members. Another trend suggested by some franchisors is the separate incorporation of additional units. For example, a franchisee decides to expand and buy additional units within a particular franchise. Each newly acquired unit is purchased and operated by a separate corporation, even though the shareholders are the same. The franchisee, by incorporating each operation separately, is protecting the overall success from being affected should one of the newly acquired units fail.

The distribution of stock in a family-owned or closely held corporation has important control and tax implications. Many franchise agreements also control stock distribution because the franchisor obviously wants to ensure that controlling interest is always in the hands of the person who is a party to the original agreement.

Control of the franchise is a matter that demands considerable foresight. Common stockholders have certain rights, and, in the event of divorce or death, these rights can affect the ability of the owner to manage the corporation. For example, stockholders as a group have the power to:

1. Elect a board of directors.
2. Adopt and amend bylaws.
3. Amend the articles of incorporation.
4. Authorize the issuance of new securities.
5. Authorize the sale or mortgaging of assets.
6. Authorize the sale or merger of the corporation.
7. Change the amount of stock to be issued.

The articles of incorporation and the bylaws may also provide certain specific rights to individual stockholders such as the right to receive dividends in proportion to their percentage of ownership by a vote of the board of directors. It is not uncommon for minority stockholders to wish to take short-term profits out of a franchise despite the long-term goals of the original owner.

In most states, common stockholders may enter into agreements that alter the basic rights. Often, family-owned corporations restrict outside interests in obtaining stock by inserting in the bylaws a first right of refusal clause.

Needless to say, the stock distribution issue is very important to the future life of the franchise. We suggest that you discuss this matter fully with a competent attorney, who is knowledgeable not only in corporate law but also in the laws concerning franchise agreements.

Since access to stock financing is somewhat limited for most franchisees, debt financing is the only alternative. Fortunately, despite the condition of the economy, there are still several possible sources.

Before investigating these sources, however, you should be aware of several aspects of debt financing. First, any money that is borrowed is not considered part of the equity base of the franchise. The holder of the debt or the lender, in most cases, does not have any rights to the increased value of the franchise should it be successful. (Exceptions to this rule of nonequity participation will be discussed later in this chapter.) Loans are usually made for a specific period of time and for a specific rate of return, although the rate may be indexed to some agreed-upon monetary standard.

Second, all debt will be assigned a priority in terms of repayment should the franchise fail and the remaining assets be distributed among the debtors. First mortgages, for example, may be in a senior or first position relative to other debt, which means they would be paid off first in event of a default. Second and third mortgages would be junior or subordinate to the first mortgage but senior to certain other types of debt. Obviously, the lower the priority of position, the greater the risk is, and this fact is usually reflected in the interest rates.

Some of the types of debt available to franchisees are:

1. *Mortgage:* A long-term debt instrument usually secured by a specific piece of land or building or group of buildings. A first mortgage holds the first position and any subsequent mortgages are second or junior to the first.

2. *Security agreement:* Sometimes called a "chattel mortgage," this kind of loan is secured by personal or nonreal estate property and usually is junior to mortgages secured by real estate.

3. *Note:* This is a short-term loan agreement requiring repayment by a specific period of time or on demand. The interest rate is usually fixed, and the repayment schedule is stipulated.

4. *Debenture:* A long-term debt without specific security, a debenture affords the holder a claim to any assets not already assigned as security for another debt.

Sources of Financing

Despite the fact that small businesses and franchisees are responsible for most of the growth of the economy and the number of new jobs, financing is still one of the most difficult hurdles. A franchisee, particularly in the early years of start-up, must face the fact that most types of debt financing will require security, and usually this will make it necessary to pledge personal assets. A common mistake made by many seeking financing is to assume that, if they have sufficient assets to pledge, then getting a loan will be easy. Remember, even though the lending source may accept your house as collateral, it does not want your house. It is in the lending business, not the housing business. Although accepting your real estate as security reduces its risk, the decision to lend you money will be based on your ability to repay the loan; therefore demonstrating that ability must be your primary focus. Before discussing the mechanics of applying for a loan, however, let's look at some of the sources.

Direct Financing or Loan Guarantees by the Franchisor

Although approximately 30 percent of franchisors will offer some type of financial assistance, very few will offer direct financing or loan guarantees. Most will offer you help in finding a bank or other lenders, and some will have leasing programs available for property and/or equipment. The Franchise Opportunities Guide, published by the International Franchise Association, will give you some information about which franchisors offer financial assistance and what these kinds of assistance are.

Commercial Banks

Commercial banking is undergoing the same dramatic changes that are affecting the entire banking industry. Although many consumer-oriented banks had commercial banking departments, the never ending series of mergers and acquisitions has changed the role of these departments and in many areas of the country has closed them to small business loan markets. Today, few commercial banking departments in the large regional consumer banks are interested in making loans under $1,000,000. However, as the merger mania continues in the consumer banking industry, numerous smaller banks have found a good place for themselves in the lending market for smaller businesses and franchisees looking for loans in the $50,000 to $1,000,000 range, together with other commercial banking services.

Commercial banks generally specialize in short-term loans that may be secured or unsecured. Most will handle the following forms of financing:

Lines of credit	Installment loans
Secured loan	Security agreements
Term loans	SBA-guaranteed loans
Receivables	Inventory

Many commercial banks are involved in the Small Business Administration Loan Guarantee program, and some are known as preferred or certified lenders because of their track record with the SBA. This program, designed to give practical financing help to small business people, offers the best opportunity for the franchisee seeking smaller loans.

Small Business Administration

Although the SBA is primarily involved in loan guarantees, it does make some direct loans. The availability is limited to franchisees in high unemployment areas who are unable to obtain guaranteed loans and to handicapped persons, Vietnam vets, and disabled veterans. The supply of these loans is limited and sporadic because they are funded by Congress.

Small Business Lending Companies

These are companies licensed by the SBA to operate under the SBA 7-A Program. They are fairly active in lending to franchisors for start-up and expansion but, at this writing, have written few loans for franchisees.

Small Business Investment Companies (SBICs)

SBICs furnish equity capital and long-term financing, but they want an equity position and often demand a role in managing the franchise.

Venture Capitalists

These are always mentioned as a source of seed money and start-up capital, but realistically they are not an appropriate source for most franchisees. First, the amount of money needed by most franchisees is not large enough to attract venture capitalists. Second, they want an extremely high return within a relatively short period of time. Third, venture capitalists will demand an equity position—i.e., part of the franchise—and often will insist on a role in management or a position on your board of directors. Fourth, they usually will want a guaranteed buy-back at a preset price, allowing them to get out within a short period of time. Most small business people who have tried this route say, "Don't waste your time."

Individual Investors

These are individuals who are looking for a place to invest money. They seldom put all their eggs in one basket preferring, instead, to loan smaller amounts to several people. The types of loans range from 90-day notes to long-term mortgages arranged through brokers or mortgage bankers. Often, an attorney or accountant knows of some of these investors. Also, there are other individual investors who are actually looking for a partnership. Depending on your personal goals, this type of investor can be a viable possibility.

Developing a Business and Financial Plan

Certainly, having a comprehensive business and financial plan is advantageous for any business, but if you are looking for either start-up financing or additional capital, it is an absolute necessity. The business plan, as it is used in a financing proposal, should have at least:

1. General information about the franchise, including products and/or services.

2. Detailed information about you and your key players.

3. The amount and type of financing requested.

4. How the proceeds are to be used.

5. Information about the potential market.

6. Potential customer profiles.

7. Financial information, past and projected.

As we discuss these topics in detail, it will become obvious to you that being a part of a franchise will not only improve your chances of securing financing but will also greatly simplify the development of your business plan. Much of the information required in terms of product, history, marketing, and business expense has already been developed by the franchisor. Consequently, your projections will be based on tangible information, not on pie-in-the-sky guesswork. The existence of a franchisor is of particular importance to those of you who are preparing a proposal for your first franchise unit. Most franchisors will be very willing to provide you with information about typical income and expense patterns. Also, since you have no previous experience on which to base your projections, their input will give your proposal the advantage of being founded on reality.

General Information About the Franchise

Normally, in giving this information, independent small business persons would have to assemble and describe, in detail, their company, its history, and the products and/or services that it intends to produce or sell. You, however, have all this information already available in your franchisor's disclosure statement. We suggest that, as part of your plan, you prepare an abstract or summary of this statement because usually it is very long. (Some will run in excess of 100 pages.) Add a clause that the entire statement is available on request.

If you already own at least one unit and if the purpose of your proposal is to secure financing for expansion or for working capital, then it will be necessary to include a brief history of your own operations.

Information About You and Your Key Players

One of the most common mistakes committed by owners who are preparing a financing proposal is to omit information about their management team and in some cases about their board of directors. Every lending or financing source is keenly interested in the depth of the management team. Each one is providing money with the expectation of being repaid, and one of the main elements in the success of any business is the strength of its management. You should provide in-depth resumes of yourself and your key staff, emphasizing general management experience. Personal information concerning family status, health, and education should also be included. Similar information about your advisory staff (attorney and accountant) should also be submitted.

It is advisable to provide a personal financial statement (business financial statements are included in another section of the proposal), and indicate what assets you would be willing to pledge if necessary.

It usually is advisable to include an organizational plan with your description of key players unless you have set this topic up as a separate category of information. Lenders will be interested in your business structure and your organizational chart.

The Amount and Type of Financing Requested

Describe the type of financing required, including the amounts and terms. It is not unusual to request two or more types of financing such as secured notes, a line of credit, and an intermediate-term loan. Include a schedule stating when the money will be needed.

How the Proceeds Will Be Used

Indicate how each type of loan will be used. For example, a line of credit may be used to increase inventory and an intermediate-term loan may be used to buy major equipment.

Marketing Information

Although the franchisor may have general marketing information, the lending source will require additional information about your particular market area and demographics, including local advertising and promotions, size of the sales force, potential accounts, and major competitors. The nature and extent of this information will depend on the type of your franchise. See Chap. 6 about analyzing markets and developing a marketing plan.

Potential Customer Profiles

Your franchisor will probably have a complete profile of your potential customers. And your market demographic study will provide the number of people within your market area who fit that profile. This information should be provided as part of the marketing plan.

Financial Information

This usually is the decisive section of your business plan or financing proposal. Even though the lender may be suitably impressed with your management credentials and the reputation of the franchisor, if the financial information that you provide does not convince the lender of your ability to repay the loan, then it will be denied. The type of information required will depend on your status as a borrower.

Borrowing for Start-Up Capital

1. *Detailed personal financial statements:* These include a description and market value of each asset, cash, and other liquid assets. Liabilities should be listed in terms of amounts and, if some are loans, the amount and times of the repayment schedule.

2. *Projected operating statement:* This, in essence, is based on your budget projections and is an estimate of your income and expenses for at

least the first year. Often, lenders will want a projected operating statement for a minimum of three years, which means that you will have to extend your budget projections since normally you will prepare a budget only a year in advance. The most important part of this section of the process is the justification for the projections. Anyone can plug into a operating statement projection some figures that will project fantastic profits, and obviously the lenders know this. Fortunately, as a franchisee, you should have access to information about similar operations from your franchisor or from other franchisees within the same franchise. This information should be submitted as justification for your estimates. Another important part of the justification process is your market demographic study. You must be able to demonstrate that your market demographics are reasonably similar to those of other successful units within the franchise.

3. *First-, second-, and third-year balance sheet projections:* These balance sheet projection must relate to your budget and operating statements. They are designed to show changes in your assets and liabilities at the end of the first, second, and third years. Generally, you do not have to provide additional information about the balance sheets of other units within the franchise to justify your projections. (An explanation of operating, or profit and loss, statements and balance sheets will follow later in this chapter.)

4. *Cash flow projections:* Again, the cash flow projections must be tied into your operating statements and your budget. Generally, lenders will not require cash flow projections beyond one year. Most require, however, that cash flows be illustrated on a month-to-month basis, rather than only at the beginning and end of the year.

5. *Break-even point (BEP) analysis:* Check with the lender before you submit the proposal to determine whether BEP information is needed or helpful. (See Chap. 11 for discussion of the BEP.)

Borrowing for Expansion or Acquisition. If you already have owned a franchise unit for two or more years, you have a wealth of information in your past financial records. Although you will still have to provide the lender with the same projections as the start-up borrower, you have a decided advantage in that you can base your projections on the operating statements and balance sheets from previous years. To be valid, these previous statements and balance sheets must have been prepared and certified by your accountant. It still may be advantageous to provide additional information from your franchisor concerning their marketing programs. Of course, you will have to produce evidence that either you or the franchisor has conducted a new up-to-date market demographics study.

Understanding Financial Statements

A never ending complaint by accountants, banking personnel, and franchisors is that too many franchisees do not fully understand financial statements, particularly operating (profit and loss) statements and balance sheets. Without understanding what the figures mean, the franchisee is often misled as to the actual worth or value of the franchise and the amount of profit or loss. Although you should ask your accountant for a full explanation of your financial statements, you should learn to know by yourself what they mean. Here is brief description of typical reports for a franchise.

Balance Sheets

A balance sheet shows the franchises's financial condition at a specific period in time. Although this report is usually rendered at the end of each fiscal period (monthly, quarterly, etc.), it can be prepared at any time if required.

Generally, you need to know the following definitions:

1. *Current assets:* These assets are cash and items that you can expect to convert to cash within 12 months. Current assets usually include cash on hand, accounts receivable, inventory, prepaid expenses, and interest due. The two categories most subject to error are accounts receivable, unless it is adjusted by bad debt, and inventory totals, which are usually overstated unless they have been verified by an actual physical count.

2. *Property and equipment:* These totals represent the book value of property and equipment necessary for the operation of the franchise. Nine times out of ten, the actual market value of property and equipment is considerably less than shown on balance sheets simply because the accountant enters the value according to a depreciation schedule that bears no relationship to the actual resale or secondary market. Although this overvaluing of an asset may not affect day-by-day operations, it becomes tremendously important if the franchise is going out of business and the owners need a realistic total of cash

and marketable assets. The equipment may be carried on the books with a value of over half its original cost but be almost worthless because there is no market for it.

3. *Other assets:* These are assets that are not in either of the first two classes. Although they are related to the franchise, they generally are not liquid and consist of such items as investments, loans receivable, and cash surrender value of insurance on the principals or partners payable to the franchise.

4. *Current liabilities:* These are liabilities that are anticipated to be paid within 12 months or at the end of the current fiscal period. These generally consist of accounts payable, short-term notes payable, accrued expenses, unearned income, the current portion of long-term debt, and taxes payable on payroll, sales, property, and income. The category causing the greatest problem is unearned income because, far too often, it is included with cash and income on the asset side but not listed as a liability. Fortunately, only a few franchises are subject to this problem unless they characteristically deal with advance deposits, payments, or tuition.

5. *Long-term debt:* Long-term debt is debt whose maturity date exceeds one year, and the total should be adjusted for the amount listed as a current liability.

6. *Stockholders or proprietors equity:* For stockholders, this total is the original plus any subsequent investments, together with retained earnings minus any dividends paid. For proprietors, this total is the amount of capital put into the franchise plus profits retained, minus any losses and moneys withdrawn by the owners.

Comparative Balance Sheets

Sometimes called the statement of changes in financial condition, this report compares the balance sheets at the beginning and end of a specific period of time, usually the beginning and the end of a fiscal period. The report identifies the differences in balance categories and, if the differences are out of the ordinary, the reasons for the changes are footnoted. This report is often required periodically by debtors.

Statement of Operations

This report, also called the profit and loss statement or the statement of income, must closely resemble the format of your budget and coincide with the budget period if the report is to be meaningful as a management tool. It is a statement of income and expenses during a specific period of time, usually a month, a quarter, or a year. It includes the following:

1. *Sales:* This total includes both cash and credit sales for the period and should be adjusted to show sales tax receipts. This is particularly important when franchisor royalties are based on total sales.

2. *Cost of goods sold:* The cost of goods sold is usually computed by adding your purchases made during the accounting period to your beginning inventory and then subtracting your ending inventory.

3. *Gross profit or gross margin:* Your gross profit is computed by subtracting your cost of goods sold from your sales. The resulting figure is your gross margin and can be used in computing your break-even point if using the markup on individual products is too cumbersome. You should be aware, however, that using the gross margin is less accurate if your product mix varies from month to month.

4. *Other income:* Income from sources other than sales can be entered here or after adjusting for sales and administrative expense.

5. *Sales and administrative expense:* Sometimes just labeled as "expenses," this category includes all the other expenses of the franchise including royalties, payroll, advertising, and the like. Again, to make this statement most meaningful, the expense categories *and their definitions* must coincide with the budget categories and must be for the same period of time. Often a question arises about the proper method of handling your compensation as owner of the franchise. For labor cost comparison purposes, the following rule is usually the best (but check with your accountant): If you are routinely involved in the management and operations of one or two units and draw a salary, then your compensation should be included under the labor cost category (prorated if necessary). If you own several units, each with a manager, then your compensation, whether a salary or draw, should be charged to a central administrative category along with other general expenses ("general" meaning expenses incurred by the central administration). These charges should then be prorated and charged to the units as an administrative expense. An alternative method is to list the compensation paid to you and other officers as a separate category.

6. *Provision for income tax:* This category is necessary for corporations but not for sole proprietorships, partnerships, or S corporations since the income in those business structures passes through to the principals and is treated as ordinary individual income.

We must repeat, at this point, that these statements are far less meaningful and accurate if they are based on a cash accounting rather than an accrual system.

The Abstract or Summary

An application for financing, in some respects, is like submitting a resume for a job. Seldom is the person responsible for the actual hiring the first person to see the resume because there usually is an initial screening process that eliminates those who are obviously not qualified. The same process exists within lending and financing institutions. An application for a loan usually is initially screened to determine whether it would be of interest to the lender, but seldom would the entire business plan be reviewed unless the lender is interested. Consequently, much as a resume requires a cover letter that condenses the applicant's qualifications, the loan application needs a summary or abstract to attract the attention of the lender's screeners and to provide them with a quick method of evaluating the proposal without reviewing the entire financing document.

The summation or abstract should be not more than two pages long and should contain:

1. The identity and scope of the franchisor and franchisee.
2. The location and principals involved.
3. The amount and type of financing requested.
4. How the proceeds of the funding would be applied.
5. A description of the market and potential customers.
6. Volume and profit projections.
7. How the loan is to be repaid.

Since in most cases the summation or abstract will be the only item that will be read doing the screening process, it is extremely important that it be professional, well organized, and concise. Today, many quick print franchises have specialized services available for producing business and financing proposals, and therefore they can prepare for you an attractive professional looking package. Obviously, if you have a contact and are able to submit the proposal in person to the lender, your chances that the proposal will be reviewed are much greater.

The Proposal
Evaluation Process

If your proposal passes the initial screening process, it will then enter the evaluation and confirmation process. Certain items of information, such as business references and history, will be confirmed, your credit will be checked, and often information concerning the franchisor will be independently verified. Your financial figures will be carefully reviewed and, in some cases, analyzed by feeding the numbers into a computer software program that will produce certain ratios. Although these ratios are important, many lenders have deemphasized their effect on the lending decisions. As already noted, the most important factors in their decision center around you—your management experience, your reputation, your business history, your organizational ability, and your ability to repay.

Financial ratios do, however, provide the lenders with a tool to aid them in determining whether an existing franchise is financially healthy—an important fact if you are applying for financing to expand or acquire additional franchises. The following ratios are most often used:

Current Ratio

This should be foremost in the mind of a franchisee who wants to sleep nights because it measures the ability of the franchise to pay current bills when they come due. This ability is expressed by dividing current assets by total current liabilities. A ratio of 2 to 1 is satisfactory, but anything close to a 1 to 1 ratio may indicate problems.

Quick Ratio

This ratio will tell how well protected you are in a cash emergency or how liquid you really are. The measurement for this, sometimes called the acid test ratio, is obtained by dividing the amount of money you can get your hands on quickly, such as cash, dependable accounts receivables, and cash value securities, by the amount of your current liabilities. Generally a 1-to-1 ratio is acceptable. Anything less could be troublesome.

Debt-to-Equity Ratio

The banking industry often uses the debt-to-equity ratio as a key indication of the company's ability to handle additional debt. It is computed by dividing the total debt by total equity, and many loan officers will apply this formula to several past financial statements to establish a trend. The upper limit will differ from bank to bank.

Return on Investment Ratio

Sometimes called net income to equity, this is computed by dividing net income or pretax net profit by shareholders equity or tangible net worth. If the return is equal to or less than the return available on high-grade investments, then your reason for remaining in business has to be questioned.

Inventory Turn Ratio

This ratio should be used on every performance center in the franchise because of the need to keep close track of how fast products or merchandise are turning over. It is computed by dividing the cost of goods sold by current inventory.

Accounts Receivable Ratio

This ratio tells how long you are letting other people use your money. Divide total credit sales by your current accounts receivable: the higher the number, the better your collection rate. To figure the average number of days that it is taking you to collect receivables, divide 365 by the number computed above. Anything above 45 indicates that you need to spend more effort on collections.

Different lending sources will use different standards or criteria when evaluating a loan. For example, banks tend to look more at the ability to repay, while finance companies tend to look at the collateral. It is always advisable to discuss the way a loan or financing proposal is evaluated with a principal of the lending institution before submitting your documentation. In some cases, the only information a lender wants at first is the summary or abstract. If its officers find the proposal interesting, they will then require that you submit the entire plan.

Financing proposals can be very complex, and your accountant and financial advisor should be involved with every step of the process. If and when the financing is approved, your attorney should review and approve every document before you sign on the dotted line.

11

Don't Trust Money: Watch It

Three Tragedies That Money (or the Lack of It) Can Bring

Let's continue to discuss money. We assume money is a principal reason for you to be in a franchise, but we hope it isn't the only one. We hope you view money as the means to other ends and will keep those ends in view; otherwise they are likely to get lost. You should go into your franchise realizing that three big dangers threaten you: One, you will fail. Two, you will take in just enough to drudgingly get by. Three, you will take in so much you become greedy. One of these three tragedies happens to most persons who launch out for themselves.

It is a very heartening fact that you are considerably less likely to fail with a franchise than if you venture into business from scratch without the backing of a franchisor's experience and name. Still, failure is not impossible. It can occur for a number of reasons: loss of capital, inadequate income, ill health, a change in traffic patterns, the closing of the nearby bellwether store in a mall. Alert management is essential to constantly guard against the danger of failure.

Also, many of the persons who keep going in business earn only meager amounts of money, often barely enough to support their families. And in the toil of doing so they fail to gain much. Quite likely they expected long hours and hard work for a while, but, when these turn into endless slogging, they become a mockery. Thousands of the persons who seek to escape from the feeling that they are slaves to bosses or bureau-cracies become slaves to themselves. And often they find they must be very harsh masters, indeed, in order to survive. This condition can be very destructive to individuals and sometimes even more so to families. Many couples become divorced, and many children estranged, because of this kind of bondage.

In contrast, also tragically, are the men and women who succeed in making plenty of money but become enslaved to it. Normally, people start out with the idea of having money as a means to worthwhile ends: living comfortably, raising fine children, and regaling and realizing them-selves in travel, studies, sports, good works, and so on. But it is dangerous to make money. It can become addictive, and few addictions are worse. Don't think it can't happen to you.

The Uses of Money

With these caveats out of the way, let's look at money more pleasantly. And let's be basic. Let's start with its uses. Do you know how many uses money has? Millions? Billions? In a way. But sort them out and you can put them into exactly six businesslike categories. Even given that there can be overlaps between them, keeping the six in mind will enable you to better see where your money is and what it is doing for you. In general, it may be said that a person should have a suitable balance or apportionment among the six categories, but what the division should be for you is something you must work out for yourself.

1. You can *spend* money. When all is said and done, the main reason for having money is to be able to spend it—or to know you have the power to spend it if you want to. This is the motive even of misers who are too stingy to spend money. Normally, to some degree or another, we spend money to gain pleasure or protect against trouble.

2. You can *save* money. This means putting it safely aside where you can get it right away when you wish to, in a savings or checking account, a safe deposit box, or even a sock at home. It gives one of life's most comforting feelings.

3. You can *speculate* with money. "Speculate" is a high-sounding word for gamble. Regardless of its pretense, it means essentially putting money into a venture over which you have little or no control and to which you may be guided more by guess than by judgment. The money may be increased or decreased, but in fact sometimes the likelihood of

decrease, or even complete disappearance, is so great that the money should be viewed, not as money gambled, but as money spent on a fling. Anyway, the desire to take a risk is so universal that it probably is accurate to say that a little speculation now and then is relished by almost everyone.

Note: A great many of the financial attractions termed "investments" today are really speculations. One of the most valuable financial skills a person can develop is the ability to discern the difference.

4. You can put money into *scarcities.* Scarcities include such items as desirable land, works of art, antiques, coins, stamps, first editions, autographs, oriental rugs, and gems. They have value because of their rarity and often because they have beauty or some other virtue. In general, money is put into scarcities by:

    a. Persons who enjoy what they are buying.

    b. Persons who want mainly to make money.

    c. Persons who truly enjoy these items, but who also hope to make money.

    The persons in the first group are particularly fortunate; therefore, if you are moved by the love of land, works of art, or any other scarcities, you may be able to doubly enrich yourself by following your own inclinations when you have the funds to do so. But remember that some so-called scarcities are really speculations or illusions.

    Some analysts might include bulky items such as precious metals in the category of scarcities, but today these items are mainly speculative commodities in which people trade but never see. In contrast, the collector of scarcities usually can physically see and live with what he or she has put money into.

5. You can put money into *investments.* An investment is a loan vehicle that provides reasonable expectation that stipulated interest will be paid and that the face value will not be subject to extreme fluctuation. Traditional investments include bonds, preferred stocks, and government and commercial papers. In addition, recent times have brought forth a number of other loan plans, some of which are genuine investments, while others have risk aspects that may not be emphasized by those who promote them. A genuine investment should be truly a secure place for money because it is issued by a reliable party, pays a suitable rate of return and will return a sum that is at least close in buying power to the amount that was borrowed.

6. You can use money as a *source*. A source can be by far the very best
    of uses for money. It is an activity in which the application of capital,
    judgment, work, or some combination of the three can produce
    money. As a franchisee, you are the owner of a source—in a far better
    position than most persons to direct your destiny and build your for-
    tune. To make the most from your source, however, earnings cannot
    be left to the attractiveness of the franchisor's good name, a good
    location, or your own hard work. They must be planned for, and
    worked for, with watchful and wary financial practices.

Today there is no shortage of financial advice in our country. Rather,
there is an excess of it. Recent years have seen the development of what
amounts to a large self-appointed financial priesthood. We do not belong
to this. We do, however, recommend that you carefully consider the
financial advice offered by your franchisor and your accountant. And we
do offer some suggestions for your consideration. All of them can help
you be watchful of your money. And money must be watched. Money not
watched tends to get into trouble.

Set Realistic Earnings Goals

You should obtain two different kinds of earnings from your franchise;
therefore you should set realistic, separate goals for each. One is your
remuneration for running the franchise. The other is the earnings on the
investment—your capital or equity—in the business.

1. The term "your remuneration" should be interpreted comprehensively.
    It should include all your pay and perquisites, direct and indirect, and
    those of all other members of your family, shareholders, or insiders
    who are more or less actively involved in running the show. How
    much should this total be? It should be at least as much as you would
    have to pay someone else to run the franchise for you. Try to be gen-
    erous with yourself, but be very careful not to take too much, either
    directly or indirectly. One of the main causes for financial troubles in
    owner-run enterprises is the fact that more is taken out than the en-
    terprise can afford. Thoughtfully determine the correct amount.

2. Your earnings on the capital should be at least as much as the interest
    you could obtain if the capital was invested in high-grade investments,
    plus enough to increase the capital so that amount you will have will
    at least stay even with the inflation rate. The rate of interest and the
    rate of inflation are variable factors, and you should watch each

closely. As an example, suppose the general anticipated rate of interest for next year is 5 percent, and suppose the rate of inflation also is expected to be 5 percent. You certainly are entitled to earn at least 5 percent on the capital, because if you did not have the capital in the business you could earn that much by putting it into top-rated investments. And you must also add at least 5 percent net to the capital during the year; otherwise it will be, in effect, decreased by inflation. To have this total of 10 percent net left after taxes, you must gross some 15 percent or more before taxes, depending on your federal and state tax levels. Thus, it is plain that your minimum requirement for pretax earnings on your capital should be somewhere above 15 percent. And you must earn more than the minimum if you are to make your capital grow.

If you expect the interest and inflation rate each to be above 10 percent, your pretax earnings should be around 30 percent. If you expect each rate to be 15 percent, then you will need to earn 45 to 50 percent. The point is that both the rate of interest and the rate of inflation have a definite bearing on the amount your business must make. You will be kidding yourself and inviting financial trouble if you don't keep an alert eye on these rates and reckon with them realistically.

Separate Your Business into Performance Centers

You cannot expect to operate your franchise at a high level of efficiency and profitability unless you are able to watch and analyze each important activity. Therefore, see to it that your operation is organized into separate performance centers and keep sufficiently separate records for each. Allocate to each center an operating budget based either on anticipated income or on a carefully considered appropriation. Then set performance goals for each center. Exactly what these centers, or divisions, should be for your particular franchise are matters for your decision, but the clarifying term is "important activity." Make enough separations so that you can keep in touch with vital performances but avoid entangling yourself with separations that are petty. In some franchises it is best to make separations according to functions, in others according to the products handled or to the accounts to which they are sold. In setting up your centers, obtain the best professional advice you can. Confer with your accountant, and you may want to ask if he or she wishes to bring in a specialist in cost accounting as a consultant. Confer, too, with your attorney and study whether it may be advisable to set up some of your centers as separate corporations. Doing so may bring substantial tax advantages, which is why many enterprises (including more than a few really quite small ones) are divided into numerous corporations.

Separation management helps you to have the proper control of every part of your business, but you cannot have proper control without proper responsibility. Therefore, in organizing each center, make some person responsible for managing it within well-defined guidelines. And, of course, in many companies a manager has to be responsible for more than one center, perhaps several. Furthermore, it is best to keep each center small—preferably a group of no more than a dozen persons who work together for a common purpose. Anyway, the manager and the group should be given the responsibility for achieving goals and keeping operating costs within budget. The manager and the group, however, cannot be responsible for events beyond their control. Furthermore, it is desirable to see to it that compensations are in proportion to responsibilities and accomplishments. In general, it can pay to give a manager and group members fair basic compensation with the incentive to earn additional compensation by achievements.

There are two sets of guide figures relating to centers: income and expenses. Usually it is not very difficult to arrive at reasonable income goals, but the allocation of expenses is often likely to require careful study. This is because a center typically has two kinds of expenses, direct and indirect. You may need to make some judicious decisions concerning these, but *fairness* is the balancing word. You want to be fair to yourself so that you can accurately measure the accomplishments of each center. And you do not want anyone in a center to feel that he or she has been loaded with an unjust burden.

In managing your overall franchise, it may be helpful up to a point to have good-natured competition among various centers. Watch this closely, however, and do not allow it to become more than a healthy business stimulant. A spirit of cooperation will do infinitely more for your franchise than internal rivalry.

Make Selling a Financial Function

This is one of the truly big secrets of making money. In many businesses, selling is regarded as an operational function. This is a great mistake. Properly viewed, selling is a financial function. Selling produces income. *Selling is the generation of money.* This fact should be impressed again and again on your organization; and especially on your sales, advertising, and promotional people. Why? Because there is always a danger that they will become preoccupied with the superficialities of their jobs and lose sight of the great financial fact that, when a company makes the right amount of correctly priced sales, all other goals are easier to meet.

Your primary sales objective should pertain directly to the earnings you require for your capital. Say, for instance, that the net worth of your franchise is $1,000,000 and you have determined that you must make at least 30 percent on this. Therefore you overall profit objective must be at least $300,000. To find out how much you will need in sales to earn this much profit, use this formula:

$$\frac{\text{Profit objective}}{\text{Percent of profit on sales}} = \frac{\text{Sales goal}}{100\%}$$

You should know, or your accountant can tell you, what overall percentage of profit on sales you can reasonably anticipate, but say it's 5 percent. Therefore, you can set up the following overall formula:

$$\frac{\$300,000}{0.05} = \frac{x}{100}$$

By cross multiplying, you will get these results:

$$5x = \$30,000,000$$

$$x = \$30,000,000 \div 5$$

$$x = \$6,000,000$$

You would be misleading yourself, however, if you stop with this overall figure. You should apply the formula to each product category of your franchise, with its varying percentage of profit. Then you will know how much volume each part must do.

Stick to a Budget

Nobody likes to hear the word "budget." It brings recollections of the picky irritation of having to make one and of the annoying frustrations of living within it. However, all who run a franchise need to have a different attitude. Viewed rightly, a budget is a best friend who can tell you what you safely can do and keeps you out of trouble. Furthermore—and this is something we often forget—a budget isn't cast in concrete: It can be changed. Like an MBO program, it should be employed as an active guide, regularly reviewed, and modified as needed. And, in line with the

MBO program, it should identify certain income and expense objectives and enable you to measure your performances. In fact this ought to be done every month, and certainly no less often than every quarter.

Your accounting system and budget must be kept in parallel; otherwise you never will be able to measure your performance against projections. This statement may seem obvious, but we have been amazed at the number of franchisees who had systems and budgets that were not coordinated, and consequently they have abandoned budgeting because they felt that the whole process was worthless. They were right, not because the principle is wrong but because their methods were wrong.

The amount of estimating or guesswork you must do in preparing a budget depends on your status. If you are just starting your first franchise unit, the amount of guesswork can be considerable, although for many items, your franchisor should be ready and willing to help. If you have a year or more of experience behind you, then you should have past records as guides. Whatever kind of franchise you own, your budget, prepared with the help of your accountant and probably others, should closely suit your franchise and plans for it. Here are some hints:

1. Remember that making budget projections and cash flow projections are two different processes.

2. The budget period should be at least six months and preferably a year.

3. Be certain that your budget period corresponds to your fiscal year.

4. The budget should be prepared month by month and, again, should correspond with your monthly income and expense reports.

5. Income should be reported for the month that it is earned, not paid.

6. Expenses are reported when they are incurred, not when the bills are paid.

7. Semiannual or annual expenses, such as property taxes and insurance premiums, should be prorated and divided by the appropriate number of months.

Budgeted Income

Sales Income

If this is your first budget and you have no track record on which to base your projections, then your franchisor is the next best source of information. Most will not give any specific unit's figures but may be willing to provide you with averages for your region. If you are expanding and already have at least a year's experience in sales, take last year's sales totals month by month and adjust them by anticipated price changes. Also be aware of trends, look carefully at your previous year's sales, and note any seasonal variations. Most business sales volumes will vary from month to month, particularly those in resort areas and college towns. If the general economy around you is in a decline, this fact should be reflected in your projections.

Cost of Goods for Sale

The cost of goods to be sold should always be related to projected sales. It may be based on profit margins or markups especially in franchises with a limited number of products, if the percentages are consistent. Another approach is to estimate the amount that will be purchased each month in relation to the anticipated sales of each product. The most important figure is your projection of how much product will have to be purchased each month because that total will be very important when projecting cash flow.

Other Revenues

This category includes all other sources of revenue such as interest, by-product sales, and any other source of income not related to the franchise's principal product or service. If any other source produces a significant amount of income, it should be listed separately. This separation is particularly important if it is based on product or service sales that are not included in royalty percentage computations.

Budgeted Expenses

Advertising

Normally, a franchise will have two categories of advertising and marketing: (1) the percentage of sales or the flat fee paid to the franchisor to be used in the franchise advertising pool, and (2) the amount you spend for local advertising. Some accountants prefer that any moneys paid to the franchisor for advertising be listed separately under fees and royalties. This practice, however, tends to obscure the total amount that you are paying in this category. Be aware that the total amount spent monthly may vary according to the season.

Automobile Expense

Include all expenses for vehicles owned by your business and also reimbursable expense incurred by either you or your employees for personally owned vehicles. Be sure to account for insurance, interest, and licensing fees.

Administrative and Office

Include all nonpromotional office expense: furniture, supplies, office equipment, telephone expense, and contract service fees, such as for payroll preparation and periodic equipment servicing. If you are a multiunit franchisee with a central office, you may wish to consider allocating all central administrative expense among your franchise units.

Building Services

Include trash removal, exterminators, janitorial services, parking lot cleaning—any fee for service contracted out on a regular basis.

Collection Expense

If your franchise is predominantly a cash business, this category is not necessary. If a substantial amount of your business is on credit, then this item will help you keep track of just how much granting credit is costing you.

Depreciation

Check with your accountant about listing this category. Usually, depreciation is a balance sheet entry, not an actual expense. If, however, you make an actual cash transfer to a depreciation or equipment reserve account, then the annual cost should be divided and allocated to each month.

Dues and Subscriptions

This category should be used only if the amount is significant; otherwise add your dues and subscription costs to your administration and office budget.

Insurance

Add up the total annual premiums paid for general liability, fire, business interruption, auto and other insurances, divide by 12, and allocate the resulting amount to each month. Generally, taxes paid for unemployment compensation insurance are included in the labor expense category even when paid to an insurance company. Check with your insurance agents about any anticipated premium increases.

Interest Expense

Add up your total annual interest charges on loans and on lines of credit, including any franchisor finance charges, divide by 12, and allocate on a monthly basis. Ask your accountant about auto or truck loan interest charges. Are they included as vehicle or interest expense in the profit and loss statement format? It generally is advisable to allow for a possible 1- or 2-percent interest rate increase when projecting yearly interest costs.

Labor

Base your projections on gross salaries and wages even though deductions will be made. Include salaries paid to you and members of your family unless your accountant recommends that owners use a drawing account. For those of you just starting your franchise, who have no historical data to use, check with your franchisor for information about average staffing levels throughout the franchise. Many accountants recommend that the labor cost category include subheadings for social security, unemployment compensation, and out-of-pocket fringe benefits expenses. These fringe benefits would normally include group medical, life, and dental insurance, and car allowances if not included under vehicle expense. They would not, however, include vacation or sicktime pay.

Professional Services

This category includes fees for attorneys, accountants, and franchise consultants. Ask your professional advisers for estimates on next year's fees. Distribute the total equally among the 12 months.

Rent

Although the amount of rent is usually a stable cost per month, don't forget any escalation clauses or base rent plus percentage of sales conditions in your rental agreement. Check with your accountant to determine the proper method of projecting common maintenance fees if you are subject to such charges. Some accountants will prefer to list charges, such as common mall maintenance charges, under maintenance or contract services.

Royalties

Royalties are usually based on a percentage of gross sales, not including sales or excise taxes. Some royalty schedules have varying percentages based on total volume. Be conservative and budget the highest percentage rate. Do not include the monthly payments if you partially financed the initial fee. Interest on such loans should be listed under the interest expense category.

Taxes, Licenses, Fees, and Assessments

These should be totaled and distributed in equal monthly amounts throughout the year. Taxes should include local and state property taxes, use taxes, and probably sales taxes although you should check with your accountant about this matter. Some prefer to register sales incomes as gross receipts minus applicable sales taxes. This is to ensure that the proper figure is used as the basis for royalty payments.

Telephone/FAX

If you are a single-unit franchisee, enter an estimate for each month. A call to the phone company should tell you whether or not to expect an increase in rates and approximately how much. If you are a multiunit franchisee, refer to the comments concerning central office expenses in the next section of this chapter.

Utilities

Since this category includes heat, air conditioning, and electricity, your estimates should correspond to variations in usage. Some accountants may be satisfied by estimating the annual cost and dividing by 12, but remember that inaccuracies in a budget can affect cash flow projections.

Miscellaneous or Other Categories

You should have a separate category for every significant expense, and in some cases you may want to break down a major item into several sub-headings or components. Remember that your budget is a control mechanism that can alert you that something may be wrong; also it is a management tool in that it places you on notice about changes in the marketplace.

The Actual Versus Budgeted Income and Expense Profile

Although your budget is a valuable planning tool, its most important function in a franchise operation is to measure performance. As already stated, budget projections, whether on the expense or income side, are objectives and you must have some method of determining whether you are meeting them. The most simple and effective way to measure performance is to compare the actual amounts with the budgeted amounts each month and note the deviations. Compare the deviations in several categories, and you can begin to spot your weaknesses and strengths. For example, if sales are below projections for two or three months and yet the cost of goods remains the same or increases, then something is wrong. If office supplies continue to climb despite discussions with your managers, there probably is a theft problem.

For comparisons to be accurate and effective, you must be certain that the person doing the books is posting them using an accrual method. You also must be sure that you and he or she have a meeting of the minds as far as the definitions of income and expense categories are concerned. For example, if your bookkeeper lists auto insurance under vehicle expense, and you have it budgeted under insurance expense, the result will be that both accounts are out of step.

You have options for comparing actual versus budgeted income and expense. The simplest method is to set up three columns for each month. For example:

	1 Budgeted	2 Actual	3 Variance
Sales	$23,000	$21,700	($1300)

If you want more comparative information, you can add columns for the following information:

1	2	3	4	5	6
Budget	Actual	Variance	BYTD	AYTD	VYTD

BYTD = Budgeted year to date

AYTD = Actual year to date

VYTD = Variance year to date

You also can add columns for comparing totals to the same month last year.

If you do your bookkeeping on computer, you should be aware that a number of small business accounting software packages include a program for generating actual versus budgeted expense profiles.

For a multiunit franchise, particularly one with a corporate or central office, a budget should be prepared for every unit and the central administration. Let us reinforce a statement that we made earlier. Corporate offices do not make money, they spend money; therefore, central office expenses must be allocated to the operating units and should be a line item in the budget. Maintaining a central office is a burden on the back of every operating location, but the unit managers must realize that central administration is a necessary cost of doing business. If each unit manager is on an incentive plan based on net profits, administrative costs, as a legitimate operating expense, should be charged against the operation before the net profit is determined.

Often multiunit franchise owners will require that each unit submit a budget variance report each month explaining, if necessary, why the actual versus the budgeted figures for any category do not match. This report not only obliges the managers to be conscious of every category but also is an excellent warning bell to draw everyone's attention to changing market or economic conditions. Often, because of consistent trends identified in the budget variance reports, budgets are adjusted to accommodate these trends. Before any adjustments are made, however, every effort should be made to bring performance up to or above the budget.

Aim for Your Break-Even Point (BEP)

Once a budget is prepared, whether it is for a start-up operation or for day-to-day operations of an existing franchise unit, your next step should be the computation of your break-even point. The break-even point is that point at which sales equal costs or income equals expenses. Prior to reaching the BEP you are not making any profits. To compute the BEP you must separate your costs into three categories:

1. *Fixed costs:* The costs that remain constant regardless of sales volume. For example, rent, property taxes, contract services, and in most cases utilities are fixed costs.

2. *Variable costs:* The costs that relate directly to the production of a product or service. The most common examples are raw material costs, components, and royalties.

3. *Semifixed Costs:* The costs, although related to sales volume, that do not increase or decrease in a direct ratio. Labor costs, for example, may increase when sales volume increases but do so in a series of steps. Let's assume that you must have a staff of four employees just to open your doors. With these four people, you can handle a daily sales volume from $0 to $3000. If the volume exceeds $3000, then you must add another employee. The addition of that one person, however, will allow you to accommodate an increase in sales of up to $1000 before any further adjustment in staffing is necessary.

The break-even point is a commonsense point. It does not have the fallacy of a pie chart. Often, franchisor literature and books on business illustrate the income and expense of a certain type of business by showing a dollar of sales as a pie with each item of expense shown as a slice or percentage of the pie. Cost of goods may be 35 percent, rent 20 percent, advertising 5 percent, royalties 6 percent, and so on. Invariably, one slice of the pie will be labeled "net profit." *Unfortunately, there is no net profit until the break-even point has been exceeded.* In fact, that pie and its percentages are only true at one point in the sales curve. Below that point, your costs per sales dollar are higher. Above that point, your profit percentages are higher.

It happens also that product and service franchises differ greatly in terms of which costs are fixed, semifixed, and variable. A fast food franchise, for example, will have a significant amount of variable costs because every hamburger that is sold represents a true cost of meat, roll, lettuce, tomato, and cheese. On the other hand, an employment agency will have few variable costs because there is no raw material involved. Service franchises, in general, have a higher level of fixed and semifixed costs.

Since, when preparing a budget, costs such as insurance, taxes, and other periodic costs are distributed among the months, developing a break-even point on a monthly basis is a simple task. First, list the amount of your monthly fixed costs: rent, contract services, basic utilities, equipment lease payments, loan payments, etc. To them, add the prorated monthly cost for insurance, taxes, and other periodic payments. The total of these two categories will give you total fixed costs for the month. To that add your semifixed costs. Compute your labor costs based on minimum staffing levels, and don't forget to include payroll taxes in your computations. Total your fixed and semifixed costs, and you will have the expenses that must be paid before there can be any profits.

For example, take a fast food franchise where the raw food normally should be 45 percent of the selling price, 55 percent is available for everything else including profit. To determine the amount of sales necessary to reach the break-even point, use the following formula: Fixed and semifixed costs divided by gross profit margin equals the break-even point:

$$\frac{\text{Fixed and semifixed costs}}{55\%} = \text{BEP}$$

Say that fixed and semifixed costs are $9000 per month, then:

$$\frac{\$9,000}{0.55} = \$16,363$$

Thus, you know you must hit the $16,363 mark before you make a dime; therefore you are impelled to reach that point as early in the month as possible.

In some franchises, pricing is controlled by the franchisor. Consequently, to determine the gross profit margin, it is necessary to determine what it costs to produce the product, not including labor. This cost will include raw material, supplies, packaging, and waste. Once the unit cost is determined, it is then possible to compute the gross profit margin by subtracting the unit cost from the selling price and dividing the result by the selling price.

A key fact about the BEP can be illustrated by using the amount of sales required in the preceding example. Assuming that your monthly sales must reach $16,363 to cover your expenses, how much profit do you make for every dollar of sales over that amount? The answer is 55 cents because at the $16,363 point you have paid the $9000 in fixed and semifixed costs. The only additional cost you incur during any subsequent sales for that month are variable costs, that is, directly related raw material and supply costs. This will be true until, at some point, the sales volume will supply costs. This will be true until, at some point, the sales volume will require additional employees. When this occurs, you must adjust your semifixed costs and recompute your BEP. You must also recompute if, under some circumstances, an increase in sales is minimal and yet additional staff is added, then the BEP may adjust to a higher figure than the current sales level.

Although, as a franchise matures, certain patterns of expenses will emerge, the amount of net profit can seldom be expressed as a consistent percentage. The break-even point may vary; therefore it should be watched, recomputed as necessary, and kept in view as an essential goal.

Watch Your Cash Flow

Another crucial projection that is at least partially based on the budget is the cash flow projection, a particularly valuable tool if you are just starting up or are threatened with a cash poor condition. The cash flow projection is used in any or all of the following ways:

1. *As a valuable tool in cash management:* Cash flow projections can indicate when you are in a position to place some of your working capital in longer-term investments. It can also indicate how to time the maturity of these investments.

2. *To monitor accounts receivable:* When collections are less than projections, something is wrong and the quicker your can find the problem, the less the impact on your overall financial condition.

3. *As a warning that you will be short of cash during some period.* Finding additional cash in an emergency just before you need it is both expensive and difficult. The longer the notice you can give yourself, the better your chances of finding money at the most favorable terms.

The amount of difficulty in developing an accurate cash flow projection will depend on whether your franchise regularly grants credit. In a franchise that operates on a strictly cash basis, the big question will be whether sales will meet projections. In a franchise that operates even partially on a credit basis, not only is the sales total critical but so also is the rate of collections. If the accounts receivable cannot be controlled, then you get a double whammy: not only have you lost the money from the sale, you also have to still pay for the product. If you refuse a sale because of poor credit, at least you still have the product on the shelf.

Projecting Cash Flow

Setting up a cash flow schedule requires certain items of information about income and expense. If you are just starting up a franchise, we strongly recommend that you work out your cash flow projections with your accountant since he or she will probably be more familiar with cash flow patterns than you are. If, however, you have an existing franchise and have been in business more than two years, you should have enough historical financial data to make reasonably accurate projections of your income and expense. We still suggest that you ask your accountant to set up the format that will be most suitable for you because there are several methods available. The items of information you will need are:

1. *Amount of cash to be received each month:* This amount will include cash sales, collections of previous month's receivables, loan or line of credit proceeds, and cash from other sources.

2. *Amount or percentage of credit sales and the pattern of collection:* For example, 75 percent of your sales may be paid for in the following month, 20 percent paid for the second month, and 5 percent paid for the third month or not at all.

3. *The payments you normally make as they occur each month:* These usually include rent, payments on debt, royalties, interest, payroll, CODs, petty cash, and other noninvoiced charges.

4. *The cost of goods plus other invoiced charges:* These may include legal and accounting services, supplies, small equipment, and miscellaneous charges.

5. *Your payment patterns:* You may find variation in these patterns based on the type of payables. For example, you may pay for goods or materials for sale within 30 days but legal, accounting, and some supply invoices frequently are not paid until 45 days after billing.

While your accountant can furnish a form that is specifically designed for you, most cash flow projections will be similar to the following:

Item	January	February	March
Beginning cash	$22,000		
Cash sales	45,000		
Receivables 75%	XX,XXX	30,000	
20%	X,XXX	X,XXX	8,000
5%	X,XXX	X,XXX	X,XXX ($2,000 in April)
Line of credit	—		
Other	—		
Total cash	XX,XXX		
Cash outlays (Standard costs)			
Rent	3,000		
Loan payments	8,000		
Payroll	14,000		
Interest	1,000		
Other			
Cost of goods	XX,XXX	42,000	XX,XXX
Other invoiced	XX,XXX	XX,XXX	7,000
Total outlay	XX,XXX		
Cash on hand	XX,XXX		

To illustrate how this form is used, assume that your sales in January totaled $85,000 of which $45,000 was in cash and $40,000 on credit. Your previous collection experience indicates that you will collect 75 percent of your receivables in 30 day, 20 percent within 60 days, and 5 percent within 90 days. You pay your vendors within 30 days but often let some other debtors go until 45 days. Now track January's transactions according to the preceding pattern. Cash sales are posted in January, the month received. Credit sales are receivables; consequently, 75 percent is projected to come in during February, 20 percent in March, and 5 percent in April. Your standard costs are those you pay during the month incurred; therefore they would be posted in January. You pay your vendors within 30 days (in February) but your other invoiced charges will be paid in March.

By adding additional columns, your accountant can also show actual versus projected figures. If cash is tight, this comparison can be of immense value because it will give you sufficient notice if additional cash is needed.

Make Your Money Work
as Hard as You Do

Persons who own a franchise realize that, for a while at least, they may have to work harder and longer than if they were working for someone else, but do so with the belief that the overall rewards make it all worthwhile. Make certain, however, that your money is working as hard as you do. There can be literally a wealth of difference in the amount of profits that dollars can make—and in many cases actually do make—and you, as the owner, must take the responsibility for this difference. You must be a good asset manager and to be so there is one key word: *activity*. To earn profits, assets must be involved in some kind of activity; they cannot be inert.

Broadly speaking, cash must be either actively turning over in the production and sales process or actively building earnings in loans or other transactions. Noncash or physical assets must be made a part of an activity that produces profits. For example, store fixtures must be made to earn the maximum by the way they stimulate traffic around them. Warehouses and stockrooms must be run efficiently and busily, with inventories moving in and out. Trucks must be operating in a way that is most productive. If, after making every effort, you cannot get a physical asset sufficiently involved in earning money, you should look for a way to get back some of the capital you have invested in it. Your options may be to rent it out, sell it off, or even dispose of it for salvage value. Under any circumstances, your physical assets should be reviewed periodically to ensure that they are still performing at a profit.

It is, however, in the handling of working capital and surplus cash that you are likely to find the most opportunities to keep your money gainfully employed. In doing so, remember that not only activity but *velocity* is important. It is an old business maxim that the faster working capital can be turned over the better. This is true only if it is turned over with a good margin. Therefore, in most franchises, the two primary objectives should still be to make enough properly priced sales and to collect receivables quickly.

The next task is to keep a keen eye on overhead expenses and particularly on inventory so that neither one will cut too deeply into the profits from sales. Sometimes a franchise owner will not be concerned about inventory because it is holding or increasing its value. However, it is commonly accepted in business that an inventory costs approximately 0.5 percent of its value each month it is on the shelf. Furthermore, it costs additional money for storage, deterioration, handling, and theft. Add these expenses to the interest on capital that is tied up, together with the loss of profits that the capital could be generating, and you can see that excess inventory is a significant cost.

Here are a few suggestion on controlling your inventory levels.

Do not depend too much on any one person, service, or computer to keep you fully informed about your inventory and the way it is handled and paid for. No one and nothing is infallible. Have a monitoring system that enables you to cross-check inventories.

In general, keep inventories as low as possible. Try to find suppliers who can be relied on to make quick, small shipments as needed.

If you do "full need" purchasing—i.e., determining a product and service needs for six months or a year ahead and then buying on a volume discount—be certain that the savings are worth not having the ready cash, the interest that could be earned from it, and the higher inventory costs.

Compare your needs and alternatives in paying for what you buy. In some cases, discounts are large enough to justify early payment. In most cases, however, payment should be made when due and not before.

It is sometimes possible to obtain favorable terms as well as favorable prices. If the seller will allow you to defer payments on goods, it could add to your profits. A good arrangement of the kind can be to buy items that do not have to be paid for until you have had a reasonable time to sell them.

Clearly mark every case of goods and supplies with the date you receive it, so that stock can be rotated correctly.

Take inventories twice as often as you have in the past.

Remain aware of nonsale inventories such as maintenance and office supplies. Usually these items are ignored and become a source of waste and unnecessary expense.

Don't forget money that is not tied up in physical assets or inventory. It should be hard at work earning interest, including money that is owed to you as accounts receivable. The cost of carrying receivables for a reasonable amount of time should be built into your pricing, but when the accounts become past due, you should commence charging interest if it is lawful to do so. You also should ensure that, when money is paid to you, it becomes quickly available for use. Specialized depository arrangements with your bank can increase you money's velocity, and an agreement to credit your account immediately for checks that are deposited can give the benefit of the float. You may have to make some type of concession with the bank for these arrangements but it can be worth negotiating for.

Cash Management Strategies

The activity of keeping money at work earning interest is loosely called "cash management." It also is called "working and surplus capital investment" or "playing the flow and the float," but it can, by any name, yield significant profits if properly done. The entire function is based on the concept that any money left in the cash drawer, in the safe, or in the checking account overnight is "dead" because it earns nothing. In fact, it may become worse than dead because, over time, inflation can reduce its value.

It is normal for a franchise to have two types of cash to handle. During the entire year it will have requirements for current cash employed in the usual flow of business: funds that are being collected, deposited, spent for expenses, and paid for goods and services. Also, at certain times of the year, the franchise may have surplus cash, funds that are in excess of needs for the next 30 days or more. The basic objective of cash management is to have money available to pay obligations as they come due, at the same time reducing dead cash to the absolute minimum.

In today's financial world there is no lack of places where money can be kept alive, even though low interest rates at this writing have reduced the options. For surplus cash not needed for 30 days or more, there still are such securities as bank certificates of deposit, commercial paper, U.S. Treasury issues, and other investments with a specific date of maturity. For current cash, there are business savings accounts, money market accounts, repurchase agreements, and secondary markets in maturing investments.

You should have a routine for managing your cash. In general, you have two choices: an internal cash management system or an arrangement with your bank. The internal system can yield more, but it requires more attention from you and perhaps one or more of your employees. An arrangement with a bank usually yields less and requires a certain minimum balance, but needs less of your time and attention.

Two reports or documents are the keys to effective cash management: the budget and the cash flow projections. If you are posting actual performances next to the projected figures you will have the capability of adjusting your projections, therefore gaining greater accuracy in forecasting when and for how long you will have funds available for one to six months' investment. To ensure that you will not assume that these investments are available cash, you should treat the purchase as an expense and, when it matures, bring it back in the cash flow stream as income.

Internal Cash Management

To install an internal cash management system you will need a combination of services:

1. A commercial checking account with no minimum balance requirements and telephone transfer capabilities.

2. A bank money market or business savings account that pays interest computed daily on account balances and has telephone transfer capabilities.

3. A standard money market account with a history of stable operations and reasonable yields, and on which you can write checks directly. You should also look for the lowest minimum check you can write and the lowest minimum balance. If you have several operating locations, also look for wire deposit capabilities. Generally, all deposits from cash sales, collections, and transfers should go into your bank money market or savings account every day.

If necessary, each day have your bookkeeper tabulate the number of checks drawn on the checking account and have the amount transferred from the money market or saving account. Try also to reduce the number of days that checks are written on the checking account to as few as possible. Also pay bills for goods and services with money market checks as much as you can, and pay invoices for amounts below the money market account minimum out of a regular checking account. By using the money market checks you will continue to collect interest on the funds during the float.

External Cash Management
Systems

Repurchase Agreements These agreements provide you with opportunity to buy a portion of the bank's portfolio of securities for a specific period of time under the condition that you agree to sell them back at the same price plus interest. You can arrange to have the bank sweep your account every night and buy "repos" with the cash over and above a required minimum balance. The bank automatically takes care of the entire transaction and credits the earnings to your account. But before you choose to use repos, there are some facts you should consider:

1. Most commercial banks require a minimum balance of $100,000 and any repos purchased must be in blocks of a minimum of $50,000 or in some banks $100,000.

2. The rate of return differs daily and from bank to bank.

3. The rate of return is usually below that of federal funds, certificates of deposit, and money market accounts.

4. Unlike money market and cash handling accounts, repo arrangements give you actual title to the securities purchased. In some states, however, the banking regulations make this title meaningless.

5. Repos cannot be used to satisfy minimum balance or other bank financing requirements.

6. Repos are designed for franchises and other businesses with a large active cash flow.

Automated Banking Services. Check with several commercial banks in your area for other automated services. Competition among banks is still intense, therefore new plans and services frequently come forth.

Short-Term Certificates of Deposit. Many banks sell short-term (31 days or more) certificates of deposit. The minimum amount of the certificate varies widely from bank to bank, but some have minimums as low as $500.

One final comment: Don't confuse money management with speculation. The funds involved are the life blood of your franchise and, despite the fact that the yields on the instruments mentioned here may not be high, they are consistent with prudent cash management principles. Limit your financial connections to banks and other firms that you have good reason to believe are thorough, sound, and cautious in their practices. Try to make your money work as hard as you do, but don't take unnecessary or speculative risks. Wall Street has an old saying worth keeping in mind: "Pigs get fat, hogs get slaughtered."

12

Be Judicious in Hiring

"I can't seem to find very many good employees anymore, and when I do find 'em, I can't keep 'em." This very common complaint expresses one of the great concerns of the franchise industry today: how to find and keep high-quality employees. It would seem, considering that unemployment is in excess of 7 percent nationwide at this time, franchisees would have an inexhaustible pool of potential employees. But this fact itself may be part of the employee turnover problem. A franchisee, knowing that he or she can always find replacements, becomes lax in recruiting and adopts the "burn 'em up and throw 'em out" philosophy, guaranteeing high employee turnover.

Many franchisees, particularly those in the fast food field, recruit entry-level teenagers, a group not known for either employment stability or productivity. Since these people can be hired at minimum wage, they are considered to be the best deal in town by franchisees who judge labor productivity mainly by the hourly rate. However, this particular labor pool presents some special problems.

First, teenagers require much more training than experienced workers. The basic elements of customer service, for example, must be taught to the novice, while the experienced salesperson slips easily into the routine. It is difficult to say just how much longer it takes to train a young totally inexperienced person, since the amount of time will depend on the complexities of the job. But it is safe to say that increased training time costs money and ineffective performance costs sales.

Second, teenagers usually lack established work ethics. First-job employees usually have little sense of how they contribute to or detract from the profit and loss statement, nor do some of them care. In many cases, there is little identity with the franchise (although a few franchises have developed a strong sense of loyalty and identity among their young employees).

Third, teenagers are strongly influenced by peer pressure. This is not to say that peer pressure is a negligible factor with older employees, but it is an especially strong influence among the young. If the manager is knowledgeable and experienced, this youthful peer pressure can be made a very positive motivator. But if the manager does not know how to deal with this type of pressure, the results can be counterproductive, even disastrous. Please know that we are not advising against the use of the younger employee, but, we are emphasizing that employing the younger worker poses some special challenges.

Most franchise owners and managers seriously underestimate the cost of training a new employee. Every step of the hiring process, from recruiting to training, involves either lost time or direct out-of-pocket expense at the management level. Equally important, the orientation and training time is a nonproductive labor cost. Even after the employee is on the line, it may be from two weeks to a year, depending on the type of franchise, before he or she becomes truly productive. In a high turnover situation, the employee is seldom on the job long enough to make back the hiring and training cost. Fortunately, you can take numerous measures to reduce turnover. In this chapter, we will discuss measures that relate to the initial hiring and training process, and other ways to reduce turnover will be considered in the following chapter.

Generally, when you begin the process of hiring a new employee, you have three objectives:

1. You want to find someone with a high performance potential, a person who is well qualified (meaning having the right skills and personality) and highly motivated. He or she should be trainable and flexible enough to be both transferable and promotable.

2. You want to find someone with a genuine long-term employment potential, thus reducing your unemployment compensation, hiring, and training costs.

3. You want to reduce your exposure to charges of discriminatory hiring claims. Recent legislation and emerging case law have made the cost of settling a discrimination claim exceedingly expensive and, if a claim is successful, you could easily become bankrupt.

We must at this point add a fourth concern, especially if your employees have access to your customers' homes, places of business, or, as in the case of hotel and motel franchises, rooms. Recently, a speaker at a National Trial Lawyer's Association meeting declared that the emerging issue of the nineties would be "Negligent Hiring Practices," a trend that is already well established. This issue involves the extent to which a franchise owner can be held liable for the actions of his or her employees. At this point, there already are numerous cases involving employer liability for acts of employees which either have been decided or settled out of court and have involved sizable awards—some in the millions of dollars. Still more are currently being litigated.

These cases involve employees who have burglarized, assaulted, raped, or murdered customers they have come in contact with in the course of their normal duties. The central issue now appears to be whether the employer made a *reasonable* effort to ensure that the employee was "low risk." That is, did the employer make a prudent effort to determine whether the employee had a background of criminal behavior or mental problems? One of the areas closely scrutinized by juries has been the hiring process to determine whether the actions of the employer were reasonable in light of the risk and the circumstances. Although the kinds of franchises described above seem to be the most highly exposed to negligent hiring claims, no franchise is completely free from liability for the actions of employees. Consequently, the selection and hiring practices of any type of franchise should be defensible in the light of current standards of reasonableness.

The Nine Basic Steps in the Hiring Process

Any reasonable hiring process should consist of nine basic steps, all of which should be adequately documented. These steps are designed, not only to produce qualified and productive employees, but also to serve as a defense against negligence.

1. Recruiting.
2. Job descriptions and specifications.
3. Evaluation of resumes and applications.
4. Interviewing.
5. Background and reference checks.

6. Preemployment tests.

7. The employment agreement (written or oral).

8. Orientation.

9. Training.

Regardless of whether you own a single franchise with three employees or 30 units with 250 employees, the following procedures should be used consistently. Any breakdown in either the routine or the documentation can produce a weak link in your chain of protection, a weakness you ill can risk.

Recruiting

When you need new employees, you have several methods of getting the word out to potential applicants. Which of these methods is are best for you depends on both your circumstances and the current labor market. You want to reach as many qualified potential applicants as possible, yet you don't want to be inundated with applications from unqualified people. Consider the following methods and their pros and cons:

Newspaper advertising: This is probably the most popular and the least effective of all recruiting methods. Placing an advertisement in a local or regional newspaper can result in 100 or more resumes or applications, including many that are from applicants not even remotely qualified. As more and more pressure against discriminatory hiring practices is applied by various state, federal, and private advocacy groups, the need to process all of the resumes and applications received by a consistent, well documented procedure is also increasing, a process that can be costly. Newspaper advertising reaches everyone—the qualified, the unqualified, and the high-risk. Because of the scope of the readership, chances are good that some of the applicants will have criminal records or a history of mental problems that will be difficult to uncover in a background check.

Trade associations and trade magazines: These media are usually low risk and applicants generally can be considered as prescreened. In the recruiting context, "prescreened" means that a higher number of the readers will be qualified because they are already in the trade or business. It does not mean, however, that the trade association or the magazine staff has checked the references or the background of their readers or members. Accepting an applicant from this source does not relieve you of that responsibility. It only means that this labor pool will probably have fewer high-risk or unqualified people.

Employment agencies: This is a source for qualified employees of varying reliability. There are some excellent employment agencies with a longstanding reputation for referring highly qualified applicants. There also are agencies with the reputation for being in business for a quick buck. Both kinds can be expensive; so some shopping around and a chat with the local Chamber of Commerce or Better Business Bureau is strongly recommended. Although applicants from an employment agency can be considered prescreened from an experience or knowledge viewpoint, do not believe any claims about a complete background check. Accepting applicants referred by an agency does not relieve you of your responsibility to verify all aspects of an applicant's employment, educational, and personal history.

Local outplacement services: Because of the state of the economy today, many industries are downsizing or merging and thus reducing their work force. As a service to their former employees, they offer an outplacement service, i.e., help and counseling in finding another job. Often these employees have been with their employers for many years and their termination is simply beyond their control. Even though you may have to completely retrain these employees, recruiting them has several important advantages: First, their employment records are at least partially accessible and reliable. Second, the chances that an applicant has an acceptable work ethic are much improved, particularly if he or she has been with an employer for several years. Third, these employees are from a comparatively low-risk pool. The chances are that, if criminal activity or mental problems had occurred during their previous employment, they would not be included in the outplacement service.

Current employees: Your current employees are an excellent source of prescreened potential applicants. Passing the word out among your employees that you are looking for people with certain qualifications is effective because no one wants to recommend anyone who would reflect negatively on his or her own judgment. This method involves no advertising costs and, since the number of applicants can be controlled, processing and hiring costs are less. A major disadvantage of this method may be that, if your current employee group does not contain minority representation, a claim of perpetuation of past discriminatory practices could be directed against you.

We must reemphasize the fact that, although some of these recruiting methods prescreen applicants to a limited extent, none of the methods relieves you of the responsibility to conduct your own prudent and reasonable background checks on *all* applicants.

Job Descriptions and Specifications

Job descriptions and specifications may not be necessary if you own and manage one or two franchise units and do all the hiring and supervising yourself. The minute, however, that you delegate interviewing and/or hiring to someone else, then written job descriptions and specifications become an important part of the hiring process.

Before continuing, we should define the terms "job description" and "job specification" and discuss the differences between the two. A *job description* states the actual functions and duties of the position. *Function* is stated broadly by such terms as administrative, equipment operations, clerical, financial, customer relations, etc. *Duties* usually are described in detail. The job description is used in several ways. First, it serves as a guide for those interviewing applicants. Second, it serves as guide and a source of information for the employee in the position. Third, it is an essential part of the employee's personnel file, especially in cases involving wrongful discharge or appeal of unemployment insurance claims.

The *job specification* defines the type of person best suited for the job in terms of knowledge, education, experience, personality, character, behavior, flexibility, assertiveness, and any other personality or character trait that would pertain to job performance. The job specification is used by interviewers and may also relate to various types of preemployment tests. For example, the job specification may require minimum scores on certain skill, knowledge, or personality tests. Be certain, however, that your job specifications do not discriminate racially or culturally.

Evaluation of Resumes and Applications

Usually a franchisee will ask an applicant to submit a resume and, if the applicant appears to be qualified, will ask the applicant to come in and fill out an application. Many of the franchisees who hire mostly entry-level younger applicants do not require a resume, relying instead completely on the information on the application. Yet a resume contains certain types of information that an application does not yield. Unlike the application, the resume requires some imagination, creativity, and even judgment to prepare. The resume provides an insight into the applicant's level of self-confidence or self-esteem, sense of organization, ability to think clearly and logically, and the ability to present information in a sensible sequence. A resume can also be used to judge an applicant's ability to spell and to use grammar correctly. The care with which the resume is prepared and presented can provide insight into how seriously an applicant approaches a job. And if the resume was prepared by one of the many professional resume writers, this does not detract from an applicant's intentions. It merely emphasizes the fact the he or she wants to make the best presentation possible.

You may, however, have to be more detailed when you interview a person who has used a professional. The resume writer was not trying to impress you; he or she was trying to impress the applicant in order to sell the resume. Increasingly, however, employers are requesting that resumes contain certain items of information and that the information be presented in a certain format. In fact, many personnel managers will not accept resumes unless they have been prepared in either the chronological or combination format.

Resumes can be prepared according to three different formats: chronological, functional, and a combinations of the two. The *chronological* format will present employment history information in a certain sequence, last employment first and the remainder in reverse order. Each period of employment should be identified by the inclusive dates of employment, the place and address, the job title and a short description of the applicant's duties. Education is identified by the school or college, degrees or diploma earned, or number of years in attendance, plus the major, minor, and grade point average. The actual dates of attendance are usually not required. (In fact, we recommend that you do not request that information because it may be construed as an effort to determine age.) Other information, such as hobbies, interests, special projects, marital status, and special skills, may also be included although, again, marital status is a protected status under the discrimination statutes of many states and municipalities.

The functional resume will provide the personal and educational information in much the same format as the chronological, but the employment information is presented in terms of job functions. The functional resume will describe the applicant's experience in management, sales, manufacturing, retailing, purchasing, and so on, but does not relate those functions to specific positions, companies, or dates. You may find that the functional resume is easier to skim, but be wary. Professional resume writers and books on resume writing recommend the functional format when the applicant has had an erratic work history and long periods of unemployment. Because of the way the employment information is presented, it is very difficult to conduct a background check. You should also be aware of the fact that many professional personnel managers simply will not accept a functional resume.

The *combination* format will include a short description of the applicant's work history in functional form (short meaning one third of a page or less) but will back up this description with a complete chronological work history providing the same information. This style of presentation is preferred by most employers and personnel managers because the resume can be skimmed to determine if minimum qualifications are met and then the chronological section can be used for the background check.

Resumes should be kept on file with the job application for at least two years, whether the applicant is hired or not. Some companies, especially those subject to affirmative action, will record the reason for rejection or the action taken on each resume and application on file. This information is very valuable if you are required to defend yourself against a claim of discriminatory hiring practices.

Interviewing Potential Employees

Have you, like so many persons, ever had the experience of being interviewed for a job by someone when the interviewer appeared more nervous than you did? Most people, including franchise owners, probably have not had the experience or the skills necessary to interview professionally. There are, however, some general guidelines and suggestions that should help you achieve the objectives of an employment interview.

The first step in developing an effective interviewing technique is to decide what information you want to obtain from the interviewee and also what information you want to give. The employment interview is a two-way process that should provide both parties with the opportunity to ask questions that involve the position and the applicant's ability.

1. The interview offers you the chance to confirm the personal and employment history contained in the resume and application, and explore in greater detail the actual duties and responsibilities in the applicant's previous work history. This part of the process is extremely important because, during this stage, discrepancies in dates of employment and other historical information can be detected and examined. Those applicants who have provided false information often cannot remember where they have lied, which in turn tips you off to the fact that this is a potential problem employee.

2. The interview provides you with the opportunity to fully explain the duties and responsibilities of the position and ascertain if the applicant is genuinely interested. Also, at this point, the conditions of employment including wages, fringe benefits, and the general work rules can be explained. If the applicant is genuinely interested, the interview can continue; if not, you have wasted as little time as possible.

3. The interview gives you the opportunity to evaluate the character and personality of the applicant and to gain an insight into his or her work ethics. Questions involving the reasons for leaving former positions, relationships with former supervisors, and a general inquiry about attitudes toward work can provide you with an overall picture of the applicant's ability to fit in with your other employees.

4. It is possible also to include other members of your staff in an interview. Sometimes, the opinions of others can either supplement or help clarify your own conclusions.

If you own one or two franchise units and you personally manage each one, then there is little doubt that you should personally interview all employee applicants. If, however, you own several units, each with its own manager, then the primary interviewing responsibility should lie with those managers. Even if you also interview applicants, the hiring decision should still be made by your managers, the people who will be supervising the employees. You may retain a veto power, but this should be used only in extreme circumstances, such as when the background check turns up unfavorable information. When you use your veto power the reasons for your actions should be carefully explained to your manager. The principle is that the interviewing and hiring authority should rest with the person who has the responsibility for the profits or losses of the unit. This is a basic rule of accountability. It is difficult for a manager or even a department head in a large franchise unit to supervise an employee who has been assigned to him or her because there is always a question in the employee's mind as to who is actually the boss. Without a clear statement, reinforced by both words and actions, that the manager has hiring and firing authority, the employee is likely to run to you every time there is a conflict with the manager.

The interview process can be separated into two distinct phases: the quantitative and the qualitative. The *quantitative phase* is usually the first because it is basically an exchange of facts; the interviewee provides the employment history and background information and the interviewer provides the job, benefits, salary, and work rule information. The *qualitative interview,* usually set up after the background check has been completed, is the one that probes the character and personality of the applicant and determines whether he or she would be appropriate for the job.

The qualitative interview may be one-on-one, by a group, or progressive. The one-on-one interview is conducted by the person with the authority to hire. The group interview is usually by several people, all of whom will have a future relationship with the applicant. The progressive technique involves having the applicant meet one-on-one successively with seveal people who will be working with the successful applicant on the job. It should be emphasized that, in both the group and progressive methods, one person still retains the hiring authority, but the input from the other members of the group should have some bearing on the hiring decision. We strongly suggest that you encourage opinions from everyone, but hiring should not be done by vote. This destroys accountability.

Background and Reference Checks

The importance of a documented background and reference check cannot be overemphasized. In one lawsuit, an employee was found guilty of two burglaries and a rape involving customers of the employer. During the original criminal trial it was revealed through testimony that the defendant had access to the homes of the victims as part of his job. It also was revealed that the employer had not made any attempt to check the employee's background before he was hired; consequently, the fact that he had several previous convictions involving burglary and rape was not discovered. The employee was convicted and, shortly thereafter, the victims brought a civil suit against the employer charging negligent hiring practices. Although the case was not yet concluded as of this writing, there seems to be little doubt that it will be costly.

Admittedly, you will find it difficult to conduct background checks on potential employees for several reasons:

First, rights to privacy laws prohibit the release of information concerning a person's criminal history to anyone other than a law enforcement agency and a few other groups with the right to know.

Second, although criminal history is public information in most states, it is only available to those who are able to physically search the files in each court jurisdiction, an almost impossible task if an applicant has lived in several areas during his or her lifetime.

Third, numerous employers have been sued because of the information they had given to other potential employers about a former employee's work history. As a result of these suits, many employers now have a policy that they will release only the dates of employment and the job title for any former employee. They will not volunteer or confirm the reason for separation or provide any information concerning job performance. Sometimes, if you can reach the former employer or supervisor on the telephone, you can obtain some valuable information from the tone of voice or certain inflections. Some persons also will tell you whether they would rehire the employee.

If you are an owner of multiple units and hire over 10 people per year, we strongly suggest that you develop a checklist to be used by those checking references and backgrounds. This list should identify the applicant, the position applied for, and the person or persons doing the checking. The list should require the following information:

Name, title, and company of the person contacted.

If unable to contact the person, the reason why.

If the contact was successful, the comments and information obtained.

Inclusive dates of employment.

Any discrepancies between the resume, the application, and the background and reference check.

Once the list is completed, it should be filed with the resume and the application—again, whether the applicant is hired or not. By following this procedure to the letter, you can demonstrate that you made a reasonable effort to check the background and the references of every applicant you have hired. However, you must be absolutely consistent. A pattern in which some applicants are checked and others are not will destroy your credibility in a court of law.

Some owners feel that checking references is a waste of time because no applicant will name as a reference a person who will provide negative information. Although this may be true, it still is worth making the calls because, again, much can be learned from voice inflection and the manner of response, particularly if the reference is questioned about how long he or she has known the applicant and under what circumstances.

Preemployment Tests

The number of franchisors who can provide preemployment tests to their franchisees is gradually increasing. At this point, however, the practice seems to be limited to those franchisors in the more complex industries. Anyway, preemployment screening devices have considerable merit. The tests or devices that currently are available include tests for aptitude, intelligence, job skills, integrity, personality, and drug use. All are available to individual franchisees who desire to improve their employee selection process.

Aptitude Tests. Although the development of aptitude tests predate World War II, their use by the military during that war contributed significantly to their popularity. Since these tests are designed to measure the degree of aptitude that an individual may have in the areas of clerical, mechanical, sales, administrative, and other skills, they have a variety of applications in the franchise industry. It should be noted that they are most accurate as predictors when the scores fall in the extremes. For example, an aptitude test scored from 1 (lowest) to 50 (highest) would be most accurate for those who clustered near either end of the range. Those clustering around the bottom would have low aptitude, those around the top high aptitude, and those around the center would be considered neutral or average. Some employment agencies are equipped to administer aptitude tests of certain types. Other types can be administered by you or a member of your staff.

Intelligence Tests. Several intelligence tests have been used for decades and are generally accepted by both psychologists and educators. Intelligence tests measure mental ability and capacity and are used in employment judgments where intelligence is crucial to performance. Although intelligence is important in most franchised industries, such tests, up to now, are seldom used.

Job Skills Tests. This type of test measures the amount of knowledge about specific subjects and may also include manual dexterity evaluations. Job skills testing is used extensively in all types of industry and may range from management skills to appliance repair. It is not unusual for companies or franchisors to develop job skills tests that apply only to their particular functions. Job skills testing is particularly appropriate for franchises requiring a high degree of mechanical ability.

Integrity Tests. Employee theft has been a problem for as long as there have been employees. For many years, one of the most often used pre-employment screening devices was the polygraph or lie detector. The polygraph supposedly detected persons who were most likely to steal. The use of the polygraph, however, has always been the center of much controversy because its accuracy and reliability have been questioned by some psychologists. In 1988 Congress passed legislation that severely limited the use of the polygraph, so right now it is not an easily available testing device.

When it became evident that polygraphs would be banned, personnel test designers scurried to develop a written test that would detect a tendency for dishonesty and soon an avalanche of these hit the market. In fact, it would be surprising if you have not already received promotional material or been personally approached by someone about these tests.

But before you accept such tests as a foolproof method of detecting potential thieves, you should know a few facts. Only a few of these tests have had the chance to stand the trial of time or obtain scientific validation. Most have not been reviewed by any accrediting agency, nor have they had sufficient exposure to be considered accurate. In fact, at the request of Congress, the American Psychological Society and the Office of Technology Assessment have been investigating the entire issue of written integrity tests, and, although some of the results of their investigations have been submitted, Congress has not yet reacted. Some states, however, have already introduced legislation to ban or severely limit the use of the integrity test as a preemployment condition. In light of these recent developments, we strongly recommend that you check with your attorney before attempting to use any test that claims to determine the degree of integrity of an applicant.

Personality Tests. Tests that measure the degree of certain personality and psychological traits have been used very effectively for decades, and most have been repeatedly reviewed and validated by both clinical and academic circles. These too, however, have recently come under fire as being intrusive and violating the rights of privacy of the individual.

But a look at the reasons for these complaints will give you some insight into the controversy and also what types of tests to avoid. Originally, personality tests were developed for use in a clinical setting, i.e., for the diagnosis and treatment of the mentally or psychologically disturbed. Since these tests were often used to identify and classify deviant behavior, many of the questions were "bedroom- and bathroom-related." As the use of these tests increased, some industrial psychologists recognized that, by modifying the questions, the tests could be used to prescreen employment applicants. Numerous tests were then developed to be used for employment purposes, and their use has become widespread during the latter half of this century. Some of them have been criticized strongly because a few of the tests still retain questions that are considered to be offensive and intrusive. Tests that contain only questions that are considered to be job-related seem to be acceptable in most states. But before you use any of these tests consult an attorney to see if it is legal in your state. You also should be aware of the fact that some are considered to be racially or culturally biased.

Preemployment and Random Drug Tests. Drug testing is the most controversial present-day employee screening activity. Several states are considering legislation to control or limit drug testing, and employees have attempted to sue employers for violation of privacy. Nevertheless, the courts are increasingly recognizing the obligation of employers to provide a safe environment for all employees, and that a safe environment includes being drug free. Therefore, in several cases the courts have upheld the right of the employer to conduct both preemployment and random drug tests.

Many of the major franchisors and retail chains now require that all employees must be screened for drug use before being employed, and some furnish detailed instructions to their franchisees and managers. If you wish to screen your potential employees for drug use, we recommend that you contact one of the laboratories that conduct the entire process including the collection of specimens. Most of the claims about the inaccuracy of urinalysis are based on problems in collection and transportation, not in the process itself. If the entire process is conducted on the vendor's (laboratory) site, you can avoid any criticism or complaints about your collection methods. It may be a little more expensive, but well worth the additional cost when you consider the time saved and the problems avoided.

The Employment Agreement

You may be reluctant to use an employment agreement because you feel it might limit your flexibility in dealing with employees. There is, however, one fact concerning employee agreements or contracts that you should be aware of. Recently, case law on employment issues has defined and emphasized the concept of "implied" employee contracts. An implied contract may exist if you as the employer or any of your managers make any statement or promise concerning conditions of employment, including fringe benefit policy, pay, or termination procedures. These statements or promises may be made verbally or in writing. In essence, you will already have an employment contract in existence when you describe the conditions of employment to a new employee. Putting these conditions in writing in the form of an agreement will significantly reduce the chance of expensive and time-consuming misunderstandings between you and your employees.

An employment agreement can be relatively simple, especially if you already have a written personnel policy. A written personnel policy is also considered to be an implied contractual agreement; consequently, you can refer to the policy in the basic agreement.

An employment agreement should include at least the following information:

Name and address of both parties.

Date of hire.

Type of hire (temporary or employment at will).

Job title and place of assignment.

Compensation and payment schedule.

Bonus or commission arrangements.

Number of hours considered to be a normal work week, time sheet requirements, and overtime approval procedures.

Probation period and conditions if applicable.

Drug testing policy, if applicable.

Schedule of compensation and performance reviews.

Progressive discipline and termination procedures.

Definition of termination for cause.

Fringe benefits including qualifications.

Employment at will and other disclaimers.

Other conditions including use and ownership of tools, uniforms, or use of vehicles.

Each party to the agreement should sign all copies, and one copy should be retained in the employee's personnel file.

Orientation

When the newly hired employee reports to work that first day, he or she is nervously encountering a new experience. The new employee does not know what to expect or what will be expected, and is understandably apprehensive. At this point, the newly hired employee is most vulnerable to first impressions—impressions of you, the franchise, other supervisors, fellow workers, and the work environment. Seldom will a new employee leave work after the first day without either a strong positive or negative image of you and the workplace. A positive image can be the foundation for a productive employee-employer relationship, one that can create a loyal employee with a "we" rather than a "me" attitude. A strong negative image may produce an employee who will take advantage of you at every chance and will have little motivation to consistently act in your best interests.

When a new employee reports to work, either you, your assistant, or the appropriate manager should schedule a sufficient amount of time to acquaint the employee with co-workers and the workplace. You or a member of your staff should briefly describe the history of the franchise and the importance of customer service to your unit or units, and also to the reputation of the entire system. The work rules, the compensation, the job description, and other conditions of employment should be reviewed.

One of the most important aspects of the orientation process is the reinforcement of the idea that the new employee is joining a team and that he or she will be expected to support and contribute to that team. There are very few franchises that do not depend on their employees cooperating with each other. Imagine a fast food operation in which all the employees act independently, and you will also imagine an example of complete chaos.

Avoid, as much as possible, leaving new employees alone for extended periods because either you or your staff are too busy to continue with the orientation. This leaves the impression that new persons are not important enough to bother with and places them in a very awkward position. There are few of us who have not experienced this type of situation when we first reported to a new job, and we all can remember our negative feelings toward both the job and the boss. It doesn't take any great effort to make new employees feel welcome, and that small cordiality will pay enormous dividends in the future.

Training

Most franchisors will stress employee training in their own franchisee training programs, and a few will even offer a training program for your employees. Most, however, will depend on you to train your employees to follow the procedures outlined in the franchise operations manual. Remember, however, that the training process serves two very important functions: First, the employee learns the nuts and bolts of the job—how to flip a hamburger or how to lubricate a car. Second, and just as important, the training program provides you with the opportunity to reinforce the value system of the franchise and to emphasize the spirit of teamwork so necessary for a smooth operation. Plenty of training is important because:

Employees need specific skills and knowledge to perform productively.

Employees' job performance reflects on the reputation of the entire franchise.

Employees are like gears in a complex machine. If they underperform, the entire operation is affected.

Employees are often required to make judgment calls. Good training provides them with the knowledge to make a proper choice among the options available to them in any given situation.

Good training gives employees enough confidence to do their job well which, in turn, will help them develop a positive attitude toward you and the franchise.

Good training is good defense. The quality of the training helps you demonstrate that you acted reasonably under the circumstances.

As with any other part of your operations, an effective training program must have clearly defined objectives. To some persons, the only objective is to train an employees in the actual mechanics or procedures involved in the job. To others, training has a broader perspective: the development of team attitude and the ability to think in terms of the best interests of the franchise.

Most franchisees use on-the-job training (OJT) techniques because other methods of teaching, such as classroom or discussion groups, are simply not feasible. Although OJT training can be one of the most effective methods, remember that this training is only as good as the trainer. It usually is best to identify one of your employees as a trainer and take the time and effort to help that person learn to train effectively. The practice of assigning the new employee to the person who happens to be on duty at the time is not only haphazard but dangerous because, in many instances, you may be ensuring that bad work habits will pass from one employee to another.

If you have a multiunit franchise, designate one unit as the training location for all new employees. By consolidating this way, you can develop one or two of your best employees as trainers, thus ensuring as much consistency through your franchise as possible.

Hiring Your Managers

In a single-unit franchisee, all your employee are close associates, and you have both a grasp and a knowledge of practically every detail of the day's activities. As you begin to add additional units, however, certain functions become remote and beyond your control, and suddenly you realize that you no longer can know or manage every detail. You now are faced with the task of selecting your alter ego—your manager.

You will want to scrutinize the background and experience of a candidate, but you may make a better selection if you are not too influenced by what the person has been or done in the past. Concentrate instead on what you want him or her to do for you in the future, in, say, four or five years. This should enable you to focus on your own future needs and what potential a candidate must have to meet those needs. With this as a starting point, then begin to explore the following areas.

You certainly should want someone who has enough specific experience and knowledge to know what has to be done and how to do it, someone who can work effectively with other people and who has the ability to think ahead in terms of change. Unless your person has the necessary specific knowledge and experience, he or she cannot do the job that immediately needs to be done, let alone look to the future. If your franchise is to succeed and presumably grow, it needs people who not only can grow with it but who, preferably, can take a leadership role in its growth. They must be flexible thinkers because conditions, threats, and opportunities are always changing.

In most franchise operations the managers work along with the other employees. This willingness to pitch in when business is brisk is an important consideration in the manager selection process. If the applicant is autocratic or dictatorial in his or her approach to supervising people, you can be sure that problems will develop to hinder the employee group's ability to function as a team. A manager should have that particular combination of confidence or self-assurance and a low-key or informal way of supervising that makes employees at least pleased but, even better, stimulated and inspired.

You probably have heard about a person's IQ (intelligence quotient), but nothing about one of the most critical factors in determining the success of a manager: the CQ or cope quotient. The cope quotient measures a person's ability to quickly and decisively handle the unexpected disturbances that occur in the normal course of doing business, and to do so without causing an undue amount of stress on either themselves or others. It has been said with considerable truth that business is largely one damn thing after another—a never-ending series of brush fires and emergencies. If these events are not met resourcefully and effectively, the best laid plans and policies will fail. The necessity to deal with stress is a practical reality in the life of any manager, and your selection process must attempt to evaluate the applicant's CQ. A review of previous experience, medical history, and work and recreational habits will give you insight into a candidate's ability to cope.

Another attribute to look for when selecting a manager is a sense of rightness, the desire to do even little tasks right and to treat other people, customers, suppliers, and employees fairly and with dignity. You might call it "integrity" but we think the sense of rightness is larger and more encompassing than integrity. It describes the way a person instinctively deals with a situation or problem, particularly when other people are concerned. Managers with a sense of rightness are sensitive to the needs of those they work with, and above all they weigh, fairly and objectively, all the factors involved in a decision.

Personnel Files

A review of the most common types of regulatory agency or court actions brought against franchisees will demonstrate the importance of a complete personnel file on each employee. A complete file is critical to your defense if charges of wrongful discharge, negligent hiring practices, violations of wage and hour law, or employment discrimination are filed against you. In fact, the Fair Labor Standards Act (see Chap. 13) specifically requires you to record certain types of information on each employee and to maintain payroll and time records at the place of employment.

Your employee personnel files should contain the following information:

The employment agreement, including a statement to the effect that falsification of information will be sufficient cause for immediate dismissal.

A copy of the original resume.

The appropriate job description including a statement that the supervisor may assign additional duties as required. This should be signed by the employee.

Any addendum to the employment agreement concerning tools, uniforms, or vehicles.

W-4 forms. If the employee changes the dependent information, retain both the old and revised copies.

Insurance applications.

Defined contribution agreements (pension plan).

Copies of all insurance claims including health and workman compensation claims. Include copies of all correspondence in reference to these claims.

Copies of performance and compensation reviews signed by the employee.

Records of any disciplinary action including copies of pertinent letters, memos, and notes of meetings.

Salary or wage history including records of increases.

Changes in job status including promotions, transfers, and reclassifications resulting in job changes.

Records of sick leave and vacation time.

Bonus or commission agreements.

Leave of absence, maternity, and leave without pay agreements.

Copies of all job-related correspondence between you and the employee.

Any agreements concerning training, including by the franchisor or continuing education related to the job.

One last comment about hiring and retaining employees. If yours is a family-owned franchise and one of your family is in a supervisory position or even is hired as a line employee, this will have an effect on nonfamily employees. Your relationships with family member employees will always be scrutinized closely. Many nonfamily employees feel that advancement in a family-owned business is nearly impossible because family members get all the promotions. It will take an extra effort on your part to present a convincing view of yourself as an owner who expects family members to pull their full share of the load and who will leave the door open to advancement to everyone regardless of relationship.

13
Have Prudent Personnel Policies

"Don't put it in writing." This is a frequent phrase among smaller franchisees when discussing personnel policy. Evidently the assumption is that, if it is not in writing, the franchisee cannot be held responsible for any claims by their employees. Unfortunately, this is a mistake. Emerging case law on implied contracts holds that any promise or statement concerning employment conditions, whether verbal or written, is enforceable in most states. Within the definition of implied contract, a written personnel policy becomes the best friend, not the worst enemy, of the franchisee. A written personnel policy declares the intent of the employer, and, if it is clearly defined and distributed to all concerned, the chances are good that it will stand up against any claim of an oral commitment or promise that conflicts with it. A written personnel policy statement or manual is indeed necessary in today's business climate for several reasons:

1. A written personnel policy is easier to communicate to the employees and with much less possibility of a misunderstanding.

2. It helps assure that the personnel policy is administered fairly. As long as the policy is well defined and commonly understood, the chances are much improved that the managers will treat employees equally according to their position and experience.

3. It fosters consistency. Operating a multiunit franchise or a single unit with two or three shifts requires consistent management. The manager of unit A or of the morning shift must give his or her employees the same information as the managers of other units and/or other shifts.

4. A written policy also ensures, as much a possible, a continuity of operations when managers are replaced or transferred.

5. It reduces the franchisee's exposure to litigation and to action by regulatory agencies. Most wrongful discharge actions are caused by managers who are inconsistent in their disciplinary and termination procedures. Managers also are responsible for most of the wage and hour violations because they do not understand how these regulations are interpreted by the wage/hour investigators.

A written personnel policy should specifically address these issues and provide detailed information to managers about the procedures to be used when disciplining or terminating an employee.

Contents of a Personnel Policy Manual

When developing a personnel policy manual, remember that this document will serve a number of purposes. It will be used as an orientation tool for new employees. It will be used by managers as a guide when questions concerning personnel policy arise. Furthermore, it will strengthen your image as a person committed to fair and equal treatment of all employees.

Some franchisors provide, either for a fee or as part of their operations manual, a recommended personnel policy, and many franchisees have found it to be useful. Most franchisors, however, are reluctant to provide any recommendations because the labor market and laws vary so much from state to state. We provide you here with a list of topics, which we recommend as basic for a manual. The list has been developed from a review of numerous personnel policy manuals used in a variety of franchised businesses, but in addition to these, it is likely you will find other topics peculiar to your business and location that should be included. Your manual should be thorough and explicit.

The History and Value System of the Franchise

By describing how the franchise began and the history of its growth, you can provide the employee with a sense of belonging to an organization that is proud of its origin, heritage, and purpose. Almost every franchise will create a value system in terms of quality and customer service in its advertising and promotion, and this theme should be reinforced in your policy manual. The manual is an excellent place to introduce the new employee to both your goals and those of the franchise.

The Description of Your Own Organization

By giving a history of how you originally became involved in the franchise, and telling about the members of your family who also are in the organization, you provide a new employee with a sense of your values and purpose. You might even include an organizational chart if you are a multiunit owner. You also may include in this section a description of the positions or jobs throughout your franchise to provide your employees with information concerning possible promotional opportunities.

Job Descriptions

Brief descriptions of the various positions in your franchise, including the chain of supervision and reporting, will help employees know the responsibilities of not only their own positions those but of others in your organization. If you are large enough to have a central office with department heads in charge of each specialty, as is the case with many multiunit franchisees, a description of the responsibilities of each will help your managers and employees know where to get answers to questions that are beyond the scope of their duties.

Compensation

This section defines the types of positions in your franchise and the method of compensation for each type. It is not necessary to provide the actual dollar amounts paid for each job category, but it is necessary to identify the compensation categories, i.e., salary, hourly rate, salary plus commission, or commission only. Eligibility and requirements for overtime should be stated. (See the section on the Fair Labor Standards Act and Wage and Hour regulations later in this chapter.) If your franchise involves the sale and repair of autos, trucks, or farm equipment, those positions subject to the special rules on overtime should be identified. An explanation as to how overtime is computed and what constitutes a work week should be given. Be aware that state laws differ in these matters, and you should check with your attorney or your state labor department for the regulations that apply to you.

As a defensive measure, it is extremely important that you set forth, in detail, the steps necessary for authorization of overtime payments and the documentation required. Certain circumstances will require you to pay overtime even if it was unauthorized and you had no actual knowledge of the fact that the employee was working beyond the normal number of hours. Some manuals will include, in this section, a description of the procedures used in compensation reviews both during probationary periods and thereafter.

Benefit Programs

Holidays. The personnel policy manual should identify those holidays on which the franchise unit is open or closed. If your franchise customarily is open during most or all holidays (for example, a fast food franchise), the employees should be alerted to the fact that they may be required to work holidays and take compensatory time off at some later date. If you have some type of holiday work schedule that is based on positions or seniority, then the basis for the schedule should be fully explained. The question of who works and who doesn't work is a constant source of conflict in many franchises and a well defined policy can do much to reduce problems between employees.

Vacation Time. The section on vacations should provide the formula for computing vacation time and accruing it. Usually, franchisees will require that a minimum number of vacation days must be accrued before any can be taken. And because most franchises have seasonal or cyclical periods of high volume, it is customary to not allow vacations during these periods. This section of your manual should also outline the procedure for requesting vacation time, including the schedule for submitting requests. Usually, in event of a conflict (two or more employees asking for the same period), either have the employees work it out among themselves or decide the conflict by seniority. The practice of accruing vacation time beyond one year is usually discouraged unless the time was accrued at your convenience or request. If so, then you have the option of letting accrued time accumulate beyond the end of the year or buying the time back.

Sick Time and Personal Leave. Many franchisees, particularly those using entry-level labor, attempt to avoid this issue completely by paying strictly by the time card. If the employee does not work, regardless of the reason, he or she does not get paid. This system may work in a high employee turnover operation utilizing minimally skilled people, but it will not work when you need people with higher skill levels and you need to improve your retention rates. Policies concerning the accrual of sick time vary considerably. Some franchises do not allow time to accrue beyond one year, but this is a policy that encourages some employees to take the time off whether they are sick not so that they will not lose it. Other franchises pay employees at the end of every year for unused sick time.

Leave of Absence Without Pay. Most franchisees prefer to leave this subject out of the policy manual preferring to handle it on a case-by-case basis. You should be aware of the fact that, in some cases, job guarantees after certain types of absences are state or federally mandated. There is legislation pending in some states to extend these guarantees to maternity leave.

Medical and Dental Insurance. This is an increasingly controversial benefit because medical costs continue to increase alarmingly. There are some group plans available to smaller businesses and franchisees that can installed on an employer-employee co-pay basis, but many of these are prohibitively expensive. Right now, medical insurance coverage is a hot national political issue and some of the legislation being drafted would require small businesses and franchisees to offer medical insurance to their employees.

Business Hours

In many cases, the franchise operations manual and the franchise agreement require that franchisees maintain standard opening hours. Since these hours are often more than eight per day, two or three shifts are necessary to meet the standards. The actual scheduling of employees and the timing of the shifts should be left up to the managers since each location may be operating under different conditions. The manual itself should not set shift hours but may set guidelines in assigning shifts. For example, many states have restrictions on the hours and the time that employees under 18 years of age may work.

Lunch Hours and Breaks

The manual may set the guidelines, especially in those states in which breaks and lunch hours are regulated, but the actual scheduling should be left up to the manager or supervisor because of varying peak traffic conditions.

Dress Codes and Appearance

Uniforms are often prescribed by the franchise operational manual and the franchise agreement. If so, your manual should stipulate who is responsible for washing or cleaning the uniforms and the number that will be issued to each employee. It also is advisable to include a policy on replacement should a uniform be damaged or lost. When a uniform is not supplied or required, it is appropriate for you to set your own dress and appearance standards as long as they are reasonable.

Office, Store, or Shop Policies

The manual should address such issues as smoking, personal phone calls, conducting personal business, and other matters of conduct on the job. These standards or policies are particularly important if most of your employees are working for the first time. Their behavior in the workplace is a matter of work ethics and many employees have not had the experience or guidance to know what is acceptable, particularly when dealing with customers.

Tools

Typically, in franchises in which tools are involved, the franchise operational manual will recommend how to handle the question of who furnishes what. The franchisee is usually responsible for furnishing the major shop equipment, but often the employees are required to furnish their own hand tools. Your policy manual should be very specific about your tool policy, and, if your employees are required to furnish their own, you should provide a secure storage place for them.

Employee Facilities

The policy manual should note what facilities are available to the employees. Typically, these facilities would include lockers, restrooms, lunch areas, and parking assignments.

Progressive Discipline and Termination

The most common area of dispute, and subsequent legal action, in the employee-employer relationship is the termination of an employee. Even in right to work states, the courts are tending toward a more liberal attitude on employee rights, and the issue of wrongful discharge is being raised more frequently than ever before. The most effective method of reducing exposure to this type of litigation is to include a progressive discipline and termination procedure in your personnel manual, and then make sure that all your managers and supervisors are familiar with the procedure and follow it to the letter. There are numerous progressive discipline techniques, but the most frequently used is the "three strikes and you're out" method. The employee is entitled to two warnings about poor performance or other problems, and at least the last one should be in writing with a copy placed in the personnel file. This last warning results in probation. Any further problems and the employee is terminated. Such procedures are not necessary, however, in layoffs due to economic circumstances. This fully documented progressive discipline and termination procedure gives protection not only against wrongful discharge claims but also against unemployment compensation insurance claims.

Termination for Cause

The progressive discipline and termination procedure is only used in work-related circumstances of a nonthreatening nature. The manual should clearly state that, in the event of theft, abusive language, or actions directed at another party, immoral or unethical behavior, the employee is subject to immediate dismissal. Any termination for cause action should be clearly documented, including statements of witnesses and/or victims, and all documents placed in the employee's personnel file.

Performance and Compensation Reviews

Your personnel procedures manual should provide for annual or semiannual performance reviews. The review should cover all aspects of the employee's performance and behavior, including both negative and the positive elements. This review may or may not be related to compensation issues; in fact, many franchisees prefer to go over compensation and benefits matters in separate meetings. Although obviously compensation goes hand in hand with performance, many franchisees feel that compensation should not play a role in disciplining or correcting employees. It can be a carrot but never a stick.

A final comment on the personnel policies manual. If the manual serves as a guide that is consistently followed by all concerned, it is a valuable employee relations tool. If it is not followed, however, the effect on the employees is worse than not having a manual at all.

Employee Compensation Policy

The consideration of employee compensation should begin with an understanding of the facts about the relationship between money and motivation. Many owners of small businesses and franchises believe that the only thing necessary to motivate their employees to peak performance is an adequate salary or hourly rate of pay. But those of us who have spent many years in labor management relations, particularly in a union setting, have learned that money actually plays a relatively minor part in employee motivation and behavior.

Employees' views of the adequacy or fairness of the amount of money they receive for doing a job are not based on any judgment that a particular job should be worth, in itself, a certain number of dollars. Employees will base their judgment on how both their jobs and their pay compare to other jobs and pay. If, for example, they judge a job to be more complex, require more skill and experience, and be more important to the business than a job performed by a fellow employee, then they expect that, in all fairness, it should pay more. Hence, the fairness or adequacy of compensation is a *comparative judgment*. How does the pay compare with that of fellow employees or with similar jobs in the same kind of business?

Most employees do not realize the impact that the market place has on pay levels. The amount of pay for a certain type of job is largely determined by the law of supply and demand. When designing or reviewing your pay schedule, the size of the local labor pool of potential employees for your positions will, in reality, establish your entry-level pay grades for all jobs. Remember, though, that in a period of high unemployment, most employees will initially be happy just to find a job, but you cannot expect that this first happiness will sustain their satisfaction for very long.

It has widely been assumed by owners and managers that a promise of more money and better fringe benefits will stimulate employee production and performance for an extended period of time. When the effects of such increases disappear quickly, the same owners and managers are puzzled to explain why their employees are not still highly motivated. Very likely it is because of management style.

This was well explained several decades ago when Frederick Herzberg published a concept called the two factor model. Herzberg, one of the pioneers in scientific management, observed that two factors determined productivity and performance: the maintenance and the motivational. *Maintenance factors* consisted of those aspects of the job, including pay, that meet employee expectations of what they were reasonably entitled to. If these expectations were not met, there is a negative effect on morale and attitude. If the expectations are met, the effect is neither negative nor positive, but neutral. Since the employee felt that he or she is entitled to a certain pay and benefit level as part of the conditions of the job, there was no added incentive to increase production or performance.

According to Herzberg, the factors that could be considered *motivational* and that will improve production and performance for extended periods of time are *largely a matter of the nature and the quality of the relationship between the employee and the employer.* The level of compensation has little to do with this as long as that level is adequate or fair in the eyes of the employee. A review of management/labor relations over recent years clearly reinforces Herzberg's findings.

The lesson to be learned is that your compensation schedule will have a limited effect on the performance of your employees. The most important elements in performance and productivity are the quality and effectiveness of your management style. This is not to say that a fair compensation package lacks importance, but your own management attitude and behavior are more important.

The Compensation Schedule

Since ultimately you will be ranking the jobs within your franchise according to their importance and contributions to profits or income, your first step is to identify each job in terms of its duties, responsibilities, title, reporting requirements, and any unusual elements. Also list the preferred educational level, work experience, and other training necessary to perform the duties adequately. If you already are operating a franchise and are intending to expand, your current employees can be very helpful in preparing these job descriptions. We suggest, however, that you tell them, up front, that you are reviewing your compensation schedule. If you are just starting the franchise unit, the job descriptions may be available through the franchisor or other franchisees.

The next step involves the ranking of the jobs in terms of complexity, skills required, difficulty, stress, and the degree of importance to the operation of the franchise. There is no real scientific way to do this; so you must rely on your own judgment. Rank the jobs in terms of the factors just listed from the simplest entry-level to those requiring the most skill and experience. You may find that often different jobs require approximately the same amount of skill and knowledge. These jobs can be similarly ranked. There is nothing wrong with two jobs being in the same pay range.

To establish the pay range for each job, first check with the franchisor to see if they can furnish any comparative data on wages. Other franchisees within your labor market may also be willing to share information. You are looking for the average wages paid to those in comparable jobs. Be careful, however, that you make comparisons based on actual job descriptions rather than on job titles, since job titles will vary considerably from one type of business or location to another. By making these comparisons, you soon can determine the average wages for each job category. Then, to establish a pay range for each category, set your entry-level at 85 percent of the average and the upper end of the range for that job at 115 percent of the average. This range will allow you to make adjustments in starting pay to accommodate previous experience and also to provide raises for employees even though they are not promoted. Obviously, the lowest end of the pay range cannot be less than the current federal or state minimum wage. Preferably, it should be higher.

Your compensation schedule should also show how raises are determined. There are numerous methods of determining pay raises but the most common are:

1. Merit increases to recognize superior performance.

2. Tenure increases to recognize longevity with the franchise.

3. Periodic performance reviews.

4. Cost of living increases tied to the cost of living index for your area.

You also may find it necessary to adjust the entire plan because of changes in the local labor market or because persons with certain skills will be difficult to recruit locally.

Your schedule should be reviewed annually or at any time you notice that you are no longer attracting the quality of employee you want. You may also notice that employee turnover is increasing alarmingly, which may mean that your starting rates are no longer competitive and you are losing employees before your scheduled pay raises have any impact. Be aware, however, that pay rates are usually less reason for high turnover than supervisory problems or the deterioration of general job conditions.

You also should decide the length of the pay period, i.e., weekly, bi-weekly, or twice a month. An example is on the 15th and the last day of the month. You probably will find that your accountant will prefer you to pay twice a month with the last pay day falling on the last day of the month because this method simplifies his or her job; it eliminates having to make computations and adjustments on the financial statements. From your viewpoint, particularly if you allow overtime, the weekly or biweekly pay period will make your payroll preparation a lot simpler since your payroll dates will coincide with the end of the 40-hour work weeks. It also is possible to pay hourly employees weekly or biweekly and salaried employees twice a month. We must caution, however, that many salaried employees are also eligible for overtime.

The Fair Labor Standards Act (Wage and Hour Provisions)

Many of the policies in your personnel practices manual will be governed by provisions of the Fair Labor Standards Act, a law originally enacted in 1938 that establishes standards for minimum wage, overtime, and the definitions of work time. Unfortunately, most of the 75,000 claims of violations of wage and hour regulations filed annually by the U.S. Department of Labor are against owners of small businesses and franchise units. Since these claims amounted to over $122 million in 1990, you do not have to be a Nobel Prize winning economist to realize that violating the wage and hour regulations can be extremely expensive.

There are several reasons why you, as a franchisee, and many other small business people are so often the targets of wage and hour investigations. First, few of you have a formal personnel department headed by a trained personnel specialist familiar with the various labor-oriented laws. Your personnel policy is administered either by you or by someone on your staff who is already wearing three or four hats. Typically, none of you is familiar with the laws and how they are interpreted and applied by wage and hour investigators and the courts.

Second, since Congress allows individual states to pass and enforce wage and hour laws that are more restrictive than the basic federal regulations, you can be caught in a situation in which you are in compliance with the federal law but in violation of the state law. In California, for example, the state law requires an employer to pay overtime, under certain circumstances, for all time in excess of 8 hours per day while the federal statutes only require overtime payment for time in excess of 40 hours per week.

Third, work flow in most franchises tends to be erratic. A normal work schedule is sometimes difficult to maintain, and the employees become accustomed to responding to traffic when it occurs.

Fourth, since most franchises have under 20 employees per unit, the relationships between owners, managers, and employees tend to be quite informal and almost familylike. Under these conditions, time cards and rigid work rules are considered to be unnecessary and, in fact, undesirable. All these reasons point to the fact that you, as a franchisee, are more vulnerable to claims of wage and hour violations than larger corporations or organizations. They also explain why you can get caught between the wishes of your employees and the demands of the state or federal government.

To reduce your exposure to claims of wage and hour violations, you and your managers must know how the following three words or phases are interpreted and applied by federal or state enforcement agencies: *exempt-nonexempt, suffer and permit,* and *burden of proof.* The definitions of these terms are found in the state and federal statutes but are subject to interpretation by local investigators and agencies. So it might be worth the time to check with a labor/management attorney for an opinion on local labor practices.

Exempt-Nonexempt

In labor terminology, the terms, "exempt" and "nonexempt" mean whether an employee is entitled to overtime.

A *nonexempt* employee is entitled to the minimum wage plus overtime. In 1992, the federal minimum wage was $4.25 an hour, and overtime had to be paid at the rate of one and one-half times the normal rate of pay for all hours in excess of 40 hours during a normal work week. Be cautioned, however, that many states have passed their own wage and hour laws, and the federal minimum wage and overtime provisions may not apply. Since the state laws must be substantially equivalent, any state law will be higher or more restrictive than the fed's. Generally speaking, nonexempt employees include those paid an hourly rate, those on commission or piece rate, and those on salary who do not meet the requirements for exempt status.

An *exempt* employee is one who is exempt by law from minimum wage and or overtime requirements. *The most common mistake by franchise owners is the assumption that all salaried employees are exempt. This assumption is incorrect and unfortunately is responsible for a significant number of wage and hour violations.* Employees are entitled to be classified as exempt only if their duties meet *all* the requirements stated in wage and hour laws. Exemption is not based on job title alone.

Four job categories can be classified as exempt: executive, administrative, professional, and outside sales. Each of these categories must have required duties and characteristics in order for the position to qualify as exempt. For example, for a manager to qualify as an executive, all the following tests must be met:

1. The employee's primary duty must be the management of an enterprise or of a customarily recognized department or subdivision.

2. The employee must customarily supervise the work of two or more employees therein. (In most states, it must be two or more full-time employees or the equivalent of two or more full-time employees)

3. The employee must have the authority to hire and fire, or recommend hiring and firing, or be a person whose recommendations on these and other actions affecting employees are given particular weight.

4. The employee must customarily and regularly exercise discretionary powers.

5. The employee must devote no more than 20 percent (no more than 40 percent if employed by a retail or service establishment) of his or her time to activities not directly and closely related to the managerial duties.

6. The employee must be paid on a salary basis at a rate of at least $155 per week exclusive of board, lodging, or other facilities.

The percentage tests on nonexempt work would not apply in the case of an employee who is in sole charge of an independent establishment or a physically separate branch establishment, or who owns at least 20 percent of the enterprise where employed.

You can easily see that the most controversial position in a franchise operation is that of the unit manager. In a multiunit franchise, the unit managers are usually exempt as long as at least 50 percent of their duties are managerial in nature, although this usually is a judgment call on the part of investigators. If you own only a single unit and still have a manager, the issue is whether you are truly an absentee owner or you exercise enough control to make the employee a manager in name only. In numerous cases on record, the manager did not qualify for executive exempt status simply because the owner was on the premises during most of the time the franchise was open for business. Another recurring issue involves primarily those fast food operations in which the manager is also on the line most of the time. Investigators usually will make their decision on a case-by-case basis. If the manager is truly responsible for the operation of the unit, the exempt status will be granted in most cases.

Similar tests are required for the other three exempt categories. As a general rule, few franchise employees would qualify for an administrative exemption because the tests require that their duties involve providing special advice to management, such as credit manager, purchasing agent, or personnel manager. There also are instances in which executive secretaries and assistants to the general manager may be exempt, but these positions usually are only found in larger organizations. You would be well advised to obtain a list of the qualifications for exemption for all categories from both the state and federal labor department offices having jurisdiction over your area since some states have more restrictive exempt requirements than the federal statutes.

In particular, if you have a franchise involving the sale and repair of autos, trucks, or farm equipment, ask your local labor department if the special exemptions for mechanics and parts salespersons allowed in the federal regulations apply in your state.

Salaried employees who are not exempt according to the preceding standards are entitled to overtime for all hours worked over 40 during a normal work week, or whatever the state standards stipulate. To compute overtime for a salaried employee, you must first convert the amount of the salary to an hourly rate. For someone paid a weekly salary, simply divide that amount by 40 to obtain the hourly rate. For someone paid on a semimonthly or monthly salary, divide the total monthly amount by 4.333 to obtain the weekly rate and then divide that figure by 40 to obtain the hourly rate. In most states there also are standard formulas for computing hourly rates for employees contracted for less than 40 hours a week for a stated salary or for those who contracted to work more than 40 hours a week. In both cases, the employee is still entitled to overtime but the amount is calculated differently. If you have employees who fall into either category, check your local labor department for the correct formula.

Suffer and Permit

Almost as many franchise owners are trapped by this definition as are caught by the definitions of the salaried exempt employee. The term *suffer and permit* refers to the fact that you, as the owner, are obligated to pay overtime to any nonexempt employees who are *permitted* to work over 40 hours during a normal work week whether they were required to work or not. This situation most often occurs in the small franchise unit operating on an informal basis and not using time clocks. Often, because of an erratic work load, employees will voluntarily work beyond the end of a shift to finish a project, or clean up the work area, even though they were not directly or indirectly ordered to do so. If you, as the owner, or your manager has knowledge of the fact, or if it is reasonable to assume that you or the manager should have knowledge of it, the employee is entitled to overtime compensation. The term *suffer and permit* essentially is labor law jargon which means *to allow*. If, in the opinion of the wage and hour investigator, the work constitutes a benefit to you, overtime must be paid.

You can offset overtime by granting compensatory time off in most states, but federal law requires that such compensatory time off must be given during the same work week in which it was incurred. Compensatory time off cannot be accumulated week by week. Each week stands alone in the computation of overtime.

Burden of Proof

The definition of the third term, *burden of proof,* is a compelling argument for maintaining adequate records. In essence, this term refers to the fact that, in a claim for back pay because of violations of the wage and hour law, the employee does not have to prove your guilt; you must prove your innocence. Despite the fact that, in this country, it has traditionally has been held that a person is innocent until proven guilty, the interpretation of the Fair Labor Standards Act provided by Congress, and ultimately upheld by the courts, is just the opposite. Typically, if a claim against you is made, your best defense is a pattern of documentation of time worked and evidence that you made a reasonable attempt to control the hours of work. This evidence should be in the form of precise written statements of overtime approval procedure and policy distributed to your employees, plus some type of time cards or records, preferably always signed by the employee.

Several other issues involved in wage and hour regulations also should be addressed in your personnel practices manual. The beginning and the end of the work week should be specified so that both the employees and managers understand when compensatory time must be offset. Generally, those franchises whose business increases on weekends may find that a Saturday to Friday work week allows the manager to respond to an unexpected need for overtime on a busy weekend and yet have the opportunity during the week to offset the overtime with compensatory time off.

The question of whether an employee should be paid while on call can be answered by defining the difference between two terms: *engaged to wait* and *waiting to be engaged*. Employees who are on call but who are free to use intervening time for their own use are considered to be *waiting to be engaged*. Consequently, they are considered to be working only when actually called to work. After the call, however, all the time spent on the job is considered working time. An employee required to report to work, even though no work is immediately available and therefore must remain on the premises until assigned to work, is considered to be *engaged to wait*. The key is whether the employee can use the time between work assignments for their own use. Usually, the labor department will decide claims involving call-in procedures on a case-by-case basis.

Records Required by
Wage and Hour Regulations

As noted, adequate records are one of the best defenses against claims for back pay because of violations of wage and hour regulations. Most claims of this kind are filed by former employees who were terminated or who quit because of a disagreement with an owner or manager. Therefore all records should be kept at least three years, and many attorneys recommend that payroll records be kept a minimum of seven years. The wage and hour law itself has a list of information that must be included in the employment and payroll records of every employee subject to the law. All these must be kept:

1. Personal identifying information including name, home address, social security number, occupation or job title, sex, and birthdate.
2. Hour and day when the work week begins and ends.
3. Total number of hours worked each work day and work week.
4. Total daily or weekly straight time earnings.
5. Regular hourly rate or salary.
6. Total overtime hours and pay for the work week.
7. Deductions from and additions to wages.
8. Total wages paid for each pay period.
9. Date of payment and pay period covered by that payment.

Records also should note any special or uncommon pay agreements including lodging, board, and the furnishing of a vehicle or equipment. If you provide any of these to one or more employees, check with your accountant for the proper method of recording these agreements for tax and minimum wage purposes.

Equal Employment Opportunity Issues

At this writing, Congress is debating several versions of civil rights in employment legislation that, regardless of the version finally passed, will significantly alter the way you recruit and hire employees. The current legislation will supplement and modify civil rights statutes that were enacted in 1964 by Title VII of the Civil Rights Act. As you probably know, discriminating against an applicant or an employee in matters of hiring, transfer, promotion, and other employment practices because of race, color, religion, sex, age, or national origin is strictly illegal. Most of you do not know, however, what standards are used by the enforcement agencies to identify discrimination in employment. Three of these standards were developed by the Equal Employment Opportunity Commission (EEOC) for their compliance manual which is used in investigations of charges of discrimination. These standards should give you an inside look at how your employment practices compare with these standards.

Disparate Treatment

Disparate treatment can be generally defined as a difference in treatment of similarly situated individuals on the basis of race, color, religion, sex, age, or national origin. Although the charging party must establish that the respondent's actions were based on a discriminatory motive, it is also important to recognize that the courts have ruled that a discriminatory motive can be inferred from the fact of existence of disparate treatment. In determining who is similarly qualified or situated, the investigating agency must first determine who is similarly situated within the context of a particular employment situation. Statistics alone cannot be proof of disparate treatment, but they can be used as an important part of the charge.

The burden is on the charging party to furnish sufficient evidence to indicate the probability or inference that an act of discrimination took place. The charging party does not have to prove the allegations since that is the job of the EEOC or its designated agency. You should note that discrimination does not have to be the sole cause of your actions—only a contributing factor—and that it is a violation of Title VII whether the act of discrimination is conscious or unconscious in nature.

Adverse Impact

In a charge of *adverse impact,* the investigating agency is more concerned with the effect or impact of an act than the actual motive for the act. It is only necessary to establish that an employment practice has the result or effect of excluding or adversely affecting one or more members of a protected class. (A protected class is one that is specifically listed in the statutes as deserving of protection because of race, national origin, etc.) The defense against a charge of adverse impact usually requires that the respondent be able to prove that the employment practice in question is a business necessity and the employee selection criteria are job-related.

Perpetuation of Past Discrimination

Perpetuation of past discrimination occurs when the effect of past discrimination is being continued by the present operation of a neutral employment system. Generally this charge involves a practice that limits or denies the availability of a job to a member of a protected class. If a respondent recruits by only announcing job openings to current employees or by advertising only in those areas or by media that fail to reach protected classes, a case for perpetuation of past discrimination may exist. Direct motive need not be proved. The charging party needs only to establish that past discrimination did occur and that the current neutral employment system is continuing that discrimination.

Obviously, if a charge of discrimination is filed against you, your first move is to contact an attorney. Be cautioned, however, that civil rights law is a highly specialized form of law, and few general attorneys have either the knowledge or the contacts for this kind of practice. Also be aware of the fact that the investigating agency will offer you the opportunity to settle or conciliate at several points during the investigation and that, in many instances, the settlement will not require you to admit guilt. Considering the amount of awards in recent cases, the option of settling before going to court may be very attractive indeed.

Unemployment Tax Appeals Procedures

Another item of expense that is affected by your personnel policy and practices consists of the premiums for unemployment compensation insurance. These premiums are assessed against your payroll under the authority of the federal Unemployment Tax Act and often are listed on your financial reports as insurance premiums. Therefore, they are generally considered to be a fixed cost. Actually, in most states, unemployment insurance is a cooperative venture between the states and the federal government, and, as with the Fair Labor Standards Act, the arrangement and procedures can vary slightly from state to state.

Under the federal law, a 6.2-percent tax is levied on the first $7000 of each employee's wages; however, employers can earn tax credit of up to 5.4 percent if their state meets federal requirements and their taxes are paid on time. The amount of the credit is based on the ratio of taxes paid versus unemployment compensation claims by former employees paid. Consequently, a low claims experience can result in significant savings.

How can you save? By understanding how the system works and how to sharpen your own personnel procedures to decrease the number of successful claims charged against your account. As in the case of the Fair Labor Standards Act, in order to obtain these savings, you must first understand how most state unemployment compensation commissions interpret and apply certain terms contained within the Act. In the federal Unemployment Tax Act, these terms are *fault* and *burden of proof.*

The term *fault* was contained in the original version of the Act and refers to the fact that the intent of Congress was to protect employees who were terminated through no fault of their own. Although the original wording and intent have not changed, the judicial system and many of the states have established their own definitions, and consequently there is now considerable variation in the definition of fault among the states.

Generally, states require that terminated employees be given a notice that sets forth the reason for the termination. From this information the claims officer will make an initial judgment as to whether the termination was the fault of the employee. For example, if the notice states that the employee was terminated because of lack of work, the claim will probably be approved and the compensation payments will be charged against your account. If, however, the notice indicates that the employee was discharged because of poor job performance or for cause, the claim probably will be disapproved. Both parties, you and the employee, have the right of appeal, and it is the appeal process that provides you with the opportunity to ensure that the claim is disapproved and not charged against your experience rating. To do so, you must be able to clearly prove that the employee was discharged for poor job performance or for cause and in most states the proof must be documented.

The issue of *burden of proof* is similar to proof under the Fair Labor Standards Act. You must prove your case; employees do not have to prove their claims. But the burden of proof does shift to employees if they quit voluntarily or involuntarily, and they must prove that quitting the job was due to some work-related cause or for some compelling personal reason. Usually, when claiming an involuntary quit, employees will be required to show that they attempted to negotiate the grievance and also explored other reasonable alternatives.

By ensuring that the progressive discipline and termination process described in the section on personnel manuals is followed to the letter and is properly documented, you have the proof required by most investigators or appeal boards if you wish to appeal an initial decision. To also ensure that you and/or a member of your staff thoroughly understand your state's procedures and the standards or criteria used in judging claims by terminated employees, it is advisable to give one person the responsibility for monitoring the way you handle terminations and notices of appealable judgments. This person should become thoroughly familiar with:

1. The federal and state unemployment tax act.
2. The state statutes concerning implementation of the act.
3. The appeals procedure.
4. The experience rating system and how to review it.
5. The state's definition of base period employer and last employer.
6. The state's criteria for voluntary quits.

The responsible person should monitor terminations, personnel files, and the system for receiving and filing right of appeal notices, as well as ensuring that payment of applicable taxes receives priority attention. In most states, the late payment of these taxes will automatically place you in the highest tax bracket.

One final comment concerning your personnel policy. When choosing an attorney, remember that most general practitioners are not familiar with the laws and statutes discussed in this chapter. The legal issues involved in the employee-employer relationship are complex, and you should be advised by someone competent in this area.

14

Help Your People to Be Their Best

Many management theorists define resources as the combination of people and material objects that are available to use for a specific purpose. We do not agree. People are living human beings and should not classified with inanimate material objects. Also, in business the abilities needed to be considerate of people and to bring out the best in them are vastly different from the abilities needed to manage inventories, equipment, and other inanimate goods. Your success and growth as a franchisee probably will be determined much more by how you manage the people who work for you than by anything that is material. Therefore, give the most careful kind of thought to how you can encourage people to do and be their best.

During the early part of this century, the business gurus were involved in what was then termed "scientific management." The driving force behind this concept was the theory that high productivity was the result of placing the right resource in the production process at the right time and in the right sequence. The right resources also included people, and the theory at the time was that, through a strict militaristic management style, people could be shaped into robotlike objects that would act with a specific purpose and a predictable level of performance. Another way of describing this theory would be to state it as a mathematical formula:

1. Place an employee in the production process at point A.

2. Add equipment at point B.

3. Add materials at point C.

4. The automatic result will be x amount of production.

By the 1940s this simplistic idea of management had begun to break down. Both business and our armed forces found that, despite all the clever rules and all the training and discipline, the human part of the equation was still unpredictable. Given two organizations with the same mission, the same number of employees, the same equipment, and the same conditions, the levels of production or accomplishment could be completely different. Realizing that they were going in the wrong direction, the management experts began to explore the subject of human behavior and motivation. Consequently, during the past 50 years, the management of people and the management of resources have taken increasingly divergent paths.

You, as a franchise owner and manager, are still faced with the same problem that confronted the managers of yesteryear: how to mix people and resources to obtain the maximum amount of products or services. Or, to express the same thought in today's terms, how to mix employees, dough, tomatoes, cheese, and pepperoni to obtain the maximum amount of pizzas at the lowest sensible cost. You have the advantage, however, of decades of experience in studying human psychology and behavior, and we expect you know that managing people involves much more than managing your inventory to ensure that there is enough dough and pepperoni for the day's business.

You may argue that managing one franchise unit with 10 employees is completely different from managing 30 units with 300 employees, and in terms of scope and complexity you may be partially right. Regardless of the size of your organization, however, you should realize that certain basic elements of management apply to any franchise or business whether it is a single fast food outlet or a megaunit corporation.

Your Role as Manager

Unless you, as a franchisee, are nothing more than a passive investor, you are or will be involved in one or more of the following functions of management.

Planning

Planning is the job of thinking ahead, giving careful thought to what you would or should do given a certain set of circumstances. It is the process of identifying a goal and then, through experience, knowledge, and creative imagination, plotting a series of actions to attain that goal. Experienced managers will know that most plans or projections are based on assumptions that may change and therefore will develop different plans for different scenarios or future happenings. They also will make periodic reviews and update the plans.

Organizing

Organizing is the collecting of people and resources to implement the plan. In reality, organizing is an almost continuous process because plans and circumstances are ever subject to change. The plan has to be firm enough to enable people to function, and also flexible enough to provide for the fact that something can always go wrong.

Directing

Directing is essentially the diplomatic job of getting everybody to work toward the same goal. Even a manager with no employees probably has to direct the activities of others such as contractors or vendors. Directing, as the gurus say, has three essential components: leadership, delegation, and communication. Some people think leadership abilities are inherent (hence the phrase "born leader"), but many of the elements of leadership have to be learned. The appearance and personality requirements of leadership may be inherited, but such qualities as fairness, confidence, and professionalism are traits that have to be acquired.

Almost all experienced franchisees will admit that, in the beginning, their most common management failure was in directing and more specifically in delegating. Delegating or assigning duties, responsibilities, and authority is an essential part of the directing process, but it is a task that franchisees have found very trying. Commonly, franchisees want to know and do everything, an impossible task as franchises mature. In some cases, things have gotten almost completely out of control before franchisees were able to let go and assign some of the work and responsibility.

Another problem commonly faced by many franchisees is the ability to properly communicate. They are not able to give employees adequate instruction about what they want done, and, even more important, they neglect to tell them the reason for doing it. *The purpose of communicating must be totally understood.* It is not limited to just giving instructions to an employee. Good communication also motivates employees, and helps them understand the nature and the importance of their roles in the franchise.

Controlling

In some respects, controlling is part of organizing and directing. An effective control system alerts the owner or the manager that something is wrong. Control systems are a necessary part of operational, accounting, and personnel management. In essence, they provide for the constant monitoring of every aspect of the franchise.

Coordinating

Coordinating is getting everything to work together to accomplish your goal or goals. And it is significant that coordinating is now recognized as the most important of all functions of management. Today's participative management practices require that the coordinating role of the manager be increased and the directive role be decreased. Since coordinating involves gaining the cooperation of semiautonomous groups to achieve an objective, owners and managers must realize that a participative management style will give employee groups sufficient power to become semiautonomous. Therefore the dictatorial or militaristic style of directing becomes ineffective and obsolete.

If you have read many of the articles and books on management published in recent times, you must be aware of the fact that American business is still in the midst of a revolution as far as management techniques are concerned. The most popular subject of business authors has been the comparison of Japanese and American management methods, and it is stressed that the American military-style organization is no longer capable of being competitive. The current situation is ironic when you consider that it was American leadership, such as that of MacArthur and Deming, that introduced the Japanese to the management style currently in use in Japan. Both MacArthur and Deming worked with Japanese government and business leaders during the post-World War II era in the reorganization of Japan's government and economy.

The more insightful business analysts have agreed that, although the Japanese work ethic is an integral part of their culture, the real reason for their success lies in their ability to truly function as a team. We Americans are known for our emphasis on individuality, an emphasis that can become all too evident in the workplace. For many years American management has encouraged competition between the employees in the same work group and based their incentives on individual performance. This accentuation of individuality is a trait unique to the American workplace. The cultures of industry in other nations (particularly Japan and Mexico) view performance in terms of employee groups. They see the production process as the effort of a series of teams, and will reward or offer incentives to these teams rather than to individuals.

These work teams are given considerable autonomy in selecting the methods of getting the job done and also are given the responsibility for quality control. Because of the success of this practice, numerous American companies, both in service and manufacturing, have reorganized their work force into teams and have changed the role of supervisors from that of managers to instructors and facilitators. Recently, General Motors provided a good example by successfully applying the team concept to their Saturn manufacturing facility. A notable example of how to apply this process to retailing is the Wal-Mart chain.

Management by Objective (MBO)

This century has witnessed the coming and sometimes going of numerous types of management systems, ranging from the highly structured scientific management of the 1920s and 1930s to the looseness of Hewlett-Packard's highly successful management by wandering around (MBWA) method. One of the most durable strategies, however, is management by objective (MBO) a term used by Peter Drucker in his book, *The Practice of Management* (New York: Harper & Row, 1954). Although originally most of his strategies seemed to be based on the large corporate organization, over the past few decades his principles have been modified and adapted for use by small businesses including franchises. Thus, today Drucker's principles are widely used and are recommended by the United States Small Business Administration in many of their publications on management.

Simply stated, Drucker declared that an organization must know what it wants to accomplish and, once this is determined, it must be communicated throughout the entire company. The MBO concept is described by some as the "why, what, how" theory, but, regardless of the name, it has proved to be highly successful in all types of companies when implemented correctly. The "mini-MBO" program has been particularly successful in organizations with from 5 to 50 employees. Here it is, concisely expressed:

Goal

The *goal* of a franchise is, in reality, its reason for existence. For the individual franchisee, the goal is often the same or similar to that of the franchisor, for example, "to become the leading auto parts franchise," although your goal may be limited to your market region. The goal is usually expressed in terms of the long term; 5 to 10 years are not uncommon. It is the "why" of the formula and is sometimes called the vision or the mission.

Objectives

Objectives are the "what" of the formula, that is, what must be done in the short term to reach the stated goal. For example, having the goal of becoming the leading auto parts franchise in the region might require the following objectives:

1. Expand the existing marketing plan to reach suburban areas.

2. Add a parts inventory for higher-priced foreign cars.

3. Expand the commercial or wholesale sales department.

4. Reduce the current level of out-of-stock items.

5. Add additional franchise units within the region.

Each objective usually has a specific time frame and is generally well enough defined to be assigned to a specific person or department. Objectives that are so broad that they encompass more than one department or person are difficult to administer. One of the secrets of an effective MBO program is being able to hold a single person or department accountable for a particular objective. When it is not possible to narrowly define an objective, then the next best move to preserve accountability by the assignment of strategies.

Strategies

Strategies are the "how" of the formula. Given any one objective, it is then necessary to determine how that objective can best be achieved, that is, what actions are necessary and who will be responsible for those actions. Strategies are at the heart of the MBO program because they become the actual blueprint of work for the employees. For example:

Objective 1

Expand the existing marketing plan to include suburban areas.

Strategies

Develop advertising to be placed in the suburban newspapers and shopping mailers.

Design a direct mailer for suburban zip codes.

Survey suburban locations for potential advertising signage sites.

But this is just the beginning. The program must be carried out in the right way. Here is an example of the wrong way: You, as the owner, determine your goal. You also decide on the objectives and to whom each objective is to be assigned. You sit down and write a memo to each person, and then stay aloof from the whole process, anticipating that others will handle the ball and make your MBO program a success.

Experience has shown that this hands-off approach has little chance of success for several reasons. First, a successful MBO program requires commitment, continuous support, and follow-through from top management. Because managing any enterprise involves the ability to detect and react to change, any MBO program that does not have a provision for continuous interaction between the top management, supervision, and line employees will not be effective.

Second, an effective MBO program must have a means by which progress toward objectives can be communicated and measured. Periodic meetings are needed for progress reports and the identification of problems. MBO programs, like any management process, must be continuously fine-tuned and adjusted to the changes that are natural in the course of any enterprise.

Third, the very nature of an effective MBO program demands at least some of the elements of participative management. Gaining the commitment of all levels of employees requires that objectives and strategies must communicated throughout the organization, and also that the communication is made a two-way street. Feedback from all levels is one of the most important keys to success. Fourth, those who are responsible for actually implementing the program (for instance, unit managers in a multiunit franchise) must be trained in MBO techniques. It is not a process that can be learned by osmosis.

Now look at an example of a successful MBO: You, as the owner, again determine the goal or goals for your organization. Since you are a part of a franchise, some or practically all can be goals shared with your franchisor, although certainly you may have some of your own.

At this point the objectives must determined. You bring in your manager or managers and, if applicable, your department heads to explain the MBO process and outline your goals. You then ask for opinions from the group on what must be accomplished to reach your goal. It may take more than one meeting for your people to become comfortable with this process, especially if you have never before involved them in decision making. Be patient. The most important thing at this point is that you convince your people that you are committed to making it work and that you are only one member of the team that will eventually, by consensus, develop the objectives. The next item to be decided will be the assignment of the various objectives to the members of the team, a process that probably will be simpler than you imagine because most of the objectives will fall naturally within the area of one person or another.

A common fault among owners and managers is to allow the program to coast from this point, that is, to assume that other persons, such as department heads, can be solely responsible for figuring out how to accomplish their assigned objectives and not need to involve anybody else in the process. This won't work. Remember that one of the most important features in the MBO system is the communicating of the goals, objectives, and strategies to *all* the employees. The best method of communicating this information is to allow the employees to become part of the process. Once your managers and department heads thoroughly understand the objectives, they in turn must take them back to their respective employees to map out what is necessary to reach their assigned objectives. This step probably will be the most difficult part of the whole process because most of your employees have never before been asked for their input or opinions. Also, your managers and department heads may be good supervisors but few may have had experience in group decision making. It may even be advisable to bring in a consultant in participative management techniques for a few training sessions on being a facilitator instead of a supervisor.

Once the supervisors and the employees are comfortable in their new roles, the strategies should then be worked out and written down. These are discussed by you and your management team, and the final MBO plan is developed. Typically, there will be several sessions at both levels, among the managers and managers with the employees, before the plan is finalized. During this part of the process, it is very important that, if any ideas or practices developed by the manager and employee teams must be rejected or discarded by you or the management team, the reasons for your action be explained in detail to everyone.

Once the plan is finalized, it is documented and a copy of the plan is given to everybody in the organization. Everyone must fully understand, however, that the MBO plan is an active plan; that is, it not only sets forth the goals, objectives, and strategies of your organization, but also provides for adjustments and change. Too, it should include a time for attaining each objective, along with dates or times for reviewing progress toward this attainment.

Here is a danger. We have seen many organizations develop an MBO plan and be so satisfied that they fail to review it. This practically guarantees that eventually the plan itself will fail. An MBO plan must be a vital, dynamic document brought up-to-date in a timely fashion. It recognizes changing conditions, makes adjustments to handle those changes, and communicates these adjustments to every person in the organization. Kept active, an MBO program can bring all these benefits:

1. Provide everyone in the organization with a sense of why they are doing their jobs, not just how to do them.

2. Provide everyone with the knowledge of how their jobs fit in with the overall purpose of the organization.

3. Initiate a sense of the importance of teamwork and cooperative effort particularly at the unit level.

4. Develop a feedback system that will give you important information from those who are actually doing the job and who are consequently the first to know when the business climate is changing. Otherwise, you may not be alerted to these changes until you see the financial statements, and considerable profit could already have gone down the drain.

5. Improve productivity because, again, people work harder and smarter when they know why they are doing their job and how they fit into the total picture.

6. Establish a measurable performance goal for every unit team.

The Improvement of Productivity

Although, as noted previously, the MBO program will help improve productivity, certain elements in the relationship between you, your management staff, and the employees impact productivity regardless of your management system and style. In many businesses they are but little understood, and hence are ineptly handled. To understand the importance of these elements it is necessary to discuss two dynamic forces that actually control the behavior of your employees, your managers and the relationship between them: (1) peer pressure and (2) the informal organization of the work group. We advise you to be much aware of them.

The Peer Group and Its Pressure

A *peer group* is a number of people with certain shared characteristics. A peer group, in the eyes of a labor relations specialist, is a number of persons who work in the same location for the same supervisor or the same company. From your viewpoint, the most important fact about the peer groups in your employ is the amount of influence or control the group as a whole has over the job performance of its members. If you have any doubt about the amount of influence or power that a peer group can exercise, remember when you were a teenager and how much the opinions of your friends influenced your behavior. If you are fortunate to have teenage children, then we do not have to remind you how much your children's friends or peers control them.

Peer pressure is not limited to the teen set. Each of us is still very much influenced by our peers, and, as we mature, the number of different groups that influence our behavior can increase. Your golfing or bowling group, the local service group of which you are a member, your church—all of these are examples of peer groups that exert pressure on you to conform to their rituals, their standards of behavior and dress, and in many cases their opinions. Your employees are subject to the same types of pressure, and one of the most influential groups in their lives is their work group. They often spend more time with their fellow employees than they do with their families, and this group will develop its own standards of behavior, its value system, and, most important, its own opinions about you and your values. It is important for you to realize how much pressure is placed on the members of the work group to conform to its collective standards and how powerful that pressure can be.

Is peer pressure a negative influence? Not necessarily. It can support a very cooperative relationship within the group. It can create very positive attitudes toward teamwork, and it can reinforce high standards of behavior and dress. Peer pressure also can be very destructive by curtailing productivity or fomenting a feeling of hostility among the employees toward their supervisors. It can impose subtle differences in status that will disrupt communication between your employees, and it can create a value system directly opposed to yours and that of your franchise. You can be certain that, if the work group in one of your units has developed a negative attitude toward you or your manager, every new employee assigned to that unit will be under considerable pressure to adopt the same attitude. These work group attitudes and standards are, in essence, self-generating. Unfortunately, it usually is beyond your capability or your managers' to directly confront and change these standards.

Negative peer pressure can be changed only through the leadership of the work group, and the term "leadership" does not, in this instance, refer to you or your managers. It refers to the leadership of what labor relations specialists call the *informal organization*, the relationship between the various work groups within a particular business.

The Formal Versus the Informal Organization

Whether you like it or not, as a franchise owner with employees, you will be constantly dealing with two employee organizational structures, particularly if you own more than one franchise unit. Your formal organization defines the chain of command and the channels of communication within your business. In fact, it is possible your organizational chart graphically portrays the authority and responsibility of you, your department heads, your managers, and your employees in both the central office and the units. What that chart will not show is the actual interaction between your employees, and between them and your managers. Yet that interaction exists and effectively forms the second organization that you must deal with—the informal organization and its leadership.

It exists because—whenever two or more people associate with one another, whether at work or socially, for any period of time—they begin to arrange themselves according to status and dominance. It is virtually impossible for members of any group, regardless of size, to share equally in influence over other members of the group. In fact, it is safe to say that all living beings act in essentially the same manner. Within a relatively short time, both humans and animals will arrange themselves in some type of pecking order, and someone will emerge as the most dominant and influential member of the group—the leader.

This leadership is neither elective nor appointive. It evolves as a spontaneous and unspoken consensus and may be based on a forceful personality, a sense of humor, or the ability to relate effectively with others. Often the leader is chosen because of his or her knowledge of the job, especially if the overall attitude of the group is supportive of management. But the choice of leadership is likely to be based on aggressiveness or assertiveness if the work group is in conflict with management over one or more issues.

Unlike a large business with many departments existing under the same roof, a multiunit franchise usually consists of a number of smaller independent operations in many different locations. This fact can be a considerable advantage because it simplifies the job of dealing with the effects of the informal organization. In the larger organization, there can be scores of informal work groups, each with its own leadership and characteristics. These groups themselves can further develop a complex system of influence and communication, particularly during a period of labor-management conflict. You, as a franchisee, will normally have only from 2 to 20 employees at each location, and usually each location will only have one or two work groups per shift. So it is far more difficult for the leader of one group to influence another at a different location because of proximity. Thus, if you do have a problem with the leadership of one group, it is easier to identify and correct it before it spreads throughout the entire franchise.

One of the frequently asked questions about work groups is how does the group affect or control productivity and performance? After all, they all report to a manager or a supervisor and it is that person's job to control and direct the employees. The answer to that question may not be to the liking of you or your manager, but the truth is that your managers and you are limited in your control over these work groups. Of course, managers may periodically exercise their authority and either fire or discipline the poor performers, but in the long run it is the employees who will either accept your performance standards or establish their own.

In significant recognition of this fact, American companies are beginning to adopt this participative management concept of work groups managing themselves, a concept long since adopted by our foreign competition. Front-line managers or supervisors are being eliminated. The work group or team selects its own leadership, assigns its own duties, decides how a job is to be done, and also assumes responsibility for its own quality control. What these businesses are actually doing is allowing the informal organization to assume some of the formal organization's responsibilities.

It is perhaps only normal for peer or work groups to develop their own identity, including standards of behavior, dress, conduct, and certain rituals, and exert considerable pressure on the members to conform. From your point of view, the question is whether this identity is in your best interest or in conflict with them. To the casual observer, the informal organization may not even exist. But when a smooth running operation develops problems, when tension in a particular location is high, when rumors are flying and absenteeism and turnover skyrocket, you can be quite sure that one of two things is happening. First, there is the possibility of a serious conflict between the manager and the leader or an influential member of the work group. In this situation, the leader attempts to convince the other employees to side with him or her, and the manager or a management policy becomes the central issue. The employees are then torn between two loyalties: to you (or the manager) as the employer, or to the informal leader of the group, one that they have selected. The results can be, and often are, chaotic.

The second possibility can be as disruptive. It occurs whenever a new employee is assigned or transferred to an existing group and the pecking order will be changed. If the new member is subdominant and a follower, there will be little change in the overall character of the group. If, however, the new member is aggressive and dominant, he or she may challenge the existing leader for that role. At this point, the group becomes quasipolitical in nature, and, as in any political conflict, there must be an issue that can be used to convince the members to join one or another. Unfortunately, since this is a work group, the most persuasive issue will be work-related, and usually either you or the manager will end up in the middle of the fight.

There is no simple formula for dealing with or directing work groups. Unfortunately, they can be as complex and complicated as the individuals who make up the groups. We do know, however, that identifying the leadership is the most important step in recognizing the basic attitude of the group, that is, whether the members are supportive or in conflict with you and your management. To determine this, you and your managers must observe and analyze the interaction within the group. Here are some suggestions for use in doing this:

Discern if there is a pattern in how the members react to another. For example, when they report to work, do they go out of their way to greet another person? Do they greet some and ignore others?

Observe who initiates the contacts.

Notice the intensity of the contacts. Try to identify those strong friendship bonds and separate those from contacts that are basically work-related.

Observe the rituals: telling jokes; what is done at the beginning and the end of work routines; kidding around.

Identify persons who appear to be dominant and how they react to one another. Also look for persons who may be influential but are not in competition for leadership. Often this will be a person with considerable knowledge about the job and the business.

Observe the nonwork relationships. Who goes to lunch together? Who is on the same bowling team?

Look for conflicts, dislikes, and antagonistic relationships. Are they based on competition or personality differences?

Identifying the make-up and leadership of a group can help you or your managers in several ways. For example, if the leaders or the influential members are antagonistic toward you or one of your managers, you can feel certain that pressure is being exerted on the other members to adopt the same attitude. This type of situation must be confronted directly. It is possible that one or more conversations will reveal and eliminate the cause of the antagonism, but, if that does not work, you have little choice but to transfer or terminate the person.

Identifying the group and the leadership can be helpful in many ways—in introducing new ideas, carrying out special projects, increasing output, and assigning personnel. For example, when a group is supportive and functioning effectively, you should be wary of assigning to it a new employee who is aggressive and may compete for leadership. Knowledge of the group and its leadership is particularly useful when installing or using the MBO system and working out the strategies to meet certain objectives.

People and Productivity

Practically every aspect of your franchise operations will impact productivity: the right choice of equipment, the correct placement of equipment, adequate inventory, the proper raw materials, staffing levels that are based on traffic or volume. All these factors ultimately concern your people. To encourage them to achieve the highest productivity and the highest-quality customer service, you must provide them with a high-quality work life. This does not mean more lockers or more chairs for the lunch room, although employees are certainly entitled to a clean, safe, healthy, and pleasant work environment. It means mainly the quality of the relationship between you and you employees. And this is something that you must work at. From time to time ask yourself, do you let them make decisions? Do you treat them with respect and dignity? Do you make it easy for them to communicate with you? Are you always fair?

The biggest mistake some franchisees have made is to try to build a future with low pay, little consideration, and high turnover. You really cannot fool employees. If you are genuinely helping them to be their best, your efforts will be reflected in their work.

15

Beware of These Financial Dangers

In working with franchisees for than 30 years, we often have encountered men and women who seemed to have the right business in a good location and yet were always struggling to survive. When we became more familiar with their business operations, we were able to identify some of the causes of their financial troubles. We found that, almost without exception, they had fallen into one or more of the several financial traps that can menace every franchisee who is not continuously alert. These common financial dangers are discussed in this chapter.

Ten Common Financial Dangers

1. Not Knowing Enough

Most franchisors provide training in the operation of their franchise, training that may appear to be all the franchisee needs to know to be successful. But even if you were supremely well-informed when you started your franchise, the business climate is in a state of constant change and you may not have kept pace with these changes. The following kinds of questions indicate why:

Are there changes in technology that benefit your competitor more than you?

Do you try to keep fully informed about technological changes that can affect your kind of franchise?

Are you fully aware of new trends that will affect your customer base?

Are there plans to make changes in your general locality that will affect your traffic patterns?

Do you regularly read trade journals and business publications to keep current on management and legal issues?

Do you keep up-to-date on the suppliers capable of filling your needs?

Do you monitor your customers' financial condition? Is one of your biggest customers and debtors heading for bankruptcy?

Successful franchisees usually live with their businesses to a considerable degree, consciously or unconsciously, most of the time. Although you should not be obsessively attentive, it still is advisable to keep your antennas out all the time and be sensitive to any information that can affect your future.

2. Inadequate Working Capital

We don't know what philosopher first said, "There is no human problem that is not made easier by the possession of sufficient money." We do know, however, that it is a profoundly true observation about business, one that will be heartily endorsed by any man or woman who is trying to run a business without adequate working capital.

A shortage of working capital may have existed from the time a franchisee first opened the doors, or it may have developed since then for a variety of reasons. Either way, the owner has the same stress and struggle to make payments when they are due, yet there are possible remedies for working capital shortages:

Increase Sales. Although this may seem obvious, in many cases simply not enough attention and effort is paid to the selling function. To be sure, a working capital shortage can be caused by the need to finance sales that are already increasing (a situation that may encourage a lender or participant to furnish additional capital). But in perhaps the majority of instances, the owner has not focused sufficiently on sales as an income generator.

Shrink the Business. Sometimes, instead of trying to increase sales, it is better to do just the opposite: shrink the business, at least temporarily, so that its requirements will be no bigger than is comfortable for the available working capital. In current business jargon, cutting back is called downsizing or rightsizing, but, regardless of the name, it is presently a common practice. Many businesses, both large and small, are growing lean by cutting expenses and limiting sales efforts to those areas that are most profitable, and furnish the best cash flow.

Make Your Money Work Harder. Make certain that your money is working as hard as you are. We have seen many situations in which the owner's money is allowed to become lazy. Better cash management and more attention to inventory levels and receivables are just a few of the ways that you can make your working capital become more productive.

Put in More Capital of Your Own. If the franchise needs an infusion of more capital, you should see if you can provide it out of your own personal assets, either as an addition to equity or as collateral for a loan. If you have the resources to finance your franchise but are unwilling to do so, you can hardly expect someone else to take the risk.

Put in Money from Someone Else. If your franchise is basically sound and you have some concrete projections, you may be an attractive prospect for an investor or lender. For more details on attracting investors or lenders, see Chap. 10 on financing.

3. Excessive Fixed Assets

Many franchise owners have developed a financial headache because too much of their money has become tied up in unnecessary fixed assets. The owner may be overextended in equipment or facilities, or he or she may have used company funds to acquire other more or less unrelated property. It used to be that an owner in this situation had only two remedies: either sell or borrow money using the excess assets as collateral. Today, however, it also is possible to convert capital assets into usable funds by selling them and leasing them back. Even company-owned property can be changed over to a leased facility.

4. Heavy Expenses

Sometimes excessive expense is due to one or two big commitments but, more often, it is due to numerous small items. Whatever the cause, the proper remedy is usually the same. The owner should cut expenses starting with himself and his family: smaller salaries or draws, fewer and smaller vehicles, reduced expense accounts, and few perks. Austerities like these, coupled with more rigorous working, will provide incentives for employees to sincerely cooperate in cutting operating costs in other areas.

5. Price Cutting

If and when to cut prices is truly a judgment call. Certainly having sales is a common business practice today, but cutting prices must be done with a true knowledge of your costs. *Many businesses, both large and small, have failed because they discounted too much.*

6. Poor Inventory Management

In many kinds of franchises the effective management of inventories has to be continuous because low inventories must be balanced against the possible loss of sales and poor service to customers, and high inventories must be balanced against costs. The Small Business Administration, in its booklet entitled "Inventory Management," gives concise reminders of the contradictory demands on inventory managers.

Maintain a wide assortment of stock, but don't become spread too thin on the rapidly moving items.

Increase inventory turnover, but don't sacrifice service level.

Keep stock low, but don't sacrifice performance or service.

Obtain lower prices by making volume purchases, but don't end up with slow moving inventory.

Have an adequate inventory on hand, but don't get caught with obsolete items.

Frequently, inventory problems are caused by not knowing enough about when and what to buy. But today this should seldom occur. Thanks to computers, keeping track of what is selling and what needs to be replenished is much simpler than it used to be. Still, even the most informative computer system cannot be relied on to tell you when a new item is likely to become a hot seller or, conversely, when a hot seller may suddenly cool. Use a computer, if you can, to help with your inventory, but never cease to watch that inventory yourself—and watch the trends before you automatically replenish items. If a product is seasonal or subject to fashion trends, it often is sensible to unload for whatever one can get, rather than be stuck with unsalable merchandise sitting on the shelf. Even some money is better than no money; in fact, keeping outdated merchandise will be just another expense.

Proper inventory management also involves proper pricing, and this becomes a matter of policy on which you perhaps should confer with your accountant. One school of thought holds that the selling price of an item should be based on the purchase price when it was brought into inventory. That is, if you pay $1 for an item and are operating on a 50-percent gross profit margin, then the item should be priced at $2. Another school, however, is more conscious of the fact that continual selling is a cycle and that, when an item is sold, it must be replaced. Consequently, this school holds that the selling price should not be based on the initial purchase cost, but on replacement cost if this is to be higher. The reasoning is that the gross profit margin is actually decreased unless the increased replacement cost is included in the selling price. Using the preceding example, suppose it costs you $1.20 to replenish the item you just sold for $2.00. Then you should figure that 20 cents of your gross profit has gone back into the cost of goods for sale, leaving you with only 80 cents gained. Hence, if your expected net profit is 10 cents on the sale, you have actually lost money on that transaction. Pricing according to replacement may not be a significant consideration during a period of low inflation and stable prices, but when inflation heats up, replacement costs must be closely considered or profits will diminish.

7. Unsound Expansion

There has always been a danger that a franchisee will be tempted into making an unwise expansion, but recently such ventures seem to be on the increase. Influenced perhaps by widespread publicity about business mergers and buyouts, some franchise owners have unwisely followed this trend. Some have done so because they mistakenly believed that "big is beautiful" and that spreading out would solve all their problems. No one can criticize franchise owners for looking over the fence to see how green the grass is, and, in fact, they may learn better ways to keep their own yard in shape. Yet, expanding a franchise deserves the same careful consideration given to purchasing the franchise in the first place.

8. Leaks and Disasters

Many franchise owners are surprisingly careless about protecting themselves against both the small profit leaks and the potential for large disasters. Items disappearing occasionally may not seem like much, but during the course of a year theft can erode much of your profits. Without proper insurance a disaster can wipe you out. Safeguard yourself with practices that discourage dishonesty, promote safety, and provide as much insurance as is reasonably possible. See Chaps. 16 and 17 for more detailed information.

9. Draining Too Much Out of the Business

Many franchises that should be financially healthy are weakened by the fact that too much of the income is imprudently drained away, resulting in chronic or repeated cash shortages. In most cases the big drain comes from the owner and his or her family who, in one way or another, take more remuneration than the franchise can afford. The right amount of compensation or remuneration can only be correctly controlled by an owner who sets a personal example of thrift and efficiency and who bases the amount of family or insider compensation on sound financial statements and projections.

10. Weak Credit and Collection Practices

Credit and collection is an area that is often identified by franchisors as a franchisee's most serious weakness, so much so that we have been asked by several to devote a section of this chapter to sound and effective credit and collection practices. Since, when granting credit you are, in essence, loaning money to a customer, we entitle this section:

Be a Careful Lender

Whenever you sell something and wait to be paid, you are doing what business pundits call "extending credit." This is a fine-sounding term that confers a kind of dignity on you, the extender, and also on the person to whom you have granted the privilege, the extendee. But if you are wise, you will think of the transaction as lending money because that is what you are really doing while you are waiting to be paid. And you will help yourself be paid faster if you keep this fact in mind.

Normally the price of what you sell should have a built-in figure to compensate you for making the loan, provided the buyer pays you within the time expected. But if payment is not made on time, the loan becomes increasingly costly, eating up the profit you hoped to make on the transaction. It may even cause you to lose money—and quite quickly, as a little arithmetic will illustrate:

Suppose that you are netting a satisfactory profit on sales, say 10 percent.

And suppose that the going rate of interest is 6 percent.

Then suppose you have sold something for $1000 and therefore expect a profit of $100.

The interest value of the $1000 is $60 per year, or $5 per month.

In other words, it will cost you $5 per month for every month you wait for your money. And it will cost you more if your profit percentage is lower or if the interest rate is higher than in this example.

This may be the least of your cost when you consider these other possibilities:

Inflation eats into the value of the money you have outstanding. If the inflation rate is 6 percent a year, it will cost you another $5 of profit a month.

If your past-due receivables restrict your cash flow, you may lack the cash to take discounts on your trade purchases.

Also, if you lack cash, you may not be able to save money on large volume purchases.

In fact, if cash is short, you might not be able to carry sufficient inventory and therefore you could lose sales.

Collection of past-due bills can entail a great deal of time, irritation, and aggravation within your franchise.

If you hire an agency or an attorney to collect past-due receivables, it could cost 30 to 50 percent of the amount collected.

If you have to write off the debt as uncollectible, the entire amount comes right off the top of your profits.

A customer who owes you a back bill may be hesitant to buy from you again and will attempt to buy from someone else.

You can and probably should, if legal, charge interest on past-due accounts, but this is no substitute for getting the bill paid on time.

If your franchise is in retailing—and most are—you may have to accept credit card charges whether you like them or not. You may be reluctant to pay the fees levied by credit card companies, but the cost of losing sales could be greater, particularly if you are operating above the break-even point. The expense of being a lender, as already indicated, is high even when the bills are paid on time. Therefore it is important that an in-house credit system be as simple and efficient as possible. Here is one that fulfills both these requirements and should be quite suitable for most franchises.

Have a Written Credit Policy, Clearly Understood by Both Customers and Employees

Develop a letter or notice to inform customers of the franchise's credit policy. This communication should set forth such details as when payment is due, the deadlines for discounts, and a statement that the customer will be responsible for collection costs should such action become necessary. Further, it is a good idea to review credit policies annually and send out a new notice or letter explaining them. In addition, all credit and installment payment literature should contain a statement of your terms.

Every employee who is concerned with processing credit applications, doing billing, and handling accounts receivables and collections should be kept up-to-date on your credit policy and also with the latest federal and state regulations regarding credit. Your attorney should be alerted to notify you when additional regulations become effective.

Perhaps the most important part of a credit policy is consistency. Your customers should come to realize through your own strict practice that your credit policy is followed to the letter and never compromised.

Always Make a Thorough Credit Investigation

Never—absolutely never—extend credit to anyone unless you have checked and made sure the person can be expected to pay promptly. It is true that recent federal laws have made it somewhat more difficult than in the past to obtain credit information, but it is still almost always possible to do so. Require a written credit application that sets forth a close personal history and includes several credit references; then be certain that all these are checked. Use one or more credit rating bureaus for this purpose. The best of them are now linked by computers nationwide and generally can provide accurate information. Recent criticism of their accuracy has forced them to refine their procedures, and at this point their reporting practices are usually reliable. Never extend credit until your information is 100 percent complete and you know the information on the application is trustworthy. Furthermore, if a normally prompt paying customer begins to lag in payments, ask for a credit recheck. Doing so may provide you with a useful warning.

Review Your Receivables Daily

The best time to do this is right after a day's receipts have been posted. Take part in this daily review yourself whenever possible. This demonstration of your personal concern can do much to spur your people in diligently pressing for payment.

Act Promptly on Delinquents

Be prompt in starting action on accounts that become past due. Three days is considered to be best, but such action should certainly be no later than one week.

Use a *collection action record*. When an account is judged to be past due, separate the record of the account from the rest of the receivables and attach a collection action record to it. The person who contacts the customer for collection should enter on the form what he or she said or wrote, and how the customer replied. This is important for three reasons:

1. Whoever next follows up on the account does not have to rely on memory or assumptions.

2. You yourself are able to keep track of the progress or lack of it.

3. The collection action record, scrupulously completed, provides a complete credit history, which can be crucial if later legal action is necessary.

Know How and When to Use the Telephone

Regardless of what may be said to you by persons who attempt to sell canned collection notices and letters, the telephone is generally the most effective collection device. It:

Demonstrates that you give close individual attention to overdue accounts.

Proves that you follow your published credit policy to the letter.

Commands attention because it is strikingly different from the kind of computerized overdue notices employed by many companies today.

Saves several days compared to an exchange of letters.

Makes it easier to resolve a customer complaint.

Is truly personal.

Whoever does the calling for you should be made familiar with the state and federal laws concerning harassment of creditors, and, moreover, it is advisable to post or circulate instructions such as these for guidance.

1. Always be courteous and businesslike. Do not use a threatening tone of voice.

2. State who you are and whom you are representing, and come right to the point about the reason for your call.

3. Record all information on your collection action record.

4. If the bill is disputed, gather all the facts to refute or verify what the customer claims. Give the customer all the information available and back it up in writing.

5. Firmly request the amount of money past due, and endeavor to obtain a definite promise for the mailing of this amount (or a smaller amount if you absolutely have to compromise) by an exact date. Emphasize that you will follow up immediately if the payment does not arrive when expected.

6. Never call before 8 A.M. or after 8 P.M. (check state law), and never on Saturdays, Sundays, or holidays.

7. If the customer claims bankruptcy, obtain the date of entry and the name of the court handling the proceedings. Do not continue collection efforts if the information is correct.

8. If you are making a second or third call, you may want to quote the company's terms concerning the involvement of attorneys or court action including the fact that the customer will be required to pay the costs of such action.

9. Reinforce your phone calls with written communications, stating again the amount overdue and confirming any promises or commitments.

10. Check to make certain that everything significant is entered on the collection action record.

Know How to Use Letters

It is sometimes impossible to reach an account by telephone. If this is the case, you then must use a letter, but, in doing so, make certain that it does not have the appearance of a mere form. Take the time and effort to have it express individuality and you can expect much better results. Generally, the first letter should be a reminder type that asks the customer to either pay in full or contact you right away. The second letter, if necessary, should restate your credit terms and the system of collection. It should be firm and set a deadline for response. Do not invite or engage in protracted correspondence.

When you write you must be especially aware of the laws and regulations, both state and federal, that govern collections because some of these laws provide for severe penalties. Here are 11 "don'ts" that collectors should keep on their desks at all times.

1. Don't try to collect if the customer disputes the bill in writing until you have answered in writing and supplied complete details concerning the debt.

2. Don't fail to answer a written complaint within 30 days.

3. Don't try to collect a bill in dispute, or close the account, for a period of 90 days after the initial complaint.

4. Don't contact a debtor who has retained legal counsel; contact the lawyer.

5. Don't try to collect additional costs or interest unless the credit agreement provides for this.

6. Don't try to collect from a legally bankrupt individual or company.

7. Don't misrepresent the identity of your franchise, yourself, or the purpose in contacting a debtor.

8. Don't permit any person or agency employed by you to use physical force, abusive language, or threats.

9. Don't publish the names of debtors or circulate their names on a blacklist.

10. Don't contact a debtor more than once a day, and don't send an excessive number of notices.

11. Don't change your credit terms without notifying your customers.

Know What You Can Do When In-House Efforts Fail

Most customers are stable and honest. When either an individual or a company becomes a credit problem, it is possible that the condition is temporary and caused by a cash flow or working capital difficulty. Try as early as possible to determine the cause of slow payment and make a judgment about it. Sometimes it is advisable to allow an old and valued customer to catch up by a special payment arrangement. This, however, should be a judgment made by either you or one of your managers, not by a clerk or a collector.

Unfortunately, in other situations accounts do not respond to your calls or letters, and you must therefore contemplate some type of collection agency or legal action. If the account is another business, the reason for default may be discontinuance, bankruptcy, or sale or merger of the business, any of which events can complicate efforts to collect. If the account is an individual, it will fall generally into one of two categories: (1) skips and constant no-pays, and (2) persons with serious financial and/or marital problems. Always consider carefully whether it is likely to be worth pressing ahead. Unless there is some evidence of tangible assets or future income that can be attached, you might be throwing good money after bad. Most legal processes are drawn out and expensive. As any good poker player knows, sometimes it is best to fold.

Remember, a collection attorney or agency may charge you as much as 50 percent of all that is collected; therefore, many franchisees hesitate to turn accounts over to them. However, two alternatives may help in collecting. The first is to have your attorney send a standard letter on his or her letterhead and to charge only a nominal fee to do so. Simply provide the text for the letter, to be kept on hand in his or her files, and to be used when you request it. Have an agreement with your attorney that, if the letter receives no response, you both will review the case before any further action is taken. If you decide to continue the collection efforts with his or her assistance, this can be done at rates agreed on in advance.

The second alternative is the small claims court. Here you or another officer of the corporation (depending on state law) can process your claim; the action is therefore less expensive than using an attorney. The rules concerning small claims court actions differ from state to state, so you should familiarize yourself with those that apply in your location.

Know Your Rights

In general, it has become important for a franchise owner to have a working knowledge of today's credit and collection laws, rules, and regulations; and it is also good to know that not all of them are stacked in favor of the debtor. The Uniform Commercial Credit Code allows you the following rights:

1. If a person signs your credit application, you have the right to contact his or her employer and verify any information submitted concerning position, pay, length of service, and prospects of continued employment. You also have the right to check personal and supplier

references, including banks and lending agencies. A credit bureau retained by you has the same rights.

2. You have the right to require and hold a secured interest in anything of value that you sell a customer until he or she has complied fully with the terms of purchase. If a buyer defaults, you have the right to repossess the goods or to demand payment of the entire balance due you immediately.

3. You can always sue for moneys owed to you on cash, charge, or installment credit terms. In most cases, a judgment in your favor will include expenses. A judgment usually remains in effect until the debt is paid or can be renewed repeatedly.

4. At your request, a sheriff or constable is required by law to satisfy your judgment or lien by selling the possessions and assets of the debtor at auction. With such a threat, most debtors choose to pay up if they can.

5. Judgments become public records, accessible to banks and retailers. Most debtors would rather pay than have a judgment entered against them because it will impair their credit for many years.

6. If a delinquent decides to return the purchase to you, you do not have to accept it, and payment remains due. It takes two to cancel a contract.

7. If you obtain a judgment against a debtor, full payment is required. You do not have to accept partial payment unless you want to.

8. You have the right to retain an agency to collect a debt or sell the debt to an agency. In either case, the agency has the same legal rights you do.

16
Protect Your Franchise from Crime

Neither your profit and loss statement nor your balance sheet will list it, but, if you are a typical franchisee, you have a hidden expense that is ranging from 1.3 to 7 percent of your total sales. It is a hidden expense because no one knows when it happens or in some cases how it happens. This elusive expense is called theft.

It is nearly impossible to be in business for any length of time today and not notice that your profits are being menaced by criminals. Crime, particularly theft, has been on the increase in American business for the past five decades. Considerable attention has been given to crime prevention techniques and systems, but even the most sophisticated alarms and locks do not prevent the most common type of business theft: theft by employees.

Crime experts divide crime against businesses into two categories: internal and external. *Internal crime* takes place when an employee commits a theft or provides information or access to someone on the outside who then does the stealing. *External crime* is committed entirely by outsiders and includes shoplifting, burglary, robbery, theft from employees, vandalism, and arson.

Internal Crime

Often one of the most difficult crimes to detect is white collar theft. It usually is committed by upper-echelon executives and managers, particularly those who work in the accounting and bookkeeping areas. According to the Research Institute of America, the typical offender is in his middle thirties, usually has a family, has been an employee for five to seven years, and has been embezzling or stealing for two to three years. Employees who steal by altering internal records can be very difficult to spot. Since they usually are trusted employees, they are familiar with all aspects of a franchise and therefore can cover their tracks by manipulating the entire network of related records. Many of these thieves, when detected, escape prosecution because owners feel that the resulting publicity would reflect unfavorably on them and the franchise. The employee is quietly released, free to victimize another employer.

Failure to prosecute is a management weakness and mistake. The most effective preventive measure against white collar theft is to emphasize your inflexible determination to prosecute any employee who is caught stealing from the franchise—*any* employee at *any* level. Have a written policy that clearly explains your determination and that emphasizes that theft of any franchise property will subject the crooked employee to immediate dismissal and prosecution. Many franchisees ask for trouble by looking the other way when employees take small items, such as tools and office supplies. In essence, these franchisees are inviting their employees to make their own judgments as to whether something is a gift or a theft. This invitation is an example of extremely poor management.

Embezzlement

Embezzlement is most often defined as "the fraudulent appropriation of money or property by a person to whom it has been entrusted." To embezzle from a business, a person must either find a system that does not have effective controls or have control of all aspects of a function so that an entire transaction can be falsified. In many cases, the employee has been given more authority than the position calls for and, because he or she is responsible for both the checks and the balances, can easily manipulate the system.

The simplest form of embezzlement is the taking of cash from a sale without recording the transaction. The cash is pocketed, and there is no direct evidence that a sale ever took place. In franchises involved in retailing and food service, exposure to this type of theft can be minimized by the use of controlled registers, prenumbered sales slips or restaurant checks, and alert supervisors. In franchises dealing with receivables, the same person should never be responsible for logging in cash and checks and posting these to accounts receivable.

Here are some other methods of embezzlement.

Lapping. Employees who receive cash payments on account can withhold part of the cash from payee A, make it up with part of the payment from payee B two or three days later, and so on. As this procedure continues, the amounts kept become larger, and soon the embezzler must keep a separate set of books to know which accounts have to be credited with amounts from future payments. These embezzlers always hope that they will be able to catch up and settle all the accounts, but unfortunately this seldom happens.

False Invoices. The employee sets up a phony supplier and periodically pays falsified invoices for nonexistent deliveries. This method is difficult to detect unless you have an independent receiving report system or you require that invoices, purchase orders and confirmation of delivery must be submitted to another party for payment approval.

Payroll Fraud. Unfortunately, this method is quite common in franchises using a large number of part-time employees. The payroll clerk simply adds one or two fictitious employees to the payroll. This is particularly common in multiple-unit franchises with a central payroll department. Note that overtime can also be inflated.

Petty Cash. The petty cash box is an open invitation to a dishonest person. Petty cash vouchers can be falsified or personal purchases can be made and reimbursed from cash. All petty cash vouchers should be inspected frequently and at unannounced times.

The Kickback. The most insidious and potentially damaging form of white collar crime is the kickback. This practice may originate from either the franchise or a supplier and unfortunately be tolerated by both buyers and sellers. It is, however, perilous to either or both. The franchise becomes exposed to the dangers of inferior products or service, to the disruption of the manufacturing process, or to damage to the reputation of the franchise because of the use of below-grade materials. A seller becomes exposed to the need to charge higher prices or to provide inferior merchandise or service. Also, once a franchise employee, having taken a kickback, comes under the thumb of a vendor a franchise can suffer in numerous ways because the employee becomes a prime target for blackmail. With kickbacks, as with other forms of internal crime, the primary defense is a firm policy that is communicated with strong emphasis to both your employees and vendors. The policy should set very specific limits on the value of products that may be accepted as samples or advertising, and outright gifts of any kind should be prohibited.

Your monthly financial statements are the best monitors to use in detecting possible embezzlement. Probe the figures because any unexpected change can be caused by changes in the economy or the business climate, by error, or by someone tinkering with the books. For example:

Inventory shortages could be the result of an error in record keeping or of falsified purchases, storeroom theft, or unrecorded sales.

A dip in sales volume without a corresponding dip in cost of goods may indicate unrecorded sales.

An increase in receivables may be the result of a worsening economy, or it may be caused by someone lapping payments.

Bad debt write-offs may be legitimate or they may be an effort to conceal the fact that the accounts had been paid but the money disappeared into someone's pocket.

An unexpected change in profit margins could indicate any number of problems including fraud.

Although your accountant should have designed your accounting system so that it provides sufficient checks and balances to reduce the possibility of fraud and embezzlement, it is wise to review the system periodically for possible abuses. Some embezzlers are extremely creative, and no accounting system is absolutely foolproof. Here are just a few of the additional steps that you may want to take to reduce your exposure to fraud and mismanagement of funds.

Arrange with your accountant to make surprise (even to you) audits of certain bookkeeping functions periodically. For example, he or she may review accounts receivables on one visit, reconcile cash and petty cash on another, and compare receiving reports or signed invoices to inventory on still another. Tell your employees about the fact that you are subject to surprise audits and that their cooperation is required. Either you or your accountant also should check your supply of prenumbered blank checks to ensure that no one has taken any from the end of the book or the bottom of the box.

If a substantial portion of your sales are on credit, enclose with your billings a self-addressed envelope directed to a post office box. Pick up this mail yourself, if possible. If not, have someone other than a bookkeeper or accounting clerk responsible for the pickup.

Always have the mail opened by someone other than a bookkeeper or receivables clerk, and have that person make a log of all moneys received. Some franchisees will make photocopies of all checks for use in posting accounts receivable and deposit the actual checks as soon as possible.

All persons placed on the payroll must have a payroll authorization, approved and signed by you or by one of your managers. The same procedure should be used to authorize overtime.

All bank correspondence, including bank statements, also should be sent to your post office box. If you do not personally reconcile your bank statement, you should at least require that it be given to you for review before it is filed. Also have your cancelled checks returned with your statement, and take the time to look through them for any irregularities, particularly for those written out of sequence.

Require that all supporting documents accompany requests for checks to be written, and examine the documentation before you sign the check. This procedure should be followed for all outlays, including payroll checks or authorizations. Tighten up your procedures to avoid paying invoices twice either by error or design.

Bond all persons who are in a position to manipulate funds and records.

Thefts by nonmanagement employees are usually of small amounts of cash or supplies, but they may involve substantial amounts of tools and inventories. Usually this kind of theft is a matter of accessibility. Few employees of a typical franchise have access to large amounts of cash or negotiable securities, but they are likely to have access to all kinds of materials and objects. Accessibility and methods of carrying away are factors that you must reckon with to discourage employee theft. To be stolen, materials must be located where employees can steal them and get them off the premises without being observed. Therefore, review your franchise's facilities and take however many of the following precautions are necessary:

Divide inventory responsibilities and verify your totals frequently.

Minimize and monitor the entrances and exits for employees.

Allow no employees to park near shipping and receiving points.

Monitor all visitors.

Check for drop points, areas where employees can leave materials to be picked up later.

Price items by machine or rubber stamp.

Permit only certain employees to price items.

Double-check deliveries to ensure that everything on the shipping list or invoice has been delivered and thus prevent collusion between truck drivers and employees. This procedure is particularly important in fast food and restaurant franchises because of the volume and frequencies of deliveries and the fact that the items stolen can be easily resold.

Supervise trash pickups. Dumpsters provide an ideal drop point when the trash crews and an employee are partners in crime.

Double-check purchase specifications with the actual items delivered. Downgrading—that is, substituting an item of lower quality or a lower count—is one of the most common elements in kickback schemes between vendors and employees. This, again, is particularly true in fast food and restaurant franchises.

Do not allow delivery personnel to deliver directly to the storeroom unsupervised. Sometimes as much goes out as comes in.

Be sure that all padlocks are snapped shut on the hasp when the door is open. It is a simple matter for an employee to switch locks and then gain access after hours.

Maintain a tight control over all keys. Know who has them and why. Do not discipline an employee who loses a sensitive key; discipline the employee who fails to report that a key has been lost.

If a sensitive key has been lost, change tumblers or locks immediately.

Avoid mastering a system if at all possible. Mastering compromises security and makes it much more expensive to change locks if a master is lost.

If you do suspect that you have an employee who is stealing, do not play Dick Tracy. Bring in the police or a private security consultant immediately. Firing an employee for theft without proof can be very expensive, particularly in those states with a record of strong "wrongful discharge" case law.

If you are using computers extensively, be aware that your exposure to internal theft is greatly increased. There are methods for reducing this exposure that are too complex to be covered here, but a computer expert can tell you what to do, and the expense of computer security should be accepted today as a normal cost of doing business. Bear in mind, however, that any system needs frequent review. Computer technology and software are continually changing, and for every new system that is introduced there already are a dozen people trying to crack it.

One of the most effective ways to control internal crime is to hire honest employees and treat them in a way that encourages continued honesty.

Every potential employee should have the information on his or her application or resume checked thoroughly. And although it may be difficult, character and employment references also should be checked before the applicant is hired.

Above all, you and your managers should set the standard by being honest yourselves. If you have a set of rules, then they should apply to everyone without exception.

External Crime

Of all the crimes committed by outsiders, shoplifting causes more losses than any other. An article in *The New York Times* stated that a retailer's losses from shoplifting can run as high as 11 percent of gross sales and result in a considerable reduction of profits—so much so that certain retail industries have made significant adjustments in pricing to cover their losses.

How Can You Recognize a Shoplifter?

Generally, you can't. Shoplifters come in all sizes, shapes, and dress. The majority of them are amateurs and can be classified as follows.

Juveniles. It is estimated that juveniles account for approximately 50 percent of all shoplifting. Some do it on impulse or just for kicks, but increasingly they are operating in gangs to make some serious money. Several will enter a place business and by sheer numbers attempt to distract the employees while one or two steal as much as possible. Often they feel that, because of their youth, the store management and the authorities will treat them lightly. Actually, the worst thing you could do is to fail to treat them as you would an adult. The best thing that you can do for yourself and for them is to pursue and prosecute them as actively as you would an adult. Specific businesses and franchises are targeted as soft touches when the juvenile grapevine flashes the word throughout a neighborhood. Your battle against shoplifting is half won if you have a no-nonsense reputation.

Alcoholics and Drug Abusers. This is a category of people who are responding to a physical need and can be dangerous and uncontrolled. Usually, because of their behavior and perhaps dress, they are easy to spot, but the real question is what to you do after you spot them. Most authorities say that you are dealing with a time bomb likely to go off, and you or your employees should call the police and let them handle it. Usually, these shoplifters work alone.

Impulse Shoplifter. Impulse shoplifters are opportunistic. If the item is there and the way is clear, they will try to steal it. Usually, they don't even need the item, but the impulse is too strong to resist. This type of shoplifter is best deterred by taking away the opportunity.

The Psychologically Impaired. Like the drug addict or the alcoholic, this category of shoplifter also steals because of a compulsion. In this case, however, the compulsion is triggered not by intense physical need, but by some psychological impulse. Usually, the impaired do not need the stolen item; in fact, in many cases, they actually have no use for it. The fact that they are psychologically impaired should not deter you from taking the same action that you would in any other case.

The Professional. Like the juveniles, the professionals generally work in groups. They usually are well trained and equipped, and they tend to concentrate on items that are easy to fence or resell. They often use sophisticated tools to aid them in walking out undetected with the loot, for example:

1. A false bottom package, often gift-wrapped, which allows them to place the receptacle over an item, lift it up, and walk away.

2. Large pocketbooks, baby carriages, knitting bags, umbrellas, and even false bandages or casts.

3. Specially designed coats or pants with hidden pockets or hooks, which hide stolen goods.

4. Loose fitting clothing, enabling them to go into a fitting room and put on several layers of stolen clothes under their outer wear.

Like juvenile shoplifters, the professional groups will often break up after they enter a store, and one or more members will distract salespersons while the others lift the goods.

What Can You Do About Shoplifting?

Shoplifting losses can be substantially reduced by launching a very aggressive and highly visible antitheft campaign. In the past, retailers were often reluctant to prosecute because of the publicity and the time required to follow through after an arrest. Public attitudes have changed as recent antishoplifting advertising has highlighted the fact that theft causes higher prices for honest consumers. No longer does the news about a shoplifter being arrested reflect on the retailer involved, and many merchants now feel that the time necessary to prosecute is well spent in getting the word out to both professionals and amateurs that their businesses are too risky to hit. A campaign against shoplifting may contain any or all of these measures:

Make it widely known to both employees and the public that, without exception, shoplifters will be prosecuted.

Train employees to watch for customers who linger around one area and handle a lot of items without making a choice

Have a professional security company train your employees on how to spot professional shoplifters.

Train key employees to be roving spotters.

Control all exits.

Display small expensive items in locked cases.

Investigate the possibility of using one or more of the security devices that are now available: convex mirrors, closed circuit TV, one-way mirrors, electronic and fall-apart price tags.

Security professionals can also help you lay out your selling space to minimize shoplifting.

Apprehending the Shoplifter

Before you begin your antishoplifting campaign, check with your attorney and the local police to determine what evidence and procedures are necessary to prosecute an offender because the standards or requirements differ from one area to another. Generally, however, you must:

1. See the person take or conceal the merchandise.
2. Identify the merchandise as yours.
3. Testify that it was taken with the intent to steal.
4. Prove that the merchandise was not paid for.

It usually is best to apprehend the person outside the premises because it strengthens your case that there was an intent to steal. Under any circumstances, it also is best to avoid a verbal accusation. Literature concerning shoplifting distributed by the Small Business Administration suggests identifying yourself and then saying, "I believe you have some merchandise that you have forgotten to pay for. Would you mind following me to straighten this matter out?"

Unless there is some plausible reason why the person did not pay, you then should proceed to call the police. You should use your good judgment in these situations because there are times when someone absentmindedly will walk out of the store without paying and will make no attempt to hide the merchandise.

Bad Checks

No business is immune from bad check passers. They will hit a major department store or a fast food franchise; it makes no difference as long as the check will pass. There are some ways, however, by which you can minimize your losses from bad checks, particularly those that are fraudulent from the beginning, not just mistakes of persons who inadvertently overdrew their checking accounts.

Generally, you will be offered six types of checks: personal, two-party, payroll, government, counter, and travelers. Each type has certain characteristics that you and your employees should be aware of.

Personal Checks

A personal check is written on an individual checking account and is usually made payable to you or the franchise. Occasionally, a personal check will be made out to "cash," a practice that should be discouraged because, if it is stolen, it is the same as cash. The person accepting the check should examine the following items:

The name and complete address of the payer should be imprinted on the check, or your employee should ask for the information and write it on the face including a current telephone number.

The name and address of the bank issuing the check should be imprinted on the face. If it is a nonlocal bank, you or your employees should obtain the local address and telephone number of the payer, and enter it on the back of the check. There also should be a series of encoded characters as now required by Federal Reserve Board banking regulations.

The check should be dated with the day, month, and year and should not be accepted if it is postdated or is more than 30 days old.

The written and the numerical amounts should be the same.

If you allow checks to be written for more than the amount of the purchase, you should have a limit on the overage. This is a dangerous practice and should never be allowed in a highly transient location.

Examine the check for legibility, and be certain that the check is signed.

Do not accept any check that looks like it has been altered or erased.

Ask for two forms of identification. (See the list of acceptable identifications later on in this section.)

Two-Party Checks

A two-party check is originally made out by a first party to a second party who, in turn, wishes to make it payable to you by endorsement. If the check is returned for nonsufficient funds, it is more difficult to collect because two people are involved. You also must take, with this kind of check, the same precautions you would with a personal check.

Payroll Checks

Payroll checks are payment to an employee for wages, but, because such checks often are fraudulent, they should not be cashed or accepted unless you know the payee. The name of the payee should be printed by a computer or a check imprinting machine and the amount should be printed with a tamper-proof screen. Although smaller companies will issue typewritten payroll checks, it is best not to take them unless you know the company.

Government Checks

The most frequently cashed government checks are social security, payroll, and tax refund checks. Unfortunately, because of their distinctive envelopes, these also are the most frequently stolen. If you do decide to take these checks, impress on your employees the fact that adequate identification is very important.

Travelers Checks

Travelers checks are very popular with those who do not wish to carry much cash, and they also are difficult to forge or alter. When accepting a travelers check, you and your employees should insist that the check be countersigned at the time of purchase and that adequate identification is presented.

Be aware that recently professional thieves have been rifling through dumpsters and trash containers for so-called obsolete checks from both consumers and businesses. Since these checks are all correctly imprinted, they easily can be forged and cashed by unsuspecting businesses. The reason that these checks are now so readily found is that so many banks have either failed, merged, or been sold to other banks. Every time a bank changes hands, its name usually is changed and new checks are issued to its customers, leaving hundreds of thousands of unused checks with the bank's former name imprinted on them. When these are carelessly thrown away intact, they easily may fall into the hands of the check forgers. The problem is compounded by the fact that, during the transitional period, checks issued by the bank whose name is being changed will still be accepted by the new bank for a limited period of time. You and your employees must be kept up-to-date on these bank mergers or sales, and treat with great care checks with the imprints of banks that are no longer doing business under their old name. It would, in fact, be prudent to contact the new bank and determine how long they will honor checks under the old name.

Identification

Although no identification is foolproof, asking for it and scrutinizing it closely will certainly reduce your exposure to loss. At least one picture ID should be required and generally should be available because most states now require a photograph on their driver's licenses. Recently, one of the major credit companies has also started to issue its cards with photographs.

Most retailers now request two items of ID, one of which must be a bank card. Almost all banks now issue these when a checking account is opened, and when a bank card is offered as ID it should be from the same bank as the check. The card should be signed and the signature should be compared to the one on the check before it is accepted. From personal observations, we would point out that the failure to compare signatures is the most common mistake employees make when verifying the identity of a check writer.

Whether you can recover money lost when a check is returned depends on the circumstances. If it is a forgery, it should be reported to the police, but unfortunately the person who wrote the check has probably left your town or state. If it is marked "nonsufficient funds," usually a call to the bank will tell you whether there are now enough funds to cover it. If not, then you must try to collect from the payer. Some states have laws that enable the business to prosecute the payer if the account is not settled within a specific period of time. Generally, if you can prosecute, you should do so in order to prevent the reputation of being an easy mark.

Banks involved in mergers and acquisitions report a significant amount of problems with many of their customers who are forced to move their accounts or who are voluntarily changing banks. Often an account is closed when there still are outstanding checks or the number has been miscalculated. If you receive a check marked, "account closed," it usually is worth the effort to contact the person and ask for a replacement check. In most such cases, the person did not intend to defraud, but merely made a mistake in calculating the balance.

If your state permits you to assess a charge on a person whose check is returned to you without payment from the bank, post near your cash register a notice that prominently declares both this fact and the amount you will charge. This can be an effective deterrent to intentional bad check passing.

One final comment: discuss the matter of bad checks with your attorney. States differ in their methods of handling and prosecuting bad check passers.

Robbery

Robbery is the most menacing and traumatic form of external crime, and, since the crime involves a confrontation, it is also the most unpredictable. The robber is usually young, inexperienced, nervous, and therefore highly dangerous. Your employees should be made aware of this type and cautioned against playing the hero. You can, however, take several measures to reduce your exposure to robbery and hold down losses if one takes place. Among the measures most generally effective are these:

Install a time delay or drop safe, and publicize the fact that no clerk can open it.

Vary your banking routine, and do not prepare a deposit where you can be seen from outside the premises.

Arrange your business layout so that your cash registers can be seen from outside.

Periodically reduce the amount of money in your cash drawers.

Design your physical security alarm system so that it can also be used in the event of a robbery.

Use extreme caution when opening and closing the franchise unit.

Use caution when answering an after-hours emergency call.

As much as possible, avoid making drops or deposits after dark.

Instruct your employees to remain as calm as possible if they are robbed and to assure the robber that you and/or they will cooperate in every way.

Instruct your employees that, during a robbery, they should notice everything possible about the robber: complexion, height, weight, clothing, voice, sex, and anything that will be helpful when the police broadcast a description.

Burglary

Small businesses and franchises are most susceptible to burglary because usually their security systems are not as sophisticated as those found in larger businesses. And burglary usually is more costly than other forms of theft because the criminals have a longer period of time to loot the premises. A franchisee can take steps to prevent burglaries.

Locks

Locks on every type of entry and exit are the foundation of any security system. Numerous types of locks are available, and we strongly suggest that you have a competent locksmith set up or review your system. Many times the locks found in a local hardware store can be picked by a professional in a matter of seconds. Your locksmith usually can tell you which ones to avoid.

One of the most effective locks is the dead bolt because the bolt is not spring-loaded, that is, it is slid into place manually. Spring-loaded bolts can often be moved by using some type of flexible material. If you use pin tumbler locks, check with your locksmith about the minimum number of pins that can be used effectively.

Entry is often made by burglars through openings other than doors. For example, windows, skylights, trap doors, and ventilating shafts are common entryways for burglars and should be padlocked or secured with pins set in the frames. Exterior doors that open outward often have hinge pins on the outside that can be easily removed. There are security devices that can be used to guard against this.

Rear and side entry doors should be not only locked but also barred. The bar can be either a sliding or drop bar but should overlap both sides of the doorjamb or frame. Double cylinder locks requiring a key on both sides may be used, subject to local fire laws. Your locksmith should know whether these are allowable.

Key Control

Having an elaborate lock system means absolutely nothing if access to the keys for those locks is not strictly controlled. Know who has keys and maintain up-to-date records on every key that has been issued to employees and contract service companies. If a key is lost or stolen, rekey the lock immediately. Code each key so that it is not necessary to attach key tags that may identify your location or the lock that the key fits. This may seem like an obvious rule but it is violated all the time. And, to repeat, do not master key or grandmaster the system because it will compromise your security.

Burglar Alarms

Like locks, several different types are available. The central station silent alarm is the best but is not available in many parts of the country. This type of alarm does not alert the burglar to the fact that the break-in has been detected because there is no audible building alarm. The alarm either alerts the police, signals a private central station, or triggers a device that calls your home phone number and allows you to listen to what is happening at your place of business. The local audible alarm is also effective but decreases the chance that the burglar will be apprehended.

Lighting

One of the most effective ways to discourage burglary is to keep both the interior and exterior of your business well lighted at night, particularly the side and back alleys. The interior should not only be lighted but also arranged in such a way that the police can see inside the store. It does little good to keep the place lighted and then block the windows with displays or signs. If you have a safe, it should be in a well-lighted area visible from the outside. Trying to hide it in a back room provides an excellent opportunity for burglars to take their time when either opening or removing it. Also, don't encourage the carry-out of a safe. Regardless of its size, it should be bolted to the wall or the floor. Safes weighing more than a thousand pounds have been removed intact from offices and stores.

It is well worth the expense, particularly if you are in a high crime area, of having a specialist in burglary and robbery prevention review your premises and buildings to spot easy access points and to recommend an overall security system and lighting modifications. Also, in addition to other protective systems, you may wish to consider using private security services and guard dogs. Be sure, however, to check with your attorney about your liability for the actions of any outside service.

17

Remember That Accidents Can— and Do—Happen

Crime can cut into your profits, but accidents can cut even more, and especially in this litigious age. A single stroke of misfortune could severely damage your franchise or even destroy it. Accidents are often more expensive than you realize because the costs are both direct and indirect. The direct costs include damage to the premises and equipment, loss of materials, medical bills, lost time, and increased premiums for workman's compensation and other forms of insurance. The indirect costs include a loss of both your time and your manager's, a decrease in employee morale, and in some cases an actual slowdown in productivity because employees have become afraid to work in certain areas or with certain types of equipment. Altogether, it is important to know what measures you can take to reduce your exposure to both mishaps and disasters.

Accident Protection and Safety Programs

To begin with, you should have an active accident protection and safety program. Most franchises work under circumstances and with types of equipment that pose a danger to employees and in many cases to customers. Although some franchises have safety programs or, perhaps more accurately, had them at one time, the major fault with most is the lack of follow-through. It is not enough to tack up a few posters and make some brochures available. An effective program for accident prevention and safety requires the continuous involvement of all levels of management and employees, together with a strong sense of commitment by both you and your managers. A safety program helps to prevent both pain and expense. One potential reason for the latter is the employer's liability legislation, which has firmly established that the employer must assume the cost of accidents as part of the price of marketing a product or a service. Also, the law in some states enables an injured employee to sue for more than the benefits accorded under workman's compensation statutes. Altogether, for compelling reasons, a safety program is very much needed to protect your employees, your customers, and your profits.

Establishing a safety program is one of the most effective ways to form a bond between employees and management. After all, safety is a vital issue and the best way to obtain employee interest and commitment is to have a safety committee. If you have more than three or four employees, the committee can be effective and if you are a multiunit franchisee, the committee approach is probably the only one that will work.

In the beginning it is best to have the committee chaired by you or another corporate officer, a person whose position underscores your franchise's commitment to the program. Depending on your organizational structure, it also may be desirable to have a representative either from each department within the franchise or from each unit. These should include both managers and line employees.

The first responsibility of the committee will be to draft its objectives and publicize them throughout the franchise. The second responsibility is to clearly write down safety policies and procedures. The basis for these can be obtained, in most cases, from equipment operating manuals and from publications issued by the National Safety Council (444 N. Michigan Ave, Chicago, IL 60611). The policies and procedures should address safety problems and needs in four areas.

1. *General layout:* A significant number of work-related accidents happen because of the poor or unsafe layout of work areas. This is particularly true in fast food, restaurant, and auto aftermarket franchises.

2. *Machinery or equipment design and safety accessories:* The best designed equipment or machinery in the world will be hazardous to operate if it does not have, or if the employees do not use, its safety accessories. Protections include belt and pulley guards, blade guards, saw guides, deadman switches, and other devices to safeguard the operator and those who may be nearby.

3. *Protective clothing:* Descriptions must be made of what is safe to wear and what isn't. For example, wearing loose clothing around moving

machinery can be as dangerous being without a hard hat on a construction site. Jewelry, belts, and flowing sleeves are just a few of the items that have caused lost fingers, arms, and even lives.

4. *Proper operating procedures:* There is a safe way and an unsafe way to perform any function in the workplace. Each of these operating procedures needs to be described.

The next step should be a careful tour of all your premises by the committee. Using the general policy and procedures as a guide, the committee should inspect anything that is relevant, noting all hazards, unsafe practices, faulty building layouts, equipment problems, and any other shortcomings. After this walkthrough, the committee should have enough information to start developing a detailed safety program. Usually this program will involve a number of measures:

Correction of existing hazards, such as missing safety devices on equipment, machinery without the proper guards, risky storage methods, and unsafe working areas.

Development of a safety education and awareness program.

Procedures to ensure that all new equipment and facilities meet safety requirements.

Creation of an internal process to ensure that the program and its measures will be faithfully monitored and enforced.

Development of a routine for follow-up on all work-related accidents or illnesses. Normally, a team within the committee should be given the responsibility for investigating every accident to find out how and why it happened. It is extremely important to get this information as soon as possible because all too often the first accident is only a warning of many others that could follow. The quick identification of the problem area or individual, followed by quick corrective action, can stop further accidents of the same type and will demonstrate to your employees that you are committed to their safety.

Inclusion of safe work practices in every training program for new or transferring employees.

Formulation of accident reporting procedures. Every accident, no matter how minor, should be reported because it may ultimately result in lost time and the need for medical attention. If accidents are not reported on an acceptable accident form, you will have some serious problems with workman's compensation laws and the Occupational Safety and Health Administration (OSHA).

Although the safety of your employees and customers must be your most important consideration, you should consider another aspect of an effective safety program. When an accident that involves either an employee or a customer does happen, there is always the possibility that legal action will be brought against you. In most cases, this action will involve a claim for damages because of negligence. When reaching a judgment in this type of suit, the courts tend to look at patterns of past practices. Hence, if you can demonstrate in court a history of a strong and effective commitment to safe operations, your chances for favorable decision will probably be better. For this reason, all actions of the safety committee should documented, and minutes taken at every meeting.

The Disaster Program

While on the surface accidents and disasters would seem to be part of the same problem, in reality the objectives of a safety program and a disaster plan are quite different. The safety program involves the development of a preventive attitude while the disaster plan must deal with the after-effects of a flood, windstorm, explosion, fire, or other catastrophe. The safety committee can logically be given the responsibility for formulating a disaster plan, but, because the two purposes are distinctly different, each should be under the direction of a separate chairperson. The disaster plan's primary objective is to cope with an emergency caused by an external and uncontrollable force or event. Therefore the plan should address such concerns as:

1. Alarm systems and electronic locating devices.

2. Notification of the proper emergency services. (In most communities today the employees must be give an understanding of the 911 service and what it covers. Usually young employees need special instructions.)

3. Evacuation of customers and employees.

4. Traffic control to ensure access by emergency vehicles.

5. Equipment and personnel for emergency first aid.

6. Emergency communications and lighting.

The disaster plan must have two major components. First are the physical requirements, such as instruction, training, emergency lighting, exit signs, practices to ensure that emergency exits are not locked or blocked, location of fire and first aid equipment, and so on. The second component is leadership and direction. Each franchise unit and location must have one or two people per shift trained in how to react to a disaster and informed about whom to call, as well as the locations of alarms, alternative exits, fire equipment first aid kits, and the utility shutoff switches and valves. Cool heads are essential, particularly in franchises that deal with large numbers of customers such as fast food, restaurants, hotels/motels, and retail stores.

Unfortunately, a particular type of a catastrophe must be considered. During the past few years, several franchises have been the location of senseless shootings. Some have been random with no real target by the shooter. Others appear to have been motivated by revenge, particularly on one or more of the employees because of a broken relationship or jealousy. Such possibilities are difficult to detect or avoid, but you must try to be sensitive to employees' personal problems and alert to circumstances that may be explosive. Check with your local police to determine what legal options you have to keep potentially dangerous persons away from your place of business.

A Reasonable Insurance Program

Normally a franchisee depends on insurance coverage to recover losses from accidents and catastrophes, but, as you must know, buying insurance can be a perplexing problem today. Obviously, you can buy just about any type of insurance to cover every possible loss, but few franchises can afford such extensive coverage. Therefore, it is advisable to weigh the following considerations and options. In doing so, remember what many people who own and manage franchises have lost sight of: The basic purpose of insurance is protection from catastrophic loss. It is virtually impossible for any business or individual to buy full protection from every conceivable loss; therefore the primary function of risk management is to determine what losses or what level of losses your franchise could absorb, however painful, and what losses would seriously affect your franchise's ability to survive.

Realistically, you probably cannot afford all the insurance you would like to have; therefore it will be necessary for you to arrive at a compromise between wants and needs. To do so, review your insurance needs, dividing the coverages into two separate and distinct kinds:

1. *Voluntary or discretionary insurance:* Protection against losses that you may not be obliged to cover, but nevertheless desire strongly to avoid. Very likely these would be of a catastrophic nature.

2. *Nondiscretionary or mandated insurance:* This includes insurance coverage mandated by federal and state laws and by your financing and franchise agreements. Usually these laws and agreements will require certain minimum coverages, but you still have the option of carrying higher amounts than the minimum.

Voluntary or Discretionary Insurance

This kind of insurance requires the most careful judgment on your part. Risk is measured in terms of exposure, and a well-designed insurance package must include an analysis of your franchise's exposure to various types of loss and the degree of that exposure. For example, a manufacturing or repair franchise would have more exposure to litigation concerning the quality of the product or repair than a distribution or retail franchise. A restaurant or fast food franchise, on the other hand, would share the exposure to liability for its products because they are altered before they reach the customer. By buying raw material and using it to make a finished product, both the manufacturer and the retailer could share in product liability. Although each business may be classified according to its activity, usually no two kinds of business have exactly the same insurance requirements. Buying insurance is like buying a tailor-made suit: It has to be custom-fitted to you.

Therefore, although most of the insurance needs of a franchise can be covered by one or two broad business owner's packages, the basic policies have to be customized by either designing the provisions of the policies to your specific needs or adding endorsements to a basic policy. Usually most business owner policies will cover:

Real property loss.

Business personal property loss.

Machinery and equipment loss.

Business income loss.

Premises and operations liability.

Product liability.

Vehicle liability.

Crime protection.

Employee negligence.

Employee protection.

Officer protection.

Each of these general categories contains 5 to 50 specific forms of coverage, and each can vary because of different retentions or deductibles, exclusions, conditions, additions, endorsements, premium formulas, and methods of settlement.

Often, an umbrella policy is useful for protection. Sometimes known as an "excess coverage policy," a true umbrella may cover you in areas where you have no primary coverage and may also cover losses in excess of your basic policy limits, although usually with high retention rates or deductibles.

If some areas of your franchise operations have very little loss exposure, you may save considerable money by insuring them under your umbrella rather than under a primary policy.

Real Property Loss

This category includes buildings, land, and the equipment that is attached to, and therefore considered to be part of, the building. The coverage may protect you from losses from natural events and disasters, such as fire, wind or rainstorm, earthquake, flood, and other damage from natural causes as well as vandalism, theft, and malicious mischief. Some policies will cover such items as wind, hail, earthquake, floods, smoke, explosion, riot, or civil commotion only if the policy includes extended coverage or the events are covered by endorsement to the policy. All policies will contain exclusion clauses that eliminate certain types of disasters or natural events from coverage. Examples of typical exclusions are acts of war, power failure, certain kinds of water damage including floods, earthquakes, nuclear accidents, or damages to electrical devices because of electrical shorts or surges.

When reviewing your coverage in the real property loss area, evaluate your exposure in the exclusion section of the policy. You may wish to extend your coverage if:

You are in a flood- or earthquake-prone area.

You are in an area exposed to tidal action.

You have computers or other types of electronic equipment that are extremely sensitive to power surges or electrical interruption.

You are in a high crime area.

You have a large plate glass area. Usually glass must be covered by a separate endorsement.

Your review should also consider amounts and methods of settlement and conditions that affect the future value of the property. Some of the conditions of contract to check are:

The amount of the coverage or settlement—depreciated cash value or replacement.

The amount of the deductible on each building and item.

The allowance for removal of debris and any necessary demolition.

Any procedure for sign-off or approval from mortgagors prior to repair or replacement.

Any automatic adjustment of ensured values based on inflation or changed market conditions.

These items are only a few of the exclusions and provisions that may be in a real property policy. Therefore, carefully review your policy to make certain your coverage is realistic in today's replacement market. Most real property loss cannot be replaced with used or second-hand material; so replacement value coverage is more important in real property loss than it would be in vehicle loss.

Business Personal Property Loss

This loss category covers such property as furniture, fixtures, equipment, supplies, manuals, manuscripts, and other property used in the normal business activities of the franchise. The coverage also includes any betterments or improvements made by you as well as a limited amount of property owned by others.

Again, the standard policy coverage may not include a number of areas in which you have exposure. Review your situation carefully to see if you need extended coverage in any of these areas:

Personal property of others.

Off-premises property.

Newly acquired or under construction personal property.

Personal effects, including valuable papers and records.

Employees' personal property (tools, equipment, etc.).

Auto, truck, or fleet coverage.

Leased or rented equipment or fixtures.

The same policy features concerning methods of settlement, and other conditions involved in real property loss are also relevant in business personal property loss. However, as noted, personal property losses can often be replaced with used property; so you can safely ensure some of your personal property at depreciated or real market value rather than replacement value. If you have highly specialized equipment, make certain that it is identified in the policy as being covered. Also, it is advisable to ensure it at replacement cost.

If any of your business personal property is used as security for loans or is financed, the loan or finance agreement will usually require that you ensure the property for at least the amount of the outstanding balance. Equipment lease agreements with your franchisor will usually have similar requirements.

Machinery and Equipment Loss

Some insurers require that boilers, refrigeration, air conditioning, and other specialized equipment be ensured by separate endorsements or addendums. Review your standard policy to identify what equipment, if any, requires a separate policy endorsement. Also, many companies write business interruption insurance because of equipment failure as part of the machinery and equipment coverage, not as part of business interruption coverage. If you are operating a franchise that depends heavily on equipment to continue to operate, consider protecting your income by including an income loss provision in this policy category.

Loss of Income Coverage

Standard business interruption coverage includes business shutdowns because of fire or natural disaster. Factors or provisions to be reviewed are the definition of income or gross earnings base, the period of time, and extra expense.

Liability Protection for Premises and Operations

As a franchise owner, you already undoubtedly are aware of the tremendous increase in litigation involving businesses, employees, and consumers. Your premises and operations insurance is the core of your defense against being forced out of business by a lawsuit. Not only does the policy itself give important protection, but so also is the inspection service that most reputable companies are willing to provide. Specially trained inspectors will review all aspects of your operations where you are exposed to loss. "An ounce of protection is worth a pound of cure" is never more appropriate than in how applies to the liability portion of your coverage.

A number of standard liability packages are tailor-made for the type of business to be ensured. In addition to the general comprehensive coverage, there are more specialized packages for owners, landlords, manufacturers, contractors, and professionals as well as for such areas as employee's benefits liability, malpractice, and truth in advertising offenses. You should carefully scrutinize the coverage for liability because the actions of an employee, particularly if your employees have access to customers' homes or places of business, can seriously menace you. As noted previously with respect to hiring practices, suits based on negligent hiring practices are expected to be the most prominent legal development of the 1990s.

There is no quick and easy way to obtain proper coverage for liability. The only way to reduce risk to the lowest point acceptable is to review your entire franchise operations with your broker or insurance consultant, and ask for a report identifying the areas of exposure and the extent or level of risk. You then should be able to prioritize your needs and your resources.

Liability and Loss—Vehicles

Although vehicle policies are quite uniform from company to company, pricing is a different matter. Prices, particularly on commercial vehicles, vary widely, and your broker should shop the market each time the policy comes up for renewal. If your franchise is seasonal, look for ways to eliminate some of your vehicles when they are idle. Be certain that your coverage also applies to employee-owned vehicles if they are used for business purposes. When leasing vehicles, determine immediately if and what coverage is provided under the lease contract. If necessary, supplement that coverage with your own nonowned vehicle endorsement.

Crime Protection

This classification covers many possible losses, ranging from robbery, employee theft, and vandalism to fiduciary liability for pension plan administrators. If your franchise is in a high crime area, you can expect extremely high premiums for forced entry and vandalism coverage. Investigate the effects of a sophisticated alarm system on your premiums, and you may find that the system will pay for itself within a short period of time.

Employee Benefits Insurance Programs

Two of the employee protection coverages are state and federal mandated and controlled, and they will be covered briefly in the nondiscretionary insurance section of this chapter. Since the remaining voluntary coverages are, for the most part, considered to be fringe benefits, remember that this category of coverage may be affected by implied or written contractual commitments to your employees. Any change that may be construed as a reduction in benefits should be reviewed by your attorney.

The types of employee insurance protection benefits available are classified as follows.

Group Hospitalization and/or Major Medical. This type of insurance was originally designed to protect the employee from catastrophic medical bills. Over the years, however, the deductibles and the stop-loss levels have been lowered, and the coverage has been expanded so that now the cost of this insurance has become very high. There is presently a concerted effort by insurance companies, employers, and government agencies to effect some type of cost containment, but at this point their efforts have been largely futile. Numerous plans are now available, including universal coverage, health maintenance organizations, clinics, and partially self-insured plans. Picking the right plan for you and your employees is a formidable task and will require some expert advice. Just a few of the group plan features that should be reviewed are:

Plan deductibles and stop-loss.

High limits.

Limits based on cause or time.

Experiences pooling.

Preexisting conditions.

Retention levels.

Premium guarantees.

Definitions.

Rating experience method.

Administrative expense.

Service and information.

Claims processing system.

Life Insurance.   Life insurance is usually provided as part of the medical package but also can be furnished as a separate benefit. Those franchisees who do furnish life insurance will usually provide term policy convertible to whole life by employees at their cost if employment is terminated.

Income Protection and Long-Term Liability.   *Income protection plans* provide income to the employee from shortly after an accident or the beginning of illness until social security disability payments take over. For this reason, income protection plans are often used in place of the right to accumulate sick time. *Long-term disability plans,* on the other hand, usually have a waiting period of 30, 60, or 90 days and are designed to be integrated with and supplemental to social security disability. Any long-term disability policy should contain two important features: First, if integrated, the social security deduction should be frozen at the first payment level to allow for cost of living adjustments. Second, it should be determined whether the policy comes into effect when the employee cannot perform his or her current duties or if no work can be performed at all.

Dental Plans.   Dental coverage usually includes one or more of three types: (1) cleaning and diagnostic, (2) routine, and (3) restorative. By covering cleaning and diagnostic costs 100 percent, you encourage employees to practice better dental health and thus reduce the need for higher cost procedures.

Management Protection.   This category includes such coverage as life insurance for key persons, proprietors, or partners. It also covers business continuation and directors' and officers' liability. This category may have some estate implications, so you should seek the advice of an insurance expert or a financial planner.

Nondiscretionary Insurance

Generally, nondiscretionary, or compulsory, insurance is mandated by four entities: the state, the federal government, your franchisor, and the financial institutions with which you have financing or loans. The latter two, the franchisors and financial institutions, will require insurance protection on both the real property and personal property used for collateral or involved in leasing agreements. In addition, a franchisor often will require that you carry product and other types of liability insurance because, if a legal action is brought against you, the franchisor may be named as a codefendant. Be aware that the minimum amount of insurance required in the franchise agreement or a financing document is not a recommendation for the full amount of insurance that you should carry; it is only designed to protect the interests of the other parties. Under most circumstances, you should carry more than the minimum amounts required by them.

The two types of insurance mandated by state and federal law are workman's compensation insurance and federal unemployment tax (see Chap. 13). Since, in both instances, the state is basically responsible for the administration of the insurance programs, there will be significant differences from state to state. Be aware, however, that you can control costs significantly in both programs if you understand how they are administered and how you are rated in terms of the type of industry and experience. It can pay you handsomely to learn the in's and out's of these two mandated insurance programs.

Some Good Practices

Insurance costs are a significant part of your nonproduction expenses. Buy carefully. Be prudent in such ways as these:

Be certain that your broker or agent obtains competitive bids each time your insurance package comes up for renewal. It is too easy to become complacent and assume that you are continuing to get the best deal in town.

As mentioned, be realistic in your assessment of exposure and risk. Increase your deductibles rather than decrease your upper limits in those areas involving relatively low risk.

Do not place insurance with a friend just out of good will. No friend worth having will object if everyone is given a fair chance to obtain your business.

Insurance companies invented fine print. All policies have endorsements, provisions, exclusions, conditions, and restrictions. Learn these before you buy the policy, not when you need the protection.

Some carriers raise the rates of individual policyholders to recover the cost of claims settlements. As a result, the customer pays not only the premium but also the amount of the claim. Check a company's record in this respect. And, if a renewal premium is substantially higher following a claim, demand an explanation. The purpose of insurance is to spread the risk and the cost. If the increase is caused by the claim, then go elsewhere for your coverage.

You may find it valuable to have the guidance of an impartial expert when reviewing your insurance needs. It usually is difficult for a regular broker to be completely unbiased, particularly when commission rates differ. An independent consultant, one who does not sell insurance, may be able to suggest more suitable coverage at lower cost.

Keep aware of safety. The best way to keep costs and your exposure to liability suits down is to reduce the number of accidents.

Consolidate the effective date of all policies. Some agents who place your insurance with several different companies will stagger the effective dates to make it more difficult for you if you wish to change agents. Insist that you have but one effective date on as many policies as possible.

18

From the Start, Protect Your Family-Owned Franchise

A franchise is particularly suitable for family ownership. With the exception of large hotel or auto dealer franchises, most franchises involve relatively small business units, and business expansion is accomplished by increasing the number of these units, not by enlarging the original. Consequently, many franchises are initially both owned and managed by husband and wife teams. If the couple decide to expand by adding more units, then often other members of the family are brought on board in both employee and management roles, and the business truly becomes a family-owned kingdom.

What You Must Protect Your Franchise Against

If your franchise is owned by you and other family members and some of these members are involved in its operation, you already are acquainted with the fact that your role as the owner/manager often conflicts with your role as a member of the family. You should be aware that a large percentage, if not the majority, of the most serious problems that develop in a family-owned franchise stem from the fact that you and your key people are closely related. When all of you are able to pull together congenially and productively, the results can be richly rewarding. When you cannot, then both the franchise and the individuals may be hurt. Numerous franchises have lost their vigor, declined, and eventually passed from the scene because of family problems. Underlying these problems is the fact that it is virtually impossible to always exclude emotion from business decisions. The maxim that a business head should never mix business and family affairs simply cannot always be followed. Unless there are no relatives who are, or ever will be, involved in the franchise, you must expect that sooner or later you may have to resolve conflicts between what is good for the franchise and what family members think is good for them. If this possibility exists, it is best to recognize it frankly and to use foresight to avert or minimize the damage to the franchise and the harm to the people involved. No matter how smoothly things may be running today, you should remain aware of the possibility of such contingencies as these:

People get married.

They also get divorced.

People get senile or die.

Brothers and sisters don't always like each other.

Children get married and have in-laws.

Children do not have an equal interest in the business.

None of the children may have an interest in the business.

You may want to sell or dissolve the franchise someday.

You may want to expand the franchise.

Children become divorced.

Protective Things You Can Do

How can you, as owner of the franchise, best defend against these contingencies? The first rule is to remain flexible. At all times, keep as many options open as possible. The next rule is to use forethought to prevent or deflect conflicts, abuses, dissatisfactions, and incompetencies, or at least to reduce their impact. In general, it can be said that the head of a family-owned franchise needs to be capable of considerably more tact than a manager running a business for some remote corporation. Usually in a family-owned business five critical factors must be interpreted and handled with one eye on the franchise and the other on the family.

1. Personnel Policy

The formulation of a sound general personnel policy is likely to be of particular importance. All too often the roles of owner/employee/family member may conflict. An older son being subordinate to a younger son or a sister, a son being subordinate to a sister's husband, or a capable child being supervised by a bumbling uncle are examples of the types of conflicts and incongruities that may arise.

The correct selection and placement of family members in a franchise often require much thought and delicacy. There will be pressures to hire an unemployed nephew or a not-so-successful cousin for a key position. The politics, jockeying, and jealousies that are likely to develop in almost any business can become intensified by family relationships. And you, as the franchise owner, can never walk away from the aftermath of having to discipline or terminate a close family member or even a more or less distant relative. Altogether, the relationships of either blood or marriage are intrinsically likely to complicate normal employer-employee relationships.

The best time to avoid the headaches and the heartaches latent in business/family relationships is to act when you first buy into the franchise. This is the most desirable time to implant in everyone's mind the policy that all decisions made concerning the franchise will be based, first and foremost, on the needs of the franchise. If you wait until the business has been in operation for some time, it will be quite difficult to establish unemotional policies about such things as job descriptions, responsibilities, authority, work schedules, procedures for handling remuneration, tardiness, absenteeism, sick and vacation time, and other necessary details.

Another fact that you must consider is that a family-owned franchise may have difficulty in finding or holding the best employees. Many qualified outsiders hesitate to be in a family business because they feel that family members will get the best promotional opportunities and other principal rewards. Yet, if you expand the franchise, good unit managers and other employees will be greatly needed, because they can be extremely valuable as the source of objective judgments and advice that can be impossible to obtain from a family member's viewpoint. It is important that you be aware of this potential problem and be sensitive to the needs of the nonfamily employee.

2. Strategic Planning

No matter how impersonal everyone may strive to be, strategic planning in a family-owned franchise inevitably tends to become much more personalized than in a publicly owned corporation. In addition to having the normal business considerations, the members of the family cannot help having concerns about future business ownership, control, and income and asset distribution. These concerns often may become more acute and more complicated when people's lives change as they most certainly will. Couples get divorced. Death comes as a surprise. All children do not become interested in the business. Siblings fight. And cocontrol or co-management inevitably fails. Two questions—Who will own what? and Who will control what?—can become very complex and distressing.

Fortunately, the options that are available in the corporate format make it possible to approach these two questions separately. Your attorney can explain how, by the discreet use of voting and nonvoting stock, you may equitably distribute business assets, but keep management and control in the hands of those most capable of these duties and responsibilities.

There also is the question of timing. When should you begin the transfer process? Again, fortunately, the matters of ownership and operations can be handled separately. The distribution of ownership may begin early and usually with the best opportunities for tax savings. The transfer of operational control can be done more deliberately to give you a chance to resolve any uncertainties.

As unpleasant as it may be to do so, some owners must face the fact that no one in the organization is capable of taking over the operation of the franchise. Then the decision whether to sell or to continue operations under the control of a formal board of directors is one that will require the best advice of trusted counselors and friends.

When serious uncertainties exist or loom in the future, you often can find the best guidelines and peace of mind from the use of frequently updated scenarios based on the usual two key questions, "What if?" and "Then what?" You will be pleasantly surprised to learn how much clarity and relief these can provide.

3. Financial Control

One of the principal advantages of a family-owned franchise is the ability to distribute benefits among family members in the form of salaries, wages, fees, dividends, and perks. Most owners are much aware of this and usually are also much aware of the fact that they must be careful not to make distributions to which the Internal Revenue Service could reasonably object. Sometimes they forget, however, that they should be equally as careful about distributions that family members may perceive as unfair and unjustified. It is a fact of human nature that many persons are easily provoked to jealousy, and few things are as provoking as the belief, or even the suspicion, that someone is getting more than his or her fair share.

Sometimes the consequence is friction, then dissension, which can be very destructive to the productive operation of the franchise.

How can this be prevented? First, try to be as fair as possible, which often isn't easy. Second, be completely candid within the family and management circles. As a general rule, no benefit, however small, should be kept secret from anyone entitled to the same benefit. To be sure, someone may object to what someone else is getting. If, however, you feel that you have been fair and a difference between the benefits distributed is justified, then you should hold your position. It is part of your responsibility to make certain that the business is not hurt because someone chooses to be unreasonable.

It is even more important to ensure that the family's total take is never more than the business can afford. Unfortunately, many businesses cease to exist because those who own them have reached too much and too often into their own cash registers. It also is unfortunate that taking too much from the register has prevented many franchisees from accumulating the capital that would have enabled them to seize new business opportunities. Human weakness causes business weakness.

4. Business Structure

Both the operation of the business and its eventual transfer can be greatly facilitated by making sure that your franchise is structured to achieve the best all-around results. But be aware that no business structure is set in concrete. Changes in the economic climate, or in your needs and circumstances in your family life, may dictate a change in business structure. You should be ever mindful of changes and review them with your advisory team periodically.

Change should be regarded as a normal process in business, just as it is in nature. It is, in fact, of prime importance for the members of your family to thoroughly understand the changes taking place so that they will readily cooperate in decisions and moves that are best for the business and for their future.

5. Operational Control

To determine who has operational control of a franchise, a person has only to look for the point at which the buck stops. This is one of the main points of concern in a family-owned franchise because sooner or later the question of succession will arise. Who is to occupy the "buck stop point."

Sometimes the problem is the classic one of the elder who does not want to yield the scepter and the heir who is eager to wield it. Sometimes there a rivalry among the heirs. And sometimes the problem is that no heir has the competence, or perhaps the interest, to rule the business. The uncertainty caused by these kinds of problems can cripple the operation of a franchise for years.

Often the problem is so difficult because no one in the family can be completely objective, and therefore the solution may best be found by obtaining trusted outside viewpoints and opinions. The first persons who are most likely to be turned to for this purpose are the attorneys, accountants, and financial advisors who are familiar with the business and the family. Perhaps most of the time their opinions will tend to be right, but sometimes it is difficult for these counselors to be entirely objective too. They are only human and the income they have at stake, and the particular friendships they hold, are likely to influence their judgment.

A family may also obtain valuable advice if it follows the modern practice described in the chapter on business structures, that is, having an advisory or quasiboard of directors. Since the board members are not family members, stockholders, or employees, and have no authority or liability, the chances are that they can be more objective in their judgment and opinions. Their function is solely to review and critique any and all franchise affairs and to offer advice. The advisory or quasiboard is a concept that could be valuable for any corporation, but it is particularly appropriate for family-owned businesses.

The Transition from First- to Second-Generation Ownership

Typically, when a man or a woman with a family starts a business or buys the first franchise, part of the dreams of success involve the possibility that this is the beginning of a family enterprise, one that will sustain the family for generations to come. Although these dreams do not disappear during the early years, the long hours and the hard work necessary to get the franchise off the ground tend to relegate those dreams to the back burner. The fact that someday, if the business is successful, it will pass on to the next generation is always in the mind of the original owner. Since the transition is years in the future, there may seem to be no need to waste time thinking about it now.

Yet, look around at other franchises and businesses owned by people who have families but are not family-run businesses in the true sense of the word, and you should be convinced that second generation involvement is not guaranteed. Although the laws of inheritance may transfer the ownership of the business to your spouse and children, nothing ensures that they will be either capable of running the business or even interested. A closer look at family-owned and -operated franchises will reveal that involvement by all or most of the family was probably not only planned but encouraged from the very beginning of the endeavor.

If you and your spouse are owners of a franchise and have children ranging in age from 3 to 16, you must be aware of the fact that their conceptions of business life will be formed by your conversations and actions at home. If you are constantly complaining about the customers, stressed out because of finances, and taking your frustrations out on them, you should not be surprised if they ultimately reject any idea of becoming involved in the business. To them, it is and always has been a source of misery. Yet the task of developing a successor should start when they are old enough to understand and begin to display certain personality characteristics. Typically, when they are between 12 and 16, their personalities have developed to the point where you can determine those who may be potential successors and those whose interests are far removed from the world of the business.

The Integration of Family and Business

The 9-to-5 employees in the corporate world and in other large organizations often believe strongly in the adage, "Don't take your work home with you." We believe that, under most circumstances, this is good advice. However, being an employee and being involved in a family-owned franchise are two very separate and distinct roles. Employees travel in two different worlds: work life and family life. Their roles at work may be entirely different from their family roles. On the contrary, the owner and spouse, and even some of the children, in a family-owned franchise may work together at least part of the day, and the line marking the difference between work life and family life becomes very blurred. In fact, since much of the time the family spends together is at the place of business, work becomes one of the family activities.

The Family Meeting

In the corporate world—in fact, in any large organization—meetings are a necessary part of their existence. Meetings are the preferred method of communicating information and gaining consensus. Because of the opportunity to hear inflections and to read body language, meetings are much more effective than memos, letters, and other more impersonal methods of communicating. They serve another very important function. Meetings provide the opportunity to observe the participants in action—their attitudes, their ability to think on their feet, their ability to express themselves, their judgment. Meetings also provide the owners and top managers the opportunity to establish and communicate the goals, values, and style of the organization. Last but certainly not least, they provide the forum from which future leaders emerge.

The concept of meetings as a communication and motivation device can also be applied to family-owned franchises. Far too many owners and their spouses expect that the rest of the family will share the same enthusiasm, motivation, and understanding of the value of the business through some type of osmosis. Yet the children, even those who may work in the franchise, often view it as just something that interferes with their other activities.

When discussing the purpose and the format of family meetings, the question often arises as to what age is most appropriate for the children to attend. We think, within reason, the sooner the better. This is not to say that younger children must be present when the financial statements or other intricate details of operating the franchise are discussed, but their presence during a discussion of the goals of the franchise, the need for honesty, good customer service, and areas of possible improvement will provide them with several advantages. First, it will reinforce the sense of family. The fact that they are sitting down with their older brothers and sisters and their parents discussing "grown-up stuff" will help them form a sense of identity. Second, learning to share value systems, providing honest products and services, doing things for people instead of to them—a sense of the need to do their part—will help them mature properly. Third, they will gradually begin to understand that operating the franchise might be vital for the family's existence.

One of the most important functions of the family meeting during the first years of the franchise's development is to work out a compromise between two different common philosophies. Most owners will feel that the needs of the business assume first priority, while other family members will feel that the needs of the family must come first. The family meeting provides the forum for understanding these opposing points of view and presumably reaching a compromise.

As the family matures, the issues under discussion may become more complex. Usually, at this point, the children may range from the late teens to the late twenties, and some may already be involved in the business.

Some of the issues are:

1. To what extent, if any, will family members beyond the immediate family be allowed to participate in future ownership?

2. How will the original owners be guaranteed lifelong financial security?

3. How will a successor be identified?

4. How will the financial interests of those not participating in the operation of the franchise be distributed and protected?

5. When and how will the transition from founder to successor take place?

6. Should board of director positions be limited only to the immediate family?

7. Should the corporate charter or the partnership agreement be modified to allow for a different method of control and ownership?

These are only a few of the matters that must be addressed in a family-owned business. Obviously, as the size of the family increases through marriage or by bringing members of the extended family into the fold, new issues will face the immediate family.

Almost all these issues will involve tax-related and legal consequences, and it is essential that professional advice be sought. It is not at all unusual for those families using the meeting method to manage their affairs to have their attorney and accountant present for at least one meeting per year.

The process of transitioning from one generation to another will be different from family to family because the circumstances will be different. However, a couple of general hints may pertain in most cases:

1. The earlier a potential successor can be identified, the better. The ability to have someone work in various positions within the franchise before obtaining a higher and more specialized education allows him or her a greater understanding of the needs of the business and the skills that must be acquired. Many of those who have gone through the succession process also recommend that the person also work in other franchises or industries to gain a sense of perspective.

2. Part of the development process requires that, if possible, a person should be given a position of responsibility within the franchise after working out an appropriate apprenticeship. In a multiunit franchise this usually involves assuming the manager position in one of the

units. If he or she is assigned to a corporate position, it should be one that complements the owner, not one as an assistant. The rationale behind this suggestion is that assisting the owner really does not provide management experience because, in most cases, the owner will continue to make all the decisions. By placing the successor in a position of authority in an area in which the owner is weak or in one the owner dislikes, the chances are better that the owner will not second-guess every decision the other makes. Generally, the position will involve, in terms of accountability, the management of a recognizable profit center.

Typically, a designated successor, after finishing secondary school, will spend the next five to ten years obtaining a higher education and relevant work experience in either the franchise or a related industry. The next five years is spent in various positions within the franchise designed to provide exposure in all aspects of operations. By the time the successor reaches his or her late twenties or early thirties, the time is ripe to begin the management portion of the training.

The most common problem found in transitioning from the first to the second generation is the reluctance of the owner to relinquish control to the successor. It is understandably difficult for someone who has built a franchise business from the ground up to step back and give complete control to a successor. Yet continued interference at the workplace undermines the authority of the successor and can cause considerable problems with the employees. It is far more acceptable, considering the needs of the franchise, for the owner who wishes to maintain some input to keep a position as an officer and member of the board of directors, and thus exercise some measure of guidance in the privacy of the board room. Although the successor may feel that even this method of input is interference, at least it is not disruptive to employee-employer relations.

Compensation during the preparation stages should be fair according to the general market. Those owners who pay the potential successor meagerly often rationalize their decisions by pointing out that the person will get his or her share of the business eventually. Yet if other children are involved, usually they too will get a share, and in some cases they will have contributed nothing to the running of the business.

The planning for the passing of control and ownership must also involve estate planning since, in most cases, the owner will retain partial ownership to provide retirement income. Upon the death of the owner, this partial ownership or stock will pass on to the heirs, and it is important that this transfer of ownership does not provide a business structure that is so fractured in terms of control that the business cannot survive.

Estate Planning

To far too many franchise owners, estate planning is something you do when it's time to retire. Yet everyone of us faces the possibility of death at any time. It is one of the scenarios we must consider ever time we make a substantial financial move or some aspect of our personal life changes. Buying a new franchise or expanding a current one involves both one's financial status and personal life and, consequently, introduces new elements that must be accommodated should an owner or principal die or become severely disabled. Realistically, the threat of untimely death must be taken into consideration when choosing a business structure, when designing an overall insurance plan and when designing a financing package. Therefore, estate planning should begin the moment you commence to buy your first franchise. Since every aspect of both your personal and business life will change many times during the next several decades, your estate plan should change also.

Planning an estate is much like developing a business plan using management by objective techniques. First, you must set your goals. For example:

1. You may want the franchise to remain in the family.

2. In the event of your untimely death, you may want to ensure that your spouse has the capital necessary to keep the business and the family going.

3. You may wish to ensure that the only child who wishes to continue the business has the capital necessary to buy out the interests of other heirs.

4. You will wish to limit tax assessment on your estate as much as possible.

Each of these goals will require that specific actions be taken to achieve them, and, again, it is the members of your advisory team—your lawyer, accountant, financial planner and insurance consultant—who will provide the advice necessary to take those actions. Their participation is necessary because every step in the development of an estate plan will in some way affect your legal status, finances, taxes, and the business structure.

Life Insurance

Life insurance has an important role in estate planning for franchise owners. One of the problems often facing families owning franchises is that the assets are not easily liquidated if the owner dies, yet funds must be available to pay taxes and estate settlement costs. Without liquid assets, heirs are often forced to sell other assets so quickly that they fail to realize fair market value.

Life insurance also can be used to provide equal treatment to heirs not interested in the franchise by distributing the proceeds to them and the franchise to the successor.

And life insurance can be used in buy and sell agreements. For example, the successor can buy a life insurance policy on the owners, paying the premiums and naming himself or herself the beneficiary. Upon the death of the owner, the proceeds then can be used by the successor to buy the franchise from the estate. This arrangement may also have some important tax benefits.

Most financial planners suggest that life insurance is only one of the tools to be used in estate planning. It is not intended to be the answer to all problems, but it can be an extremely valuable asset, especially if the owner should die prematurely.

Using the Family Corporation as a Distribution Device

The family-owned corporation is perhaps one of the most flexible methods of distributing control and ownership. You will remember from our discussion on business structure that a corporation is a separate entity and, unless personal assets have been pledged in a financing agreement, they need not be used to satisfy obligations of the corporation. Also, the legal existence of the corporation is not threatened by the death of a shareholder.

The corporate structure is often used to transfer the estate from one generation to another. Since only the shares of stock owned by a deceased shareholder are subject to probate, none of the specific items involved in the operation of the franchise is tied up in court.

By gradually transferring stock to younger family members as gifts, owners may transfer ownership and yet diminish tax consequences provided the gifts are valued below IRS tax-free gift limits. Owners may still maintain complete control as long as they retain over 50 percent of the stock.

As noted, by using combinations of common, preferred voting, and nonvoting stock, owners may pass on control to successors and yet ensure that the other remaining heirs have an ownership interest.

We cannot overemphasize the fact that estate planning is complex and should be continuous. You will be well advised to rely heavily on your advisors to ensure that all your goals are met.

Appendix

Franchise Rule Summary

The Franchise Rule, which is formally titled, "Disclosure Requirements and Prohibitions Concerning Franchising and Business Opportunity Ventures," was adopted in response to widespread evidence of deception and unfair practices in connection with the sale of the types of businesses covered by the rule. These practices often appear when prospective franchisees lack a ready means of obtaining essential and reliable information about their proposed business investment. This lack of information reduces the ability of prospective franchisees either to make an informed investment decision or otherwise verify the representations of the business' salespersons.

The Rule attempts to deal with these problems by requiring franchisors and franchise brokers to furnish prospective franchisees with information about the franchisor, the franchise business and the terms of the franchise agreement. Franchisors and franchise brokers must furnish additional information if they have made any claim about actual or potential earnings, either to the prospective franchisee or in the media. All disclosures must be made (i) before any sale is made and (ii) by means of disclosure documents whose form and content are set forth in the Rule.

The Rule requires disclosure of material facts. It does not regulate the substantive terms of the franchisor-franchisee relationship. It does not require registration of the offering or filing of any documents with the Federal Trade Commission in connection with the sale of franchises.

A. Businesses Covered by the Rule

Either of two types of continuing commercial relationships are defined as a "franchise" and covered by the Rule.

The first type involved three characteristics: (1) the franchisee sells goods or services which meet the franchisor's quality standards (in cases where the franchisee operates under the franchisor's trade mark, service mark, trade name, advertising or other commercial symbol designating the franchisor ("mark") or which are identified by the franchisor's mark; (2) the franchisor exercises significant control over, or gives the franchisee significant assistance in, the franchisee's method of operation; and (3) the franchisee is required to make a payment of $500 or more to the franchisor or to a person affiliated with the franchisor at any time before to within six months after the business opens.

The second type also involves three characteristics: (1) the franchisee sells goods or services which are supplied by the franchisor or a person affiliated with the franchisor; (2) the franchisor assists the franchisee in any way in respect to securing accounts for the franchisee, or securing locations or sites for vending machines or rack displays, or providing the services of a person able to do either; and (3) The franchisee is required to make a payment of $500 or more to the franchisor or a person affiliated with the franchisor at any time before to within six months after the business opens.

Relationships covered by the rule include those which are within the definition of "franchise" and those which are represented as being within the definition when the relationship is entered into, regardless of whether, in fact, they are within the definition.

The Rule exempts (1) fractional franchises; (2) leased department arrangements; and (3) purely verbal agreements. The Rule excludes (1) relationships between employer/employees, and among general business partners; (2) membership in retailer-owned cooperatives; (3) certification and testing services; and (4) single trademark licenses.

B. The Disclosure Document

All franchisors must furnish the document described in this section. The disclosure document requires information on the following 20 subjects:

1. Identifying information about the franchisor.

2. Business experience of the franchisor's directors and key executives.

3. The franchisor's business experience.

4. Litigation history of the franchisor and its directors and key executives.

5. Bankruptcy history of the franchisor and its directors and key executives.

6. Description of the franchise

7. Money required to be paid by the franchisee to obtain or commence the franchise operation.

8. Continuing expenses to the franchise in operating the franchise business that are payable in whole or in part to the franchisor.

9. A list of persons who are either the franchisor or any of its affiliates, with whom the franchisee is required or advised to do business.

10. Realty, personalty, services, etc. which the franchisee is required to purchase, lease or rent, and a list of any persons from whom such transactions must be made.

11. Description of consideration paid (such as royalties, commissions, etc.) by third parties to the franchisor or any of its affiliates as a result of the franchisee's purchase from such third parties.

12. Description of any franchisor assistance in financing the purchase of a franchise.

13. Restrictions placed on a franchisee's conduct of its business.

14. Required personal participation by the franchisee.

15. Termination, cancellation and renewal of the franchise.

16. Statistical information about the number of franchises and their rate of terminations.

17. Franchisor's right to select or approve a site for the franchise.

18. Training programs for the franchisee.

19. Celebrity involvement with the franchise.

20. Financial information about the franchisor.

The disclosures must be made in a single document. The document may not include information other than that required by the Rule or by state law not preempted by the Rule. However, the franchisor may furnish other information to the prospective franchisee which is not inconsistent with the material set forth in the disclosure document.

The information in the disclosure document must be current as of the completion of the franchisor's most recent fiscal year. In addition, a revision of the document must be prepared quarterly whenever there has been a material change in the information contained in the document.

The disclosure document must be given to a prospective franchisee at the earlier of either (1) the prospective franchisee's first personal meeting with the franchisor, or (2) ten days prior to the execution of a contract or payment of money relating to the franchise relationship.

In addition to the document, the franchisee must receive a copy of all agreements which he will be asked to sign.

C. Earnings Claims

The Rule prohibits earnings representations about the actual or potential sales, income, or profits of existing or prospective franchisees unless (i) reasonable proof exists to support the accuracy of the claim, (ii) The franchisor has in its possession, at the time the claim is made, information sufficient to substantiate the accuracy of the claim, (iii) the claim is geographically relevant to the prospective franchisee's proposed location (except for media claims) and (iv) an earnings claims disclosure document is given to the franchisee at the same time that the other disclosures are given. The earnings claims document must contain six items:

1. A cover sheet in the form specified by the rule.

2. The earnings claim.

3. A statement of the bases and assumptions upon which the earnings claim is made.

4. Information concerning the number and percentage of outlets that have earned at least the amount set forth in the claim, or a statement of lack of experience, as well as the beginning and ending dates, of the time period covered by the claim.

5. A mandatory caution statement, whose text is set forth in the Rule, concerning the likelihood of duplicating the earnings claim.

6. A statement that information sufficient to substantiate the accuracy of the claim is available for inspection by the franchisee (except for media claims).

D. Acts or Practices Which Violate the Rule

It is an unfair or deceptive act or practice within the meaning of S5 of the Federal Trade Commission Act for any franchisor or franchise broker:

1. to fail to furnish prospective franchisees, within the time frames established by the Rule, with a disclosure document obtaining information

on 20 different subjects relating to the franchisor, the franchise business and the terms of the franchise agreement [§436.1 (a)];

2. to make any representation about the actual sales, income or profits of existing or prospective franchises except in the manner set forth in the Rule [§436.1 (b)-(e)];

3. to make any claim or representation (such as in advertising or oral statements by salespersons) which is inconsistent with the information required to be disclosed by the rule [§436.1 (f)];

4. to fail to furnish prospective franchisees, within the time frame established by the Rule, with copies of the franchisor's standard forms of franchise agreements and copies of the final agreements to be signed by the parties [§436.1 (g)]; and

5. to fail to return to prospective franchisees any funds or deposits (such as down payments) identified as refundable in the disclosure document [§436.1 (h)].

Violators are subject to civil penalty actions brought by the commission of up to $10,000 per violation.

The Commission believes that the courts should and will hold that any person injured by a violation of the Rule has a private right of action against the violator, under the Federal Trade Commission Act, as amended, and the Rule. The existence of such a right is necessary to protect the members of the class for whose benefit the statute was enacted and the Rule is being promulgated, is consistent with the legislative intent of the Congress in enacting the Federal Trade Commission Act, as amended, and is necessary to the enforcement scheme established by the Congress in that Act and to the Commission's own enforcement efforts.

E. State Franchise Laws

The Commission's goals are to create a minimum federal standard of disclosure applicable to all franchise offerings, and to permit states to provide additional protection as they see fit. Thus, while the Federal Trade Commission trade regulation rules have the force and effect of federal law and, like other federal substantive regulations, preempt the state and local laws to the extent that these laws conflict, the Commission has determined that the Rule will not preempt state or local laws and regulations which either are consistent with the Rule or, even if inconsistent, which would provide protection to prospective franchisees equal to or greater than that imposed by the Rule.

Examples of state laws or regulations which would not be preempted by the Rule include state provisions requiring the registration of franchisors and franchise salesmen, state requirements for escrow or bonding arrangements and state required disclosure obligations exceeding the disclosure obligations set forth in the Rule. Moreover, the Rule does not affect state laws or regulations which regulate the franchisor/franchisee relationship, such as termination practices, contract provisions and financing arrangements.

The following states have franchise disclosure laws:

California	North Dakota
Hawaii	Oregon
Illinois	Rhode Island
Indiana	South Dakota
Maryland	Virginia
Minnesota	Washington
New York	Wisconsin

F. The Uniform Franchise Offering Circular

The Uniform Franchise Offering Circular (UFOC) now is accepted in satisfaction of the disclosure requirements in the 14 states which have franchise registration and disclosure laws. The UFOC format is not identical to the disclosure format described in the Rule. For example, there are minor differences in language on similar disclosure requirements; there are subjects about which the UFOC requires more disclosure than the Rule, and subjects, where the Rule requires more disclosure than the UFOC. Even though the two documents are not identical in language, they are quite similar; in any event, both documents are designed to achieve the same result regardless of any minor variations in the means to reach that result. Accordingly, the Commission will permit franchisors to use the UFOC format in lieu of the disclosure document provided by the Rule. This alternative use is limited to the UFOC version adopted by the Midwest Securities Commissioners Association on September 2, 1975 plus any modifications thereof which do not diminish the protection accorded to the prospective franchisees which may be made by a state in which such registration has been made effective.

Certain provisions of the rule still will control even if the UFOC format is used in lieu of the Rule's disclosure document, such as: (i) the persons required to make disclosure; (ii) transactions requiring disclosure; (iii) the timing of the disclosure; and (iv) the types of documents to be given to prospective franchisees.

The Commission's decision to permit use of a state disclosure document in lieu of its own document does not constitute Commission deferral to state law enforcement. The Commission is expressly providing for concurrent jurisdiction between the Commission and the states in appropriate instances. The Commission's action does not and is not intended to deprive the Commission of its responsibility to determine whether particular franchisors have complied with the Rule.

Bureau of Consumer Protection
Federal Trade Commission
Washington, DC 20580

Index

About the Authors

KIRK SHIVELL is founder of Management Methods, Inc., which as a consulting firm began studying franchised businesses nearly a quarter century ago. He has written and edited a variety of advisory publications for franchised businesses.

KENT BANNING, formerly a research director with Management Methods, is a successful business writer with a range of expertise in business services, education, real estate, and management. He is author of the *Handbook of Residential Property Management,* also published by McGraw-Hill.